SEXUAL HARASSMENT IN ORGANIZATIONAL CULTURE

A Transformative Approach

Debbie S. Dougherty

University of Missouri

Bassim Hamadeh, CEO and Publisher
Todd R. Armstrong, Publisher
Anne Jones, Project Editor
Abbey Hastings, Production Editor
Asfa Arshi, Graphic Design Assistant
Trey Soto, Licensing Specialist
Natalie Piccotti, Director of Marketing
Kassie Graves, Senior Vice President, Editorial
Jamie Giganti, Director of Academic Publishing

Printed in the United States of America.

BRIEF CONTENTS

DETAILED CONTENTS

ABOUT THE AUTHOR

Debbie S. Dougherty (PhD, University of Nebraska, 2000) is a professor of communication at the University of Missouri. For more than 20 years, she has been one of the premier scholars studying sexual harassment, with publications in places such as *Harvard Business Review*, *Human Relations*, *Journal of Communication*, *Human Communication Research*, *Communication Monographs*, *Management Communication Quarterly*, *Journal of Applied Communication Research*, and *Sex Roles*. She has also provided training and development on sexual harassment and culture in a number of organizations, including the National Park Service, the U.S. Army, and the University of Southern California, among others. She has been extensively utilized as a resource for news sources, such as *The New York Times*, *Newsweek*, *Forbes*, and *The Oprah Magazine*. Dougherty's work as a scholar and consultant has earned her a number of awards, including the NCA Applied Communication Scholar Award, The Jack Kay Award for Engaged Research, the *Management Communication Quarterly* Article of the Year Award, the Norman K. Denzin Qualitative Research Award, the Excellence in Education Award, and the Gold Chalk Award for graduate student mentoring.

In addition to her work as a scholar and consultant, Dougherty lives on a sheep farm with her family and enjoys reading science fiction and doing home renovations.

INTRODUCTION

This book is centered on a long-running problem that has vexed organizations across time: Why can't we prevent sexual harassment that has damaged individuals, organizational teams, organizations, and their larger constituents? Millions of dollars have been poured into solving this problem, yet, as the #MeToo movement made clear, sexual harassment continues to be a destructive force in organizational settings. Why is this? I have spent my career as a scholar, educator, and organizational consultant trying to address this problem. This book is the outcome of that work.

Current solutions to sexual harassment tend to be overly simplistic and overly optimistic. We all want a fast and easy solution to this problem, right? A cursory understanding of the problem does suggest easy, linear solutions: Create a policy. Create training. Create clear reporting structures. If sexual harassment was simply a structural problem, these solutions would have solved it by now. Sexual harassment is not simple. It is not simply structural. It is not just a misunderstanding. Instead, it is complicated. It is woven into the very fabric of many organizational cultures, making it difficult to recognize and even more difficult to manage.

To effectively address sexual harassment, you need to have a complex understanding of organizations. In this book, I not only describe what sexual harassment is, I also walk you through a transformational model of organizational culture (Trans-MOC) that will help you understand how sexual harassment is woven into organizational culture through communication. This model is unique in that it focuses not only on how organizational cultures are created, but also on how those cultures can be transformed through careful and thoughtful communication. I am well aware that this perspective goes against much of the prevailing dogma about organizational culture as fixed and unchangeable. My work suggests otherwise, and I will walk you through how cultural evolution can occur.

This book was written for organizational change agents and aspiring change agents who are serious about addressing sexual harassment. As such, this book will be useful in a variety of contexts, including as a classroom textbook, as a coaching guide, or as a leadership toolkit for understanding and addressing problems that are woven into an organizational culture. In particular, this book is for those people who care deeply about creating a better, more just, and humane organization.

Unique Features

I was asked to write this book because of my experience combining research, teaching, training, and consulting. There are several unique features that make this book special. First, this book takes an interdisciplinary approach to addressing sexual harassment. Although I am an organizational communication scholar, I draw in theories and research from an array of fields, such as communication, sociology, psychology, gender studies, management, nursing, and health. As such, this is truly an interdisciplinary project that both draws from and contributes to a number of different fields.

Second, I was asked to write a textbook, and I have taken that charge seriously. As a result, you will find a succinct discussion of topics that can help build knowledge beyond simply understanding sexual harassment. For example, in Chapter 2, I articulate the various functions of communication. I also provide an overview of organizational communication. In Chapter 3, I describe three foundational theories of organizational culture. From there, in Chapter 4, I show how the transformational model of organizational culture was formed from this historical base. While this material focuses on culturally woven sexual harassment, it can serve as the foundation for managing other wicked problems in organizations.

The third and maybe most unique feature of this book is that I center an organizational problem and then present theories and research that will help the reader understand that problem. In my experience, textbooks are usually focused on a scholarly area instead of an organizational problem. For example, an organizational communication textbook will provide theories of organizational communication. A gender studies textbook will provide theories of gender and maybe theories of sexuality. This book is different because I start with a problem and then carefully select material that sheds light on that problem.

Finally, this book has a practical application. Regardless of what domain I am working in, people want solutions. My undergraduate students constantly ask how they can use academic knowledge in their daily lives. My graduate students want to know how they can use knowledge to not only build their own research, but to help organizations solve problems. My clients want to know how to prevent or stop sexual harassment from occurring in their organizations. This book shows how to apply knowledge to address a big social problem.

Pedagogical Highlights

The overarching pedagogical structure of this book builds on a three-tiered learning process of discovery, skill development, and organizational engagement. Discovery is the way we actively engage with knowledge to learn about and understand our world. Skill building is developing capacity to intervene in an organizational culture. Engagement is planning and executing organizational interventions. These three processes are most effective when they are intertwined. I use three pedagogical strategies to make this happen.

Think About It Boxes

Think About It boxes ask readers to absorb information in a physically engaged way. Most of these boxes are composed of activities I have done either in my classroom or during training, speaking engagements, or consulting activities. The goal is to have the reader interact with the information in each chapter. Each Think About It box includes three to five discussion questions that are designed to help the reader in discovery, skill development, and/or organizational engagement. For example, in Think About It 9.1, I present one of the training documents that I use to help organizational members discover, build skills around, and engage with their organization's espoused, enacted, and aspirational values.

Visual Features

Because learning happens best when multiple senses are engaged, I provide numerous visual representations of important concepts and ideas. Some visual representations are pictures, such as the picture of weeds in my garden in Chapter 4 (Think About It 4.3). These images help readers create mental connections, which should both enhance learning and increase connections between ideas. Other visual representations include graphs and figures that are designed to help readers mentally map the processes being discussed. These graphs and figures can be for smaller processes, such as the linear model of sexual harassment in Chapter 1 (Figure 1.1). The figures can also be larger process models, with the most important process model being the transformational model of organizational culture (Trans-MOC), which is used to visually represent cultural transformation, starting in Chapter 4 (Figure 4.2) and continuing all the way through Chapter 9 (Figure 9.2).

Real-World Examples

I use copious real-world stories and examples throughout the book to help the reader understand how sexual harassment is created through communication and woven into organizational cultures. Some of these examples are very personal, such as the story I tell in Chapter 5 about a perplexing interaction my oldest daughter and I had with stranger in a shopping mall, to illustrate the power of binary logics underlying culture. Some examples are from the media, such as the stories from a number of media outlets that describe Larry Nassar's "God-like" status in gymnastics. Many examples come from my research, such as the story in Chapter 8 from a study participant who told me about her boss, who came up behind her at a party, pushed her against a wall, and grabbed her butt. Despite the clear-cut sexual harassment of this experience, this woman insisted that her boss was flirting because "it happens all the time." These stories are featured throughout the book and provide a visceral connection between the information presented and its real-world impact.

Ancillary Materials

Instructor resources are available to adopting instructors. For more information on these materials and about adopting this textbook for your classroom, please contact adopt@cognella.com. In the meantime, feel free to take a look at my website, https://www.debbiedougherty.com/

Acknowledgments

I need to acknowledge the contributions of a number of people. First, Todd Armstrong, my editor at Cognella, has been an essential source of support. This book was written during a pandemic. Through all of the trauma and challenges that come with doing academic work while caring for both an elderly parent and minor children, my editor has cheered me on, understood my delays, welcomed my changes, and been understanding of my forgetfulness. I am grateful to him for not giving up on me when my 1-year deadline to complete the book became 18 months, then 2 years, and finally, 2.5 years. He is an excellent editor and I recommend him to others seeking to write a book.

I also want to acknowledge the unflagging support from my family. They remain supportive of me, despite all of the talking I have done the last few years about sexual harassment, equity in the workplace, writing books, and the challenges of growing a garden (a metaphor that becomes important later in this book!). My youngest child, Freya, has informed all of her friends that I am "the best Mom ever," which is a ringing endorsement from a 10-year-old. My husband has encouraged me to go on a number of writing retreats over the last several months so that I can focus just on my writing. I am blessed, no question about it.

My students, both graduate and undergraduate, also need to be recognized. They have listened to me talk about the Trans-MOC model and provided delicate wisdoms that have made this book better. They have read and loved various early chapters of this book, giving me confidence in the work that I am doing. A special shout out to Tyler Sorg for putting his confidence in the Trans-MOC model as a grounding theory for his dissertation project.

I cannot tell you how much I appreciate my colleagues for their absolute confidence in my ability to finish this project. I am surrounded by really smart, good people who push me to think and write with both care and joy.

Finally, I wish to acknowledge my clients, who have entrusted me with their organizations' well-being. My clients' willingness to reach beyond the obvious, to trust me, and yet to also push me to do better, has enriched my lifeworld and has helped me be a better teacher, scholar, and organizational change agent.

WEB-BASED RESOURCES: ACCESSING QR CODES AND LINKS

The author has selected some supporting web-based content for further engagement with the learning material that appears in this text, which can be accessed through QR codes or web links. These codes are intended for use by those who have purchased print copies of the book. You may scan them using a QR code reading app on your cell phone, which will take you to each website. You can also search for the link using a web browser search engine. Readers who have purchased a digital copy of the book can simply click on the hyperlinks beneath each QR code.

Cognella maintains no responsibility for the content nor availability of third-party links. However, Cognella makes every effort to keep its texts current. Broken links may be reported to studentreviews@cognella.com. Please include the book's title, author, and 7-digit SKU reference number (found below the barcode on the back cover of the book) in the body of your message.

Please check with your professor to confirm whether your class will access this content independently or collectively.

Chapter 1

Sexual Harassment in the Workplace

An Overview of the Problem

By the end of this chapter, you should be able to do the following:

1. Understand sexual harassment as an important problem.
2. Distinguish between acute sexual harassment and predatory sexual harassment.
3. Understand how sexual harassment has traditionally been addressed and how that approach has failed.

- Google
- The National Park Service
- University of Southern California
- Fox News
- National Public Radio
- European Institute for Gender Equality (EIGE)
- The Weinstein Corporation
- The Iowa State Senate
- Penn State
- Michigan State

- Uber
- Presentation High School
- McDonalds
- The U.S. Army
- The U.S. Navy
- The German Military
- U.S. Congress
- The United Nations
- The Catholic Church
- A Madrassa (Islamic School) in Bangladesh
- United Kingdom Parliament
- European Parliament
- So many more...

These organizations are diverse, representing different sectors, different functions, different nationalities, and different goals. What do these organizations have in common? They have all been in the news in recent years due to reported problems with *predatory sexual harassment* that appears to have become woven into their organizational culture. All organizations are likely subject to the occasional incident of sexual harassment. This behavior is disruptive and painful and, if addressed quickly, can be stopped. For many organizations, however, predatory sexual harassment is not an occasional behavior. Instead, it is hidden and nourished within an organizational culture that has gone rogue, at least when it comes to unwanted sexual attention. It has become predatory and has singular destructive capacity. It is this entrenched problem that this book addresses.

Predatory sexual harassment is nurtured in an organizational culture that has gone rogue.

I first felt compelled to study sexual harassment in 1991 as I watched the televised inquisition of Anita Hill, a woman who accused then–Supreme Court nominee Clarence Thomas of sexual harassment. I was both angry and perplexed as I watched U.S. senators attempt to shred this woman's reputation. What would cause these highly respected men to treat this woman as if she were weak, immoral, a liar, and emotionally unstable? Listening to conversations around me, I realized that others viewed Anita Hill through a similar lens. Yet, as I watched Anita Hill, it was clear to me that she was, in fact, strong, honest, ethical, and emotionally stable. These conversations about Dr. Hill, by people with no real knowledge about the event or the people involved, were given an extraordinary amount of social power. It was the people who were not present during the harassment, but who had much to say about the behavior—the people in the background—who drew my attention. It was clear that they had uncharted power that I needed to better understand.

As a result, my research over the last 20 years has focused not just on targets and harassers, but also on those who are in the background of the organization—the bystanders and coworkers who use their words and other symbols to create the meaning of sexual harassment. Communication scholars have long articulated the clear relationship between sexual harassment and organizational culture (e.g., Dougherty, 2001a; Dougherty & Sorg, 2020; Keyton et al., 2001, 2018). I have built on this body of work to create a cultural approach to managing sexual harassment, which I have presented through consulting, training, workshops, and speeches around the world. I have been repeatedly told by my clients that my unique approach to entrenched organizational problems gives them hope that they can finally create productive change in their organizations. It is this body of work that I present for you in this book.

I begin by introducing sexual harassment and its more insidious offspring, predatory sexual harassment. I describe the destructive capacity of predatory sexual harassment. I then share how the problem has been conceptualized over time, as well as why this conceptualization has failed to produce useful outcomes.

Sexual Harassment—A Big Problem

Sexual harassment is not a new problem, nor is it a Western problem. It is a global problem that causes widespread damages. In his book *The Sexual Harassment of Women in the Workplace, 1600 to 1993*, historian Kerry Segrave (1994) documents sexual harassment in the workplace worldwide. Segrave reports, for example, that women serfs, indentured servants, and slaves were regularly raped by their "masters," impregnated, and then punished with extra servitude to the masters who raped them.

Segrave identifies similar practices in the United States, England, France, Australia, Russia, and India. During the industrial revolution, Segrave provides evidence of sexual harassment as an historical problem in Pakistan, Venezuela, Peru, Malaysia, South Africa, El Salvador, Canada, Mexico, and so on. In this meticulously researched book, Segrave both identifies specific instances and provides evidence that these instances represent a much larger problem with sexual harassment. In my own research undertaken to write this book, I discovered reports of sexual harassment in six continents and numerous countries that have been documented in the last 10 years. The Catalyst organization's (2018) international research on sexual harassment illustrates the intercontinental nature of sexual harassment, finding that in Canada, 43% of women and 12% of men have experienced sexual harassment. In the European Union, 40% to 50% of women reported being targeted with sexual harassment. In India, although the overall numbers are not available, there were 444 complaints filed against the 79 largest companies. In the United States, where sexual harassment has been illegal since the 1960s, only 25% of people who are targeted report sexual harassment due to the fear of backlash and retaliation (Catalyst, 2018). In some countries, women who report sexual harassment are killed or jailed. In most countries, women who are targeted are labeled as immoral by both the legal system and by society at large (Segrave, 1994).

"Nusrat Jahan Rafi was doused with kerosene and set on fire at her school in Bangladesh. Less than two weeks earlier, she had filed a sexual harassment complaint against her headmaster." (Mir Sabbir, BBC Bengali, 2019)

Sexual Harassment Defined

Sexual harassment is defined differently in different countries, with different legal implications. In England, for example, sexual harassment is illegal because it is a threat to human dignity. As a result, all harassment, from street harassment to workplace harassment, could be treated as illegal behavior. In the United States, workplace sexual harassment is treated differently under the law because it places an economic burden on the targets of the behavior (Hogler et al., 2002). For example, people who are harassed are more likely to lose their employment, be unable to secure promotion, have their wages threatened, and experience high levels of physical and psychological health issues that make it difficult for them to continue to work. As a result, the United States defines sexual harassment as follows: "Unwelcome sexual advances, requests for sexual favors, and other verbal or physical conduct of a sexual nature constitute sexual harassment when this conduct explicitly or implicitly affects an individual's employment, unreasonably interferes with an individual's work performance, or creates an intimidating, hostile, or offensive work environment" (EEOC Fact Sheet, 2009).

The U.S. courts have recognized two types of sexual harassment. According to Catherine MacKinnon (1979), the first type, **quid pro quo**, translates to "this for that" and represents a direct exchange of sex for rewards, or the withholding of rewards (e.g., promotions, raises, etc.) when sex is withheld. The second type, **hostile environment sexual harassment**, is by far the most common form and is a key means through which sexual harassment becomes woven into an organizational culture. An organization is considered to have a hostile environment if the sexual harassment is pervasive or intense. A third type of sexual harassment is not routinely recognized by the courts, but is very real, nonetheless. **Third-party sexual harassment** occurs when a person who is not the target is negatively impacted by the behavior—such as by not getting a promotion that was given to a target due to compliance with quid pro quo harassment.

Researchers, lawyers, and practitioners owe much of our knowledge to research and theorizing by Catherine MacKinnon. I can only imagine the loneliness and isolation that must have accompanied her work in the 1970s, when most people did not want to acknowledge that sexual harassment was a problem.

Because of laws and litigation, corporations and other organizations "became suddenly attentive when court rulings established their legal and financial liability" (Wood, 1992, p. 351). As a result, our society has gone from a time when predatory sexual harassment was viewed as normal, and even as romantic (Wood, 1992), to a time when the #MeToo movement rocked not only U.S. cultures, but also had an important international impact. These outcomes are consistent with Justine Tinkler's (2008) argument that laws change how we think about behaviors over time. Yet, despite the ongoing legal efforts to stop sexual harassment, the behavior continues to be a destructive process in contemporary organizations.

Predatory Sexual Harassment

Not only am I a scholar and a consultant, I am also a farmer. My family raises sheep. One of the things you learn quickly as a sheep farmer is that sheep get sick. A lot. As the designated sheep medical practitioner in the family, I have learned a lot about different types of illnesses. None of them are good, but the infections I dread the most are from *anaerobic bacteria*. Unlike most bacteria, which need oxygen to grow and develop, anaerobic bacteria thrives in dark spaces without oxygen. **Predatory sexual harassment** is the anaerobic bacteria of organizational life: It is persistent and normalized in the organization; it is diffused across the workplace with multiple targets; it is organizationally supported; and it operates in a field of carefully crafted silence.

Predatory sexual harassment is the anaerobic bacteria of organizational life.

Not all sexual harassment rises to the level of predatory sexual harassment. For example, some years back, my aunt, who was a schoolteacher, told me about a man who called her "honey" in a meeting. She felt that this was sexual harassment and that it was inappropriate. Although I am not sure if it rises to the level of sexual harassment, it is clearly gendered language that is disdainful in content and intent. I called her back a few months later to see how this situation had evolved after she confronted her colleague. She told me that he had not repeated the behavior. This is the ideal outcome of a sexual harassment complaint. Person A acts. Person B complains. Person A stops the behavior. This is what one would expect from a healthy organizational culture. I call this type of incident **acute harassment**. It is not predatory and it is not the type of behavior I will discuss in this book. What makes this different from predatory sexual harassment? First, it is neither persistent nor normal in this organization. Second, it did not escalate over time. Third, the behavior was not supported by the organization. For example, my aunt did not feel compelled to remain silent in the face of this behavior. As a result, the behavior by this man was irritating, but it was not destructive. In contrast, predatory sexual harassment *persists*, *escalates*, is *normalized*, *silences the targets*, and is *incredibly destructive*, not only to the targets, but to the team and to the organization as well.

Destructive Outcomes of Predatory Sexual Harassment

There are thousands of studies that have confirmed the disastrous outcomes from sexual harassment. These outcomes include negative impacts on the target of sexual harassment, on team members and colleagues, on organizational stakeholders, and on the organization. This destruction crosses generations and organizational forms. Researchers describe negative consequences beginning in elementary school (Hlavka, 2014) and continuing as workers age (Ohse & Stockdale, 2008). In short, sexual harassment is really bad on every level and for every person it touches.

The reality is that the research is so overwhelming, that it was psychologically challenging for me to comb through it to find the studies that will help you understand the depth and breadth of the problem. To illustrate the destruction wrought by sexual harassment, I focus on harms experienced by the targets of harassment, organizational teams, the organization, and on external organizational stakeholders.

Individuals Who Are Targeted

The most well-documented damage from sexual harassment is at the level of the target. The negative outcomes include chronic mental health conditions, lowered life satisfaction, damaged identity, feelings of isolation, lowered job performance and commitment, and physical illness that occurs with prolonged stress (Chan et al., 2008). Perhaps the most clearly documented outcome to the target of sexual harassment is **post–traumatic stress disorder** (PTSD) (Lawson et al., 2013; Palmieri & Fitzgerald, 2005; Stockdale et al., 2009). Although PTSD is most commonly associated with soldiers who have been to war and with victims of violent crimes, unwanted sexual attention not only amplifies trauma among military veterans (Roberge et al., 2019), but is a distinct cause of PTSD (Stockdale et al., 2009). The American Psychiatric Association defines PTSD as "a psychiatric disorder that can occur in people who have experienced or witnessed a traumatic event such as a natural disaster, a serious accident, a terrorist act, war/combat, rape or other violent personal assault" (American Psychiatric Association, n.d.). This condition is not only produced through a single traumatic event, but can also come from repeated exposure to a trauma over time. The common outcomes of PTSD include lower life expectancy, drug and alcohol abuse, and physical symptoms such as increased blood pressure and chronic pain. You might ask, how is it possible that a target of sexual harassment can experience the same symptoms and outcomes as a soldier who has been to war? I believe that most people think of sexual harassment as a one-time action that is relatively harmless, like my aunt who was called "honey" by a male coworker. Instead, it is more realistic to think of predatory sexual harassment as small behaviors that escalate over time (Knapp et al., 2019), leaving targets in constant fear for their safety and wellbeing. Take, for example, Anna's experience with sexual harassment. Anna, a participant in one of my studies, was a surgical technician at a large hospital in the Midwest:

> I had a [medical colleague] here. He was a very nice man. I always thought of him as a big teddy bear. And he was always nice and friendly to everybody. And one day I started working evenings, and there are very few people in surgery in the evening. And so you find yourself alone in hallways. He was very large man. And um, he started getting touchy-feely with me. And I thought, "I don't like this. I don't like this." I was terrified and I didn't say anything to him. I was scrubbing for a case and I couldn't do anything. You know, your hands are supposed to be sterile and you can't do anything. And he came up behind me, put his arms around me, and I was just, "oh my gosh." And he started kissing my neck. I turned and looked at the desk, and there were people sitting at the desk. I mean, they didn't think anything of it. And I'm going [to the people at the desk] "excuse me," you know, "hello." Trying to do everything I could to get out of that situation, because I was terrified. And I ended up just going into the room where he was going to be coming anyway. I went in there and did the surgery and later went to my sister-in-law and said, "What do I do?" I mean, this guy scared the piss out of me. And I'm going to be working evenings. He's going to be there. What if he catches me down the hall where nobody's at? He's a large man, he could take me in a heartbeat.

Anna, like most women I have spoken to over the years, viewed herself as strong and tough. She was confident that, if she was targeted, she would respond swiftly and strongly to the behavior. When it happened to her, she was caught by surprise, perhaps because the behavior had escalated over time and because she had made a decision to trust this "teddy bear" coworker. When her trust was violated, she experienced immediate and long-term fear that this man would hurt her and there was nothing she could do to stop him. Note her language. Anna was not just afraid. She was "terrified." Researchers would label Anna's reaction as *psychological distress* (Chan et al., 2008). This label may be clinically accurate, but I believe it obscures the intensity of Anna's lived experience as a target of sexual harassment.

The destructive impact of sexual harassment is *cumulative and circular*. What I mean by this is that the more frequent and intense the sexual harassment, the more damage experienced by the target (Roberge et al.,

2019). In addition, the outcomes of sexual harassment make targets more vulnerable to being targeted (Ford & Ivancic, 2020). For example, in college students, sexual harassment produces depression. Depression is a risk factor for sexual harassment, making these students at higher risk for future incidents of sexual harassment (Wolff et al., 2017). In addition, sexual harassment tends to isolate those who are targeted from their coworkers. Isolation is a risk factor for sexual harassment, meaning targets who experience isolation in their workplace are more vulnerable to being targeted, once again, with sexual harassment. Sexual harassment that is woven into the cultural fabric of the organization, such as that listed above, will produce more long-term negative impacts than sexual harassment that is occasional and incidental.

Organizational Teams and Third Parties

There is less written about the destruction done to a team or other colleague groups. However, the work that has been done is convincing. Theresa Glomb and colleagues (1997) call this type of harm **ambient sexual harassment**, predicting that the impact goes beyond the targeted employee. For example, women observers of gender aggression toward men, such as when colleagues challenge a man's heterosexuality by calling him "gay," experienced increased levels of anger and fear. Increased levels of anger led to a host of negative psychological, physical, and organizational outcomes (Dionisi & Barling, 2018).

Destructive outcomes occur to colleagues in general (Glomb et al., 1997), but also to teams. Raver and Gelfand (2005) discovered that ambient sexual harassment was associated with increased team conflict and decreased team cohesion. This relationship between ambient sexual harassment and team conflict and cohesions ultimately led to decreased financial capacity. In other words, sexual harassment is associated with the decreased fiscal viability of an organization. When one person is targeted, research suggests that the productivity of the entire team is reduced by as much as $22,500 per person, per team (Willness et al., 2007).

Organizations

There are also documented impacts at the organizational level. Targets experience lower job satisfaction and commitment, reduced productivity, job withdrawal/stress, and an increased likelihood that they will leave the workplace (Chan et al., 2008). Many of these impacts are hidden costs that organizations may recognize as a problem, but do not recognize as direct damage from sexual harassment. One quantifiable outcome of sexual harassment is in employee turnover. Targets of harassment are nearly seven times as likely to change jobs as employees who have not been targeted (McLaughlin et al., 2017). The cost of hiring and training new workers is 16% to 20% of their annual salary. The cost rises to 213% if it is a manager being replaced (Boushey & Glynn, 2012). In case you are wondering, these negative impacts are far larger for sexual harassment than for other forms of workplace aggression (Dionisi et al., 2012).

If the harassment escalates to the level of a lawsuit, there are a number of fiscal impacts for the organization, even if the organization ultimately wins. Interestingly, it is this scenario that most organizations seem to worry about the most. Sexual harassment policies and training are typically geared toward protecting the organization from this type of damage. However, as this chapter demonstrates, given the extensive destructive impact of sexual harassment, the legal consequences may be the most unlikely and least problematic outcome of sexual harassment. The most destructive components tend to be less quantifiable.

At the organizational level, the least quantifiable but likely the most destructive outcome is to the organizational brand. An **organizational brand** represents the texture of how an organization is recognized by its stakeholders. An organizational brand includes emotional, moral, and product factors that constitute how we think, feel, and talk about an organization. For organizational stakeholders, a brand IS the organization. When a brand becomes tainted, for stakeholders, the entire organization is tainted. Sexual harassment emotionally, morally, and physically taints an entire organization. In one study exploring brand damage due to sexual harassment, it was discovered that not only does sexual harassment negatively impact brand attitude and image, but it also impacts people's willingness to work for an organization tainted by it (Sierra et al., 2008). The significant and direct negative effects found for each of these relationships offers preliminary evidence that sexual harassment undermines brand development and recruiting. Hence, firms seeking to grow their brand's value and hire effective employees must be equipped to prevent and solve their sexual harassment quandaries (Sierra et al., 2008, p. 186).

Probably the most well-known illustration of brand damage is the Weinstein Corporation, whose founder, Harvey Weinstein, targeted numerous aspiring women actors. Prior to the public exposure of his behavior, the Weinstein Corporation was a very successful production company. Due to the harassment, it no longer exists. The Weinstein brand is now closely tied to predatory sexual behavior.

Organizational Stakeholders

It should be clear by now that the ramifications of sexual harassment extend far beyond the target person. At the larger stakeholder level, ever since the advent of the #MeToo movement, shareholders have been actively filing lawsuits against corporations for things like "breach of fiduciary duties" and violation of "federal securities law." In short, these stakeholders recognize that organizations have a responsibility to their shareholders and that sexual harassment violates that responsibility (Hemel & Lund, 2018). Beyond this sort of impact, however, is a deeper and more personal level of damage that can occur as a risk of sexual harassment.

Think About It 1.1 The U.S. Army, Trust, and Recruitment

In April of 2020, SPC Vanessa Guillén, an Army soldier at Fort Hood, a beloved daughter and sister, was abducted and murdered by a male coworker. She disappeared in the middle of a workday, never to be seen alive again. To understand her abduction and murder, you need to consider the larger context within which this event occurred.

In 2019, Vanessa was targeted twice by her supervisor with what seems to me to be clear violations of sexual harassment policy. First, she was asked to engage in a three-person sexual encounter by her then-supervisor. Later that same year, the same supervisor watched her as she went to the bathroom. Both times SPC Guillén reported the supervisor up the chain of command. Another woman soldier also reported the same supervisor. Leadership did not pursue an investigation of the sexual harassment, allowing a "toxic leader" to remain in a position of authority (Fort Hood AR 15-6 Investigation Executive Summary, 2021).

In 2020, Army SPC Aaron Robinson reportedly kidnapped and killed SPC Guillén. What do we know about this predator? We know that he was previously reported for sexually harassing another woman soldier. We know he kidnapped and murdered SPC Guillén. We know that she never reported him for sexual harassment. Why would she? More specifically, why would Guillén trust the Army to protect her after its failure to follow its own policies and procedures?

The Army leadership think a lot about their values and goals. Their ultimate goal is to be ready for war at all times. They have identified trust as the key to readiness. For example, then–Army Chief of Staff, General Mark A. Miley, publicly stated,

> [Readiness] is the very essence of Mission command and it's all built upon that single word that's in the doctrine, the bedrock of the Army Ethic, which is trust. I trust that you will achieve the purpose and you will do it ethically and legally and morally ... and that takes an immense off-the-charts level of character.

"Trust" is such a core component of the Army's training that it appears numerous times in multiple outlets. For example, the word "trust" is listed 198 times in the

ADRP 1: The Army Profession (2015), which is one of the Army's foundational reference manuals. For the Army, trust is a big deal.

How might sexual harassment impact trust in the U.S. Army?

Discussion Questions

1. We know that brand damage due to sexual harassment can cause people to avoid working for an organization. What happens to readiness when well-suited individuals avoid the military because of the taint associated with the Army brand?
2. We know that sexual harassment damages teams. What happens to readiness when Army teams do not trust each other due to predatory sexual harassment?
3. We know that sexual harassment causes PTSD. What happens to readiness when soldiers who already have PTSD due to predatory sexual harassment are sent to war?
4. We know that sexual harassment infects the atmosphere of the organization. How does this atmosphere impact the trust of those people the Army is supposed to protect?

Take health care, for example. One common emotional response to sexual harassment is fear, not just by the target of the behavior (Dougherty, 1999), but among the larger group (Dionisi & Barling, 2018). Sexual harassment is very common in health care, especially as directed toward women nurses (Vargas et al., 2020). Harassment in this context comes from both coworkers and patients. This harassment leads to reduced patient care (Mcguire et al., 2006) and to increased destructive stereotyping of patients by nurses (Dougherty et al., 2011). For example, nurses labeled patients who harassed them as *biker guys* and *little old men*. To me, the little old men stereotype is perhaps the most useful example of potential harm. The nurses in this study explained to me that men who harassed them were usually older men who were not fully mentally present, kind of like children. In this version of reality, these "little old men" could not help themselves from grabbing a breast or pinching a rear end. I asked these nurses to describe these little old men and found that the age range varied dramatically, with the youngest "little old man" being about 17 years old. What are the implications of the "little old man" stereotype? If nurses believe a patient is mentally incapacitated then they will be unlikely to treat them as mature adults who are able to make good decisions for themselves. They are likely to treat them as children, which can negatively reduce the dignity of patients who are already in a vulnerable position.

Think About It 1.2 Impact on Patient Care

Let's return to Anna's example (earlier). Anna was a surgical technician who was scrubbing for a case when a large male coworker came up from behind, grabbed her, and started kissing her neck. She tried to get the attention of workplace bystanders, but they acted like this was acceptable behavior.

Now imagine that this is you. Raise your hands in the air and touch nothing. After all, you have just scrubbed in for surgery, which means that you are sterile and ready to work. Keep your hands up, no matter what happens. There is a vulnerability to being in this position. In fact, I suspect that most readers did not put their hands up, or only put them up part way. Why do you think that is?

So your hands are in the air and a large male assaults you and will not stop. He is grabbing your breasts, kissing your neck. Your heart starts beating faster. The physiological need for fight or flight sets in. You flee into the surgical room. You are terrified. What happens to your body when you are terrified? For most people, the aftermath of terror is physical shaking. Let's assume for a moment that this surgical technician is shaking. She is about to assist with surgery.

Discussion Questions

1. What could go wrong?
2. Would you want to be the patient in that room, at that moment, with that surgical team?
3. How might this type of impact translate to other forms of organization, such as schools or the military?

Traditional Approaches to Managing Sexual Harassment

So far in this chapter I have provided the definition of sexual harassment, discussed the extent of the problem, and outlined the extensive damage done by sexual harassment at the individual, team, organization, and external stakeholder level. I now turn to a discussion of the traditional ways in which sexual harassment has been addressed in organizations. I think it is fair, however, to premise this section with the recognition that these traditional approaches have been a categorical failure. They do not stop, prevent, or provide a particularly effective intervention for sexual harassment. As you read the next section, you should be able to identify at least two reasons for this failure. First, traditional approaches treat sexual harassment as a simple problem that occurs between two people. However, although sexual

Traditional approaches to managing sexual harassment fail due to practitioners' tendency to oversimplify both sexual harassment and communication.

harassment may be enacted by two people, the problem itself exists at the cultural level of the organization.

Second, the traditional approach treats communication in simplistic ways. Although there are at least four forms of communication (provision of information, message production, communication as performance, and the construction of meaning—all of which will be discussed in greater detail in Chapter 2), the traditional approach reduces communication to the **provision of information**, the sharing of knowledge, facts, or details. In the case of predatory sexual harassment, the provision of information involves sharing what constitutes sexual harassment, how it should be reported, and the consequences of the behavior. Sharing this type of information is critically important.

The problem occurs when communication is treated ONLY as sharing information. I will discuss the multiple forms of communication in more detail in the next chapter, but for now, understand that communication as information provision is the most simplistic way of thinking about communication. As a result, an information-centric approach to managing sexual harassment oversimplifies a complex communication problem. These problems are most apparent in the traditional **linear model** of sexual harassment.

Linear Model of Sexual Harassment

Most scholars and human resource personnel view sexual harassment as an interpersonal problem that has a relatively linear trajectory. The assumption is that a perpetrator enacts unwanted sexual behavior toward a target. In this model, if things work well, then the target reports the behavior to an appropriate representative of the organization, who then investigates, and an outcome occurs. The model looks something like this (Figure 1.1):

FIGURE 1.1: Linear Model of Sexual Harassment

The linear model is based on three highly simplistic assumptions about the nature of sexual harassment:

- **Assumption One:** Sexual harassment is an interpersonal problem—something that occurs between two people—a perpetrator and a target. In this model, the perpetrator is usually, but not always, male. The target is usually, but not always, female.
- **Assumption Two:** Since most organizations have sexual harassment policies, the model assumes the perpetrator/target interaction is enacted in a rule-governed space. The policy dictates how the target should report the behavior, how the reporting authority should proceed with an investigation, and the eventual consequences of the investigation.
- **Assumption Three:** Organizational training will provide the information necessary to prevent sexual harassment from occurring and provide direction for reporting and stopping the behavior when it does occur.

Communication is an unacknowledged assumption undergirding this model. Specifically, communication in this linear model is assumed to be the simple provision of information. Some experts make the language of communication explicit in their remediation models of sexual harassment, such as *the five informational domains* (Hobson et al., 2015) that can be used to evaluate organizations' sexual harassment policies and practices. Other adherents to the traditional or linear model articulate the solution to sexual harassment as simple awareness of the consequences of sexual harassment: "To prevent devastating physical and psychological injuries from occurring, employees need a legally compliant workplace sexual harassment policy to ensure that potential harassers are aware of the consequences of misbehavior and to encourage complaints if harassment does occur" (Penrod & Fusilier, 2010). These notions of "information" and making harassers "aware" are hallmarks of the assumption of communication as the provision of information. The limited assumptions about communication represent a limitation with the scholarship more broadly. The unfortunate assumption that communication is simply the provision of information is key to understanding why the linear model of addressing sexual harassment has failed to adequately manage the problem. I will now discuss each component of the linear model and describe how communication as the provision of information undergirds it.

The five informational domains include having a sexual harassment policy, a complaint filing procedure, training, complaint investigation, and corrective action, which are remarkably similar to the model I present in Figure 1.1.

Policy

The provision of information assumption of communication can be seen in the recommendations regarding policy. The Equal Employment Opportunity Commission (EEOC) explains that policies can help employees understand and comply with sexual harassment rules and expectations, providing a checklist of information that should be included in such policies (EEOC Checklist, n.d.). Researchers echo this expectation, arguing that sexual harassment policies

- need to be clear as to what constitutes wrongdoing,
- need to be highly visible,
- must have adequate support from management,
- must include a statement that violations will be treated seriously and promptly enforced, and
- support broader goals of gender equality (McDonald et al., 2015).

Of course, it is important for policies to specify all these things. Yet research demonstrates that having a clear policy is not adequate to stopping sexual harassment, especially if sexual harassment is woven into the fabric of the culture (Dougherty & Goldstein Hode, 2016). Erica Kirby and Kathleen Krone's (2002) award-winning study demonstrates how organizational policies designed to create gender equity are circumvented by organizational members. Sexual harassment policies themselves tend to be reinterpreted in such a way as to reinforce organizational culture. My colleague, Marlo Goldstein Hode, and I asked organizational members at one large governmental organization to read and then talk about the sexual harassment policy (Dougherty & Goldstein Hode, 2016). Although the policy was intended to be a clear directive as to what constitutes sexual harassment and how it should be reported, we discovered that organizational members reshaped it during conversations such that it reinforced the culture of harassment that characterized this organization. For example, the policy clearly stated that sexual harassment was *unwanted behavior*, placing the focus on the perpetrator's behavior. Yet, organizational members reinterpreted the policy as *perceptions of behavior*. This shift in language shifted the focus away from the perpetrator of the behavior and onto the perceivers of the behavior. In addition, although the policy was written in neutral and emotion-free language, the organizational members interpreted the policy through a highly emotion-laden lens, blaming targets for perceiving behavior as sexual harassment and thereby poisoning the atmosphere of the organization. This interpretation of the policy was not the goal of the policy framers. Clearly, communication about the policy went beyond the simple provision of information.

Training

The next step in the linear model is to train organizational members about the policy. Sexual harassment training is mandated by many states. Further, although not mandated by the federal government, legal precedent is that, for organizations to protect themselves from litigation, each organization must require training about the policy (Buckner et al., 2014). Specifically, it is recommended that training indicates what constitutes sexual harassment and how it should be reported, as per the organizational policy.

Despite the reality that most organizations have implemented training, research is mixed regarding the effectiveness of that training. On one hand, the research suggests that training can be effective, such as by increasing sensitivity to sexual harassment (Buckner et al., 2014; Hunt et al., 2010). Learning outcomes appear to be similar for both online and in-person training in higher education settings (Preusser et al., 2011). In contrast, there is also evidence that sexual harassment training may actually decrease a supervisor's ability to identify sexual harassment when it occurs and has no impact on their ability to make judgments about appropriate actions to take (Buckner et al., 2014). Although sexual harassment training does provide information about the contents of sexual harassment policy, current iterations fail to address the complex communication environment within which sexual harassment occurs.

Perpetrator

Most perpetrators of sexual harassment are men. I get a lot of pushback from this statement, so I wanted to address it early in this book and with a certain firmness. Why is the perpetrator usually male? Because sexual harassment is not about sex. It is about power. Historically, men have gained power through **aggressive heterosexuality**, the forceful demonstration by men that they are heterosexual by aggressively sexualizing women (Dougherty, 2006; Rich et al., 2012). Women do not historically gain power through similar enactments (Dougherty, 2006). I am not making a claim that women are somehow superior to men, nor am I making a claim that all men are perpetrators. However, in the context of sexual harassment and predatory sexual behavior, men are usually the perpetrators (McDonald, 2012).

When utilizing an information definition of communication, it is assumed that providing the perpetrator with information will stop the behavior from occurring. This informational perspective assumes that the perpetrator is simply confused and made a mistake. The belief is that a consistent policy with training should fix this problem. In my research I have discovered that the "good guy made a mistake" assumption about perpetrators is a common interpretation by other organizational members. Note how this interpretation plays out in these quotes from my previously unpublished data:

> **Study Participant 1:** I mean, sexual harassment; it could be a lot of things. There are numerous things that I've seen people describe as sexual harassment. I've been around sexual people. ... So, you don't know what it is until someone tells you that "you've sexually harassed me."
>
> ****
>
> **Study Participant 2:** You need to let the individual know that was taken like that and correct your behavior. I mean, if you tell me that I'm wearing my hair color green and it's affecting your ability to work, I can change my hair color. I can do things to change myself to not affect you and your job and stuff. But if somebody doesn't tell you, you don't know.

These organizational members are confident that perpetrators are good people who unknowingly made a mistake, stipulating targets must directly confront the harasser so perpetrators can change their behavior. The linear model of sexual harassment provides information to organizational members that is designed to prevent "good people" from inadvertently committing acts of sexual harassment. A few years ago, during training for one large government organization, one of my savvier women participants interrupted me and said, "Why don't these people already know this behavior is wrong? I mean, we know it is wrong without being told. Why don't they know? Are they just not as smart? Or do they do it because they know it is wrong?" I agree with her. Why don't they know? Most of the behavior is egregious, including comments about coworkers' body parts, sex acts they would like to perform on coworkers, objectifying symbols like pictures of naked women, or domination-style sex jokes. How is it possible that these perpetrators do not know that this behavior is inappropriate in a workplace?

Although there is an assumption that most perpetrators are good people who made a mistake, there is also a recognition that harassers may be predators inadvertently hired by the organization. Within the linear model, appropriate policy, followed by training targets how to report the behavior, should allow for the elimination of this person from the organization.

Target

I made a decision to use the word "target" instead of "victim" some years ago, when I realized that the victim label was laden with stigmas and stereotypes that further victimize those who have been harassed. Victim language is loaded language that makes it difficult for targets to move forward in the workplace (Dougherty, 2017). By using the word "target," I attempt to remove the stigma.

Targets of harassment are more diverse than perpetrators. Although targets are mostly women, gay men and other vulnerable people are also likely targets (McDonald, 2012). These people are targeted in such a way as to emphasize their femininity and related low social power (Clair, 1994; Scarduzio et al., 2018). For example, their body parts are described in sexualized ways, they are grabbed and touched, they are threatened with sexual aggression. This is called **objectification**, meaning that the behavior strips them of their humanity by treating them as objects. When men who identify as heterosexual are targeted, they are typically exposed to different types of behaviors. They are often shown pornographic images that make them uncomfortable, or they are called names that call into question their heterosexuality (Chiodo et al., 2009).

When communication is treated as the transmission of information, it is assumed that if targets are given the right information and training, they will report the behavior to the appropriate authorities. However, despite the fact that sexual harassment policies and training are ubiquitous in organizations, targets are unlikely to report the behavior (Bergman et al., 2002). Why? Because sexual harassment is not just a factual and informational experience. It is laden with power, emotions, stigmas, stereotypes, and judgments of people who have been targeted (Dougherty & Goldstein Hode, 2016). As a result, reporting the behavior is highly risky and unlikely to produce a positive outcome.

Reporting

Based on the linear model, if a person is targeted with sexual harassment, they need information on how to report it. There has been a considerable amount of effort by human resource departments to find the right process to get targets to report (McDonald et al., 2015). Despite this effort, studies consistently show that reporting rarely occurs. When it does occur, reporting rarely results in helpful outcomes for the reporter, and in fact, reporting is often destructive to the reporter (Bergman et al., 2002). The destructive capacity of reporting is not a product of the reporting itself. Instead, it comes from how the reporter and the report are treated by investigators (Bergman et al., 2002). Trust is a particularly important factor in reporting. Although most targets do not report sexual harassment, those who do often have lower trust in organizational reporting mechanisms due to unsatisfactory outcomes (Vijayasiri, 2008). To combat this problem, researchers suggest that policies provide clear reporting protocols and that multiple reporting agents are identified (Buchanan et al., 2014). What fascinates me about these suggestions is that they are often also accompanied by the recognition that the main problem is not a lack of clear information, or even that the reporting mechanisms are too narrow. Instead, these scholars recognize that reporting is stymied by the culture or climate of the organization. For example, Bergman et al. (2002) note that "fostering a climate that does not tolerate sexual harassment should alleviate many of the problems faced by organizations. First and foremost, climates that do not tolerate sexual harassment are associated with lower levels of sexual harassment" (p. 238). The authors note that research across time supports the conclusion that climate is the difference between success and failure in sexual harassment remediation. Vijayasiri (2008) similarly notes that reporting outcomes is a product of organizational cultures of trust. Although not addressing culture or climate specifically, McDonald et al. (2015) identify as a limitation of the linear model research that it fails to adequately account for gendered organizational practices "that allow sexual harassment to persist" (p. 52). Clearly, something beyond communication as the provision of information is impacting the reporting process. Something bigger and more profound is happening here.

Investigation

Based on the linear model, a report should lead immediately to an investigation. Research suggests that sexual harassment complaints should have time limits, be confidential, engage in due process, and prevent victimization (McDonald et al., 2011). McDonald and colleagues (2015) identify complaint handling as "a deficit in organizational practice" (p. 51). These authors identify two reasons for these problems. First, managers tend to treat sexual harassment complaints as an interpersonal issue that is based on personality. As a result, the power differences and injustices that accompany sexual harassment are not attended to. In addition, because of the legal component of complaints, they are typically treated as disconnected from context, which fails to account for the systemic and cultural factors that almost always contribute to sexual harassment. This can lead to unfortunate outcomes.

Outcome

The ultimate goal of the linear model is for sexual harassment policies, training, and procedures to lead to outcomes that are just and fair. The most useful model I have seen (Figure 1.2) suggests that positive outcomes lead to more trust, which increases willingness to report (Vijayasiri, 2008).

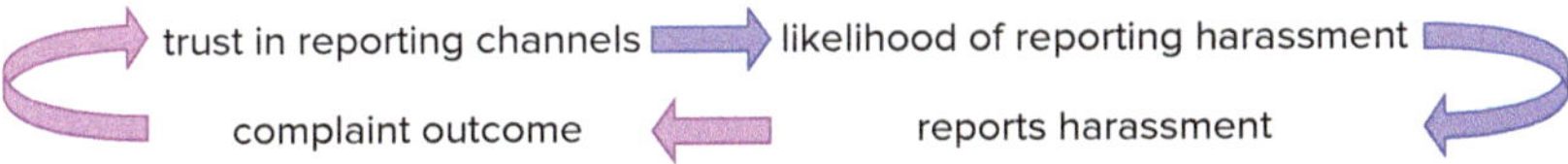

FIGURE 1.2: Vijayasiri's (2008) Possible Causal Cycle Relating Reporting and Trust

However, even in the military, which has long-established processes for dealing with sexual harassment, formal complaints, on the rare occasion when they are filed, only result in consequences for the harasser or in a positive change to the organization about half of the time (McDonald et al., 2011). Equally likely are consequences to the targets for filing a complaint (McDonald et al., 2011). Other study findings are less positive. Bergman et al. (2002) discovered that reporting "often triggers retaliation" and can increase the destructive impacts of sexual harassment on the individual (p. 237). These authors conclude that, given these findings, the most reasonable response to sexual harassment is to not report the behavior. Scholars recognize the destructive outcomes of reporting sexual harassment, arguing that negative outcomes need to be addressed by supporting the targets of the behavior (McDonald et al., 2015). Clearly, creating positive outcomes is not a simple matter of providing the right information in the right order, as suggested by the linear model of managing sexual harassment. Although this information is important and should be provided to organizational members, it is insufficient. Organizational change agents need to think in more complex ways if they are to evolve their culture in more productive directions.

Recap and Looking Forward

Predatory sexual harassment is irrational and nonsensical behavior. It is damaging at every level of the workplace, leading to destructive ends for the target, teams, organizations, and stakeholders. How, then, given the vast amount of research, legal, and organizational remediation activity, is it possible that sexual harassment continues to be a persistent and significant problem in contemporary workplaces? In my experience as both a scholar and as a consultant, there are three reasons why the linear model has failed to solve sexual harassment. **First**, the model oversimplifies a complex problem. The issues are neither linear nor straight. **Second**, predatory sexual behavior is laden with various forms of communication that go far beyond the simple provision of information. **Finally**, as many scholars have mentioned, sexual harassment is not a product of interpersonal conflict. It is interwoven into organizational cultures through communication.

Variants of the linear model have become increasingly sophisticated, with internal feedback loops and a recognition that sexual harassment represents a cultural and systemic problem (McDonald et al., 2015; Vijayasiri, 2008). Although these models represent a clear improvement from the linear assumptions that guide most work, they are still built on a primarily *information provision assumption of communication*. As such, the models focus on how managers can inject change into the organizations by providing and managing information about and around sexual harassment. Although these models may be useful to human resource personnel who are creating a framework for managing sexual harassment, they are less useful for addressing the larger cultural and systemic issues that produce and reproduce sexual harassment over time. Specifically, these models do not recognize that sexual harassment is entangled with communication in complex and interwoven ways. As I will describe in Chapter 2, not only is communication the key means of prevention and remediation, *sexual harassment IS communication*. Beyond communication as information, the very act of sexual harassment inserts meanings as to what is good, right, valuable, and appropriate in an organization. In the next chapter, I define communication and organizational communication so that you can begin to absorb the complexity of predatory sexual harassment in the workplace.

Credit

Fig. 1.2: Source: https://www.brandeis.edu/investigate/teen-sexual-harassment/pdf-articles/vijayasiri-underreporting-sh-the-importance-of-organizational-culture-and-trust-2008.pdf.

Chapter 2

Organizational Communication and Sexual Harassment

By the end of this chapter you should be able to do the following:

1. Understand communication as the complex interplay between information, messaging, and meaning making.
2. Recognize the ways in which organizations are created through communication.
3. Assess the ways in which communication creates predatory sexual harassment.

> *"Dr. Dougherty, we have tried everything. We have done everything right. And still, we are hearing about sexual harassment in Organization X. What are we doing wrong?"*

When I receive a phone call from a potential new client, usually they have tried everything in the standard sexual harassment management toolkit. They have a policy, member training, and leadership training. Some have started programs to support targets. One organization even began a character development program for its members. My first step is to draw a map of their sexual harassment intervention efforts. Here is one that I did for one of my clients (Figure 2.1). It is a simple map, yet it reveals a

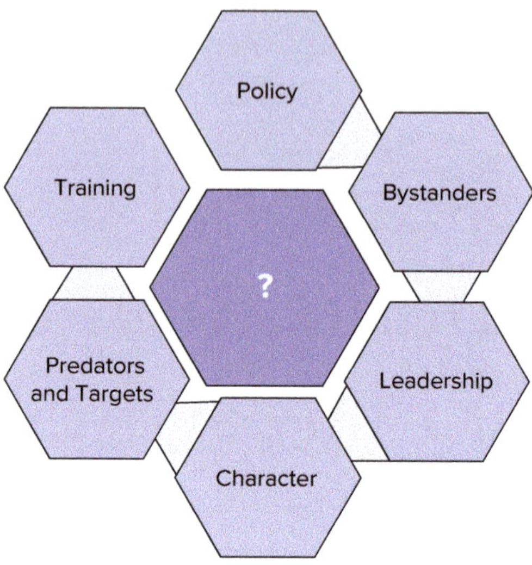

FIGURE 2.1: Map of Sexual Harassment Intervention Efforts

glaring oversight. There is nothing that draws these efforts together. Each effort is distinct, without clear connections. What is missing? Most sexual harassment remediation efforts are missing a complex understanding of communication as a means of connecting the various remediation efforts (Figure 2.2). Without this complex thinking about communication, most sexual harassment remediation efforts will fail. In this chapter, I explore the fundamentals of human communication, both generally and organizationally, with the expectation that this type of thinking will help organizations be more sophisticated in how they approach sexual harassment.

What Is Communication?

Communication is one of those topics where everyone thinks they know what it is, when in reality, few people understand its complexity. Take, for example, the eager undergraduate students who tell their professors that they like to talk a lot, so they should be communication majors. Of course, communication is more about listening than it is about talking.

Most people view communication as the simple exchange of information. Yet, as any organizational member can tell you, providing information does not ensure that the workplace will run smoothly. Communication is so much more than the simple provision of information. To help you understand its complexity, I will discuss *communication as information sharing*, *communication as message production*, *communication as enactment*, and

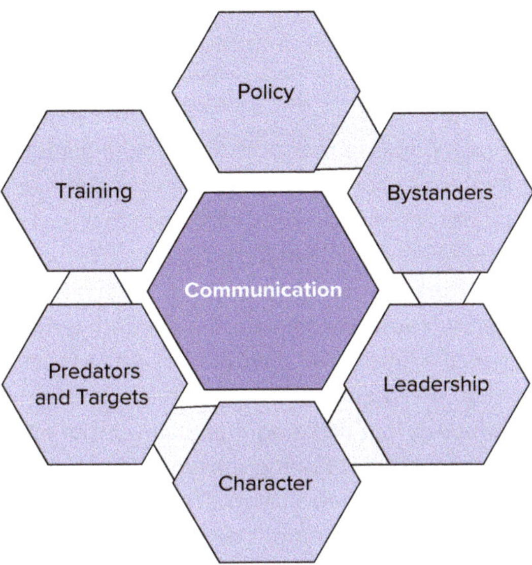

FIGURE 2.2: Communication Connecting Sexual Harassment Interventions

communication as meaning making. It is only when all four functions are considered that organizational members can begin to productively confront entrenched organizational problems such as sexual harassment.

Communication is so much more than the simple provision of information. It is the engine that gives meaning to our society and the organizations that make up that society.

Communication as Information Sharing

As seen in the previous chapter, most sexual harassment scholars and practitioners tend to treat communication as the simple provision of information. Indeed, sharing information is a core function of communication. Failure to share information can lead to organizational underperformance and even to failure. In short, it is an important way of enacting communication. A basic model of communication as information sharing looks something like this (Figure 2.3).

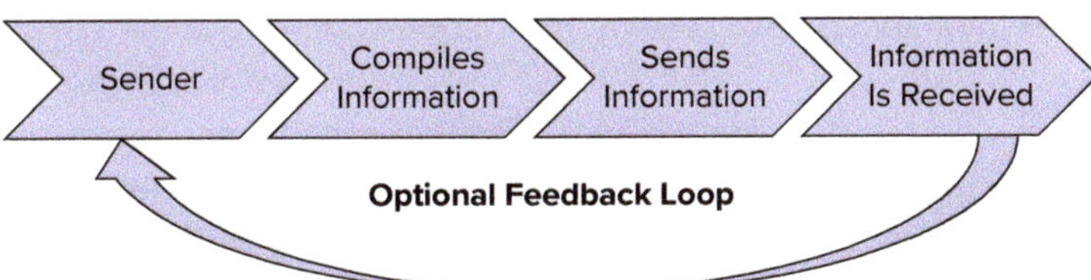

FIGURE 2.3: Communication as Information

This is a basic pipeline model of communication as information. Like a water pipe, information flows one way, from the source to the receiver. The **sender** in this model is the person who is responsible for compiling and sending relevant information. Although this seems like a relatively simple matter, it has been my experience that most organizational members assume that the responsibility for sending information lies with someone else. Critical information is not shared because there is no designated sender. I personally recall a time, when I worked as an associate dean of research, when one administrator admonished me for not showing up to a meeting. I explained that although I give the appearance of being a psychic, I actually am not so gifted. I therefore need people to tell me when, where, and why there is a meeting. The administrator turned to another person and said, "I thought you sent this meeting invite." That person looked astonished and said, "That is not my job." Designating a message sender is a simple, yet important task that is often overlooked by organizational managers.

In this model, the sender's first job is to **compile information**, which should be accurate, adequate, and timely. Although, again, this seems like a simple mandate, providing accurate, adequate, and timely information can be challenging. Consider the problematic of accurate information.

Accurate information is critically important if sexual harassment policies are to be effective. For example, the most common form of policy statement is called **zero tolerance**. It usually sounds something like "there is no place for sexual harassment in [organization X]" or "organization X will not tolerate sexual harassment in any form." The zero tolerance policy directive may be given with the greatest of sincerity, but usually by the time an organization makes such a statement, it is precisely because sexual harassment has been not only tolerated, but accepted as an organizational norm. As a result, zero tolerance statements are typically a type of wishful thinking that represents an inaccurate understanding of the problem and its solution.

Zero tolerance statements are seldom accurate information from organizations with predatory sexual harassment. In fact, sexual harassment has not only been tolerated in these organizations, but accepted as an organizational norm.

Once the sender compiles the information, the *information is sent*, a process which includes channel, level of message (individual versus mass receivers), and sensory engagement (can the receiver see, smell, touch, hear, etc., the information)—although let's be honest, most organizations do not think about sending information with any level of sophistication. Like most communication-related phenomena, sending information has more complexity than one may expect. Think about **channels**, for example. If communication as information sharing treats communication as a pipeline, the channels are the various types of "pipes" or routes through which information is transmitted. Each channel has **technological affordances**, which is the various carrying capacity for a particular technology. These affordances can be social, emotional, cultural, and cognitive. As a result, considering which channels to use involves various forms of tradeoff, some of which are not obvious, and yet, are profoundly important. For example, face-to-face training may be more effective than online training, but it is not very efficient in terms of reaching large numbers of people. Online training may be able to reach more people, but it is unlikely to engage multiple senses in the same way as face-to-face training, and it certainly cannot observe people's reactions as a form of emotive feedback.

Most information-based models treat *the receiver* somewhat like a sponge. According to these models, if you send the information in the proper format, it should be absorbed by the receiver. If it is not absorbed, then the models assume the information was not properly formatted or the receiver was not paying attention. These assumptions fail to account for the complex humanity of the receiver. The reception of a message will be impacted by personality, by the context in which the message is sent, by the status of the sender, by social power, by emotions, and by the organizational culture.

It is not always clear if a receiver has absorbed the information that was sent. The more sophisticated information models will include a *feedback loop* to ensure that the receiver knows the information. In face-to-face settings, a sender can observe facial expressions and adjust the information to be more effective. In online settings, there are often short tests to see if the receiver can recite back the information that was sent. Often, the receiver needs to keep taking the test until a certain percentage of answers are correct. Unfortunately, feedback loops do not account for the emotional responsiveness of the receivers (Think About It 2.1).

Think About It 2.1 Receiver and Sexual Harassment Training

When I was working with a large government organization (identity hidden at the request of organizational managers), I asked organizational members to describe the sexual harassment training they had received. I was curious as to why, after years of mandated training, they knew so little about their policy. Instead of describing what they learned during the training, the men in this organization told me about walking into the room where the training was being held, then sitting down with their backs to the trainer. At the end of the training, they stood up and walked out. Technically they had completed the required training, but in reality, they likely absorbed little information that day.

Discussion Questions

1. What information was being sent by the men to leadership?
2. What kind of feedback were these workers sending to the trainer?
3. Was this feedback useful for sending the information more effectively?
4. In contemporary times, most sexual harassment training is online. How do organizational members circumvent training in online settings?

Communication as Message Production

Messages are communication designed to produce a desired change in an individual. Those changes can be attitudinal, behavioral, normative, or perceptual. In short, messages are intended to persuade people. The most effective messages are receiver oriented, account for the context, and are culturally sensitive. Obviously, not all messages are carefully considered or effective. Many messages are sender focused, with little attention paid to how that message will be received. As a result, these ill-conceived messages can have significant unintended consequences. A basic model of communication as message production might look like Figure 2.4.

> Messages are communication designed to produce a desired change in an individual. Individuals are people who act alone. What does this mean for organizations where people act together?

Based on this model, there are three basic concerns that should be considered when crafting messages—context,

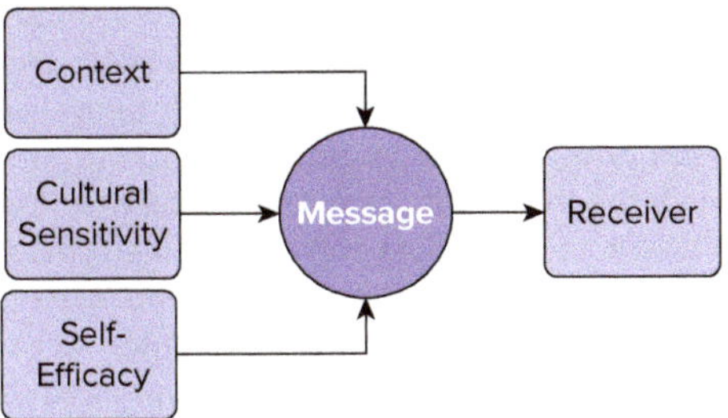

FIGURE 2.4: Communication as Message Production

cultural sensitivity, and self-efficacy. In the **context** of sexual harassment, most messages are not well conceived. Take, for example, no tolerance messages that inevitably come from managers when sexual harassment happens. This message is intended to persuade organizational members that they should not harass and that they should take the sexual harassment policies seriously. However, these messages typically are not **culturally sensitive**, failing to account for the *cultural logics* within which sexual harassment occurs. We know, for example, that sexual harassment may seem irrational from outside of the organizational culture, but there is a cultural logic within which this behavior is enacted. Sexual harassment accomplishes something that may be organizationally destructive, but is culturally productive (Dougherty, 2001a). For example, as illustrated in Think About It 2.2, in some organizations, sexual harassment creates a sense of camaraderie among workers—excluding the targets, of course. Zero tolerance messages that do not address the relationship between organizational culture and sexual harassment will fail to create productive change.

Think About It 2.2 Sexual Harassment and Employee Camaraderie

During an interview with an employee at a harassment-prone health care organization, a man told me that sexual behavior in his workplace was different than in other organizations. "In what way?" I asked.

> [The health care context] has a lot to do with it. I mean, you know. Tension, stress. How we choose to relieve it, uh. I don't know if it's good or bad, a good or bad example or not, but the old television show *M*A*S*H*. Certainly exaggerated. But the kind of camaraderie doctors and nurses show, and auxiliary staff showed in that series. That's kind of the feeling I have for around here. There's familiar. Familiarity breeds comfort as well as contempt. And I think the more people interact and joke with each other or, sometimes shock—try and shock each other, which is kind of hard to do with some of the people around here, it is a good way and a healthy way of relieving some of that tension and stress.

Consider the hit movie and television show *M*A*S*H.* This show is about a United States Mobile Army Surgical Hospital during the Korean War. The movie's primary characters are two male surgeons who are irreverent, funny, sarcastic, and sexually attractive to all but one woman character. Major Margaret Houlihan is the highest-ranking nurse in the movie and her job is to be in charge of the nursing unit. She is a powerful character. Like most powerful women characters of that time, she is treated in the movie as shrill, mean, overcontrolling, and uptight. She is also the unending target of the sexual harassment by the male surgeon protagonists. There is one scene in this film where she is taking a shower and the men pull down the walls of the shower, leaving her standing naked in front of the entire M*A*S*H unit, all of whom are pointing at her and laughing while she screams and tries to cover herself up. In this moment, her power is stripped from her and used to create a strong sense of camaraderie among her coworkers.

This is the show referenced by the male employee as a reason why sexual behavior is more acceptable at his large health care organization.

Discussion Questions

1. What is the context in which sexual harassment occurs in this specific organization?
2. What are the cultural conditions in this organization that need to be considered in message production?
3. What self-efficacy tools are needed to overcome barriers to change in this organization?
4. How would members of this organization likely react to a "zero tolerance" message?
5. Every generation has some sort of cultural manifestation of the type of movie exemplified by *M*A*S*H.* What are the cultural manifestations (movie, television, music, etc.) for your generation?

Even when organizational members can be persuaded that sexual harassment exists in the organization, that it is bad, and should be stopped, getting individuals to take desired actions can be challenging. Specifically, people need to feel like they have the **self-efficacy**, or the personal ability necessary to overcome barriers to taking required steps. For example, reporting sexual harassment takes an immense amount of courage, especially if there is a punitive history toward those who report the behavior. A good message, then, will help instill courage in organizational members.

Overall, messages are an important form of communication that can be used to stop or prevent sexual harassment. However, as the previous discussion suggests, effective messaging around sexual harassment is not a simple matter of sending out persuasive information and expecting change. Why is that? Because messages target individuals—people acting alone. In contrast, predatory sexual behavior in the workplace is a cultural phenomenon, which is created by people acting together. As a result, it is necessary to have communication that targets the larger culture, and not just individuals in that culture. Communication as messaging is necessary, but it is not enough to address the larger system within which sexual harassment is woven.

Messages target individuals acting alone. In contrast, predatory sexual harassment is created by people acting together.

Communication as Enactment

In 1962, John Langshaw Austin revolutionized communication theorizing with his book, titled *How to Do Things With Words*. In his book, Austin introduced **speech act theory**, which shifted the trajectory of communication studies by acknowledging that words are actions and those actions accomplish social coordination. For example, the words "I do" in a wedding ceremony create a marriage. The words themselves act, and that action creates society. According to Austin, words act in different ways, accomplishing different social roles and goals. Conceptualizations of communication as enactment have evolved from Austin's work in increasingly sophisticated ways. Some of the most common inheritances include practice theory, communication as constitutive, communication as performative, and communication as enactment. I have selected the word **enactment** to encapsulate this body of theorizing for the simple fact that my clients find this term easier to grasp than the other framing options.

Communication as enactment was described by Karl Weick (1995) as the way in which people talk their social environment into existence, and then reproduce that environment through action. To illustrate how enactment works, I utilize Gust Yep's (2020) theorizing on communication as performativity. Yep begins his theorizing with the clear recognition that communicative performances are embedded in both culture and in systems of power. As you will see later in this book, sexual harassment is also embedded in both culture and in systems of power, making this conceptualization of communication as enactment particularly relevant to this book.

According to Yep, communication as performance is both about *being* and about *doing*. **Performance as being** means that we perform our existence as individuals and groups in a specific society. **Performance as doing** means that through our actions we create our membership and belonging in the social world. Both aspects of performativity are situated within a particular historical and geopolitical system and are enacted within embedded systems of power.

So how does performativity work? According to Yep, performativity is about both ordinary actions as well as unusual interactions. In this way, culture is an ongoing process of enacting norms and practices within larger social structures and systems that, over time, create the illusion that the performance is a natural and universal system. Yep calls this naturalizing process **hardening performances**, in which culturally specific practices are treated like a universal performance, thereby maintaining and perpetuating hegemonic power relations. This hardening process occurs in three points on a continuum.

Gust Yep is a premier intercultural communication scholar who has had a profound impact on how scholars understand the relationship between communication and culture.

1. **Sedimentation** refers to the normalization of certain individual and collective performances as more desirable in a cultural system. Current sexual harassment policies that focus on legal issues and assume communication as information became sedimented in different organizational cultures when they were identified as best practices for addressing sexual harassment.

2. **Calcification** refers to the normalization of particular individual and collective performances as taken for granted in a cultural system. Standardized policies have become ubiquitous across organizations, meaning that these policies are now considered normal and taken for granted.

3. **Ossification** refers to the normalization of certain individual and collective performances as unquestionable in a cultural and/or global system.

> Standardized sexual harassment policies are now found in organizations globally, despite the reality that sexual harassment is defined and enacted differently in different cultural milieus.

Through these hardening processes, we can see how human performances that are used to construct a particular cultural reality come to be seen as universal and morally correct. Although communication as enactment shows us how words do things, it does not address the complex question of what all this means.

Communication as Meaning Making

Communication is information. Communication is also message production. Communication is enacted. But none of these forms of communication is adequate to solving important organizational problems. It is also important to consider the ways in which communication is the creation of meaning. As one of my cleverer training participants once quipped, "What does meaning even mean?" Great question. There are multiple definitions, the most common being *the expression or representation of words or conversational exchanges.* What is fascinating about this definition is that words can mean different things to different people, depending on a number of factors, including the context within which the conversation occurs, the culture through which the conversation is spoken, the larger discourses that people draw on to understand their world, and the personal experiences of the individuals engaging in the interaction. These differences represent **language convergence/meaning divergence (LC/MD)**. We use the same words, but they often mean something different to different people. Often people are unable to agree on what sexual harassment means (Dougherty et al., 2009). A second common definition of meaning is *the importance or value that is produced through our interactions with our social world.* Meaning is not just cognitive or intellectual. It is also entwined with values and emotions. In short, **meaning** is how we come to know our social world, what is important in that social world, our place in that world, and how to interact within it.

"What does meaning even mean?"

The idea of communication as meaning making can be traced back to Peter Berger and Thomas Luckmann's (1966) notion of social constructionism. The basic idea of this theory is that we communicate in interaction with our physical world. That interaction creates a meaningful social world. That social world provides guidance for how to behave and interact with other people. Berger and Luckmann use childhood socialization in a family to illustrate the process through which we are taught to interact with others, creating a shared sense of what it means to be part of our families. Social constructionism has been an important undergirding for many of the theories that help us understand communication in our social world, such as sensemaking (Weick, 1995) and organizational culture (Pacanowsky & O'Donnell-Trujillo, 1982). I will discuss these theories later in this book. For now, there are two important considerations.

First, meaning making is not something people do by themselves. Instead, meaning making is accomplished with other people. For example, when I have done research in organizations, one of my persistent observations is that people talk differently in groups than they do in individual interviews. As one woman proclaimed, the group interaction helped her "figure stuff out" that she had not thought of on her own. When I asked a man about his sexually graphic group discussion about women colleagues, he proclaimed, "That is just how guys talk when they get together." Clearly, there is a difference between how people think about a concept when they are alone and how they make a concept meaningful during interactions with others. Specifically, sexual harassment and other important social problems are produced through communication between multiple people. More significantly, people communicating together make meaning of their organization. These meanings provide the foundation and the fuel for organizational cultures. In turn, organizational cultures power predatory sexual harassment. For that reason, it is necessary to understand communication as meaning making when considering culturally embedded problems.

Meaning making is not something people do by themselves. Instead, meaning making is accomplished with other people.

Second, meaning making is the primary means through which organizations learn and evolve. Meaning making is an important way through which organizations identify problems, learn how to address those problems, create stability, and produce change. Clearly, this type of communication is the key to resolving entrenched organizational problems, such as sexual harassment.

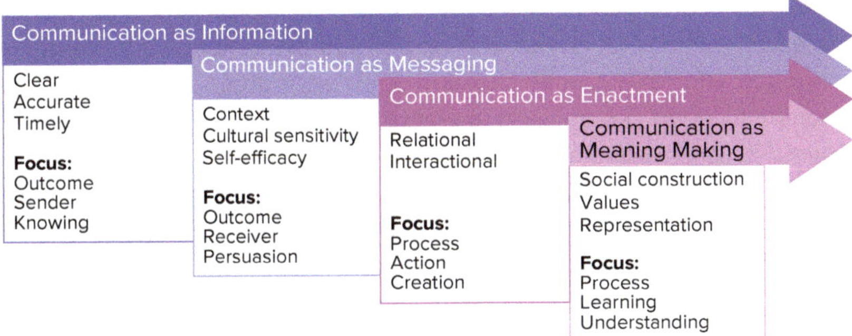

FIGURE 2.5: Communication Building Blocks

Communication Building Blocks

Instead of thinking of each formation of communication as distinctive, with some being superior to others, I personally find it more useful to think of these four forms of communication as building blocks to a holistic communication platform. (See Figure 2.5.) Communication as information and as messaging primarily focuses on *the outcome* of the communication. For both forms, communication fails when the preferred outcomes do not occur. Interestingly, communication as information primarily focuses on the sender of the information, while communication as messaging primarily focuses on the receiver of the message. In contrast, communication as enactment and as meaning making are both *process* focused. The emphasis is on the ongoing flow of communication and what it accomplishes. For communication as enactment, the end point is action—what people do in relation to their material worlds. As far as I can tell, although enactment-focused scholars occasionally mention meaning making, it is usually discussed as a natural outcome of enactment and therefore not of primary concern. In contrast, communication as meaning making focuses on the ongoing production of meaning. Here the focus is on how communication creates, recreates, rejects, and contests an ongoing and evolving array of meanings. All four of these forms of communication should be recognized as building on each other.

An example of communication building blocks can be applied to sexual harassment. Organizational members often claim that they don't know how to report sexual harassment. Providing this *information* is necessary if the organization is to use *messages* to persuade organizational members to report sexual harassment, either as the target or as the bystander. This type of change will be necessary for organizational members to *enact* their culture differently so that preferred *meanings* in the form of values and representations can be created and maintained. In this way, the organization can learn how to understand and stop predatory sexual behavior in the workplace. Ultimately, when building upon each other, these four forms of communication can be used to create shared values, create a sense of community, and weave a web for change.

I am concerned that I may have made it sound simple to use communication to solve sexual harassment in the workplace. Let me be clear. It is not simple. Although the building blocks model is helpful, it does not address many of the larger problems that drive sexual harassment in the workplace. Try it out in Think About It 2.3.

Think About It 2.3 Applying the Building Blocks Model of Communication

Do you remember Anna, the woman who was sexually harassed in front of bystanders as she prepped for surgery? During the course of a focus group interview, she had a conversation with a coworker, "Donna," about another man in the same organization who was accused of harassing a nurse. Below is an excerpt from that conversation:

> **Anna:** Another (sexual harassment case) was, I did work with a male surgical tech. If you knew him, *he was a very friendly guy. It didn't bother him a bit to give you a hug.* And there are guys that I work with that, I can walk up to them and say, "you know, I just need a hug today." And they'll give you a hug. Total friends. My husband knows them. I do it in front of my husband. It's nothing. But, this certain man, he was a, a very touchy-feely kind of person. I never took it as sexual. He knew how far he could go with anybody. That's kind of the way he was. He would feel you out—not literally. *He would check you out before and see how far you would let him go. Because he would probably go to the extreme if you would let him.* But if you wouldn't let him, he would not do it. And, I had told him before, "nope, that's where you stop. You don't mess with me that way. I'm married and I don't take that." But he was fired from an RN [Registered Nurse] who came down and worked with him and said "he's doing these things to me and they're wrong." And they brought him to the office and said "look." *He was a very good tech.* Everybody knew how he was. The manager of the department messed with him the same as everybody else did. I mean, it was just, that's how he was. And they told him, "if you deny these claims, we can't fire you because you're saying it didn't happen, she's saying it did, so we have to get into it." And he said "well, it did happen. It did happen. I'm not going to deny it because it did happen. But I didn't think I was doing anything wrong." So

he was fired because he didn't deny it. *I didn't think that was right.* Um, I don't know what you guys feel about that, but.

Donna: I think firing is probably inappropriate. If he felt he wasn't doing something wrong, that's probably more of a counseling issue. Obviously, he read the person wrong. Or maybe he's got some boundary problems to begin with that need to be addressed.

Anna: I totally agree. And that was my problem. He did have issues of his own. His wife works here. I mean, *he was married.* I don't know, it was kind of an all-around bad situation. I don't think he should have been fired.

Donna: I think people kind of get really, *because sexual harassment is kind of the hot button thing* right now, I think there are people who are going to call things sexual harassment that maybe aren't.

Anna: Mmhm.

What fascinates me about this excerpt is that this male coworker and the male coworker who targeted Anna are described in relatively similar language, yet the preferred outcome for these two individuals is very different.

Discussion Questions

1. What is the information, the message, the enactment, and the meaning Anna and Donna are sharing/creating in this excerpt?
2. How does each form of communication serve as a building block for the next?
3. What information, message, enactment, and meaning making would you share with Anna and Donna if you were the internal organizational communication officer?
4. What challenges would you face as you communicate?

I suspect that you found the challenge in Think About It 2.3 difficult, primarily because you do not know the context or culture of this organization. Organizations are a mush pot of rules, policies, trainings, habits, norms, rituals, and so on. Trying to engage with just two people who are encased in this organizational milieu feels pointless when faced with the larger problem of the organization. Clearly the process of managing sexual harassment is far more complicated than the building blocks model of communication implies. The problem is that the model does not account for the interwoven nature of communication and organization. It is therefore necessary to understand the interplay between communication and organization.

Unfortunately, most organizational members have an outdated and unhelpful understanding of what organization means and how we communicate in the organization. This old style of thinking about communication and the organization inhibits the management of many important organizational problems. In the next section, I will walk you through different generations of thought regarding what constitutes an organization and how we communicate.

What Is Organizational Communication?

Most chief communication officers in organizations are trained in external organizational communication, better known as public relations or strategic communication. These people are trained in how to communicate with external publics. While this role is absolutely important, the skills necessary for a public relations specialist are not the same skills needed for an internal organizational communication specialist. In fact, I often find that I need to accomplish two challenging tasks when I begin training and consulting: First I need to train the chief communication specialist as to what constitutes internal organizational communication, and second, I need to train them in these skills while managing their disbelief that their knowledge is not adequate to the problem they are tasked with solving. As one of my clients told me, "I need you to help our 'coms' people understand organizational communication without damaging my relationship with them." That was a tall order. I am not sure that I was successful. Obviously, I am not going to be able to train public relations people to do internal organizational communication, but this section of this chapter will help the chief communication officer understand what type of skills they should be looking for when hiring their internal organizational communication officer, who will be faced with addressing entrenched organizational problems such as sexual harassment.

So what is organizational communication? The answer depends on your dominant mental model for what constitutes an organization. Depending on how you conceptualize "organization," communication could mean the simple top-down flow of information, a two-way flow of information, or communication as the core of what constitutes organizations. The following discussion has been essential in my training as I help organizational managers think in more complex ways about the role of communication in the creation of entrenched organizational problems, as well as the solutions to those problems. Essentially, there are four generations of thought as to what counts as an organization. Each generation of thought brings a new complexity to the notion of organizational communication.

TABLE 2.1: Four Generations Conceptualizing Organizational Structure

	Theory	Communication
Generation 1	**Classical theory:** Organizations are rigidly structured and hierarchical.	Top-down communication that is focused on providing information to perform a task.
Generation 2	**Human relations:** People can be motivated to work harder by helping them achieve their human needs. These theories are paternalistic, treating workers like children.	Communication is both task and social. Upward communication is encouraged, but only downward communication is given any importance when it comes to solving important problems.
Generation 3	**Human resources:** People want to work and can work for the best interest of the organization.	Hire the right people, and let them be creative.
Generation 4	**Communication constitutes organizing:** Communication creates and sustains the organization.	We create the organization through our actions. Policies, trainings, rituals, and everyday interactions interact to produce the organizational culture.

Generation 1—Classical Theory

Historically, organizations were shaped radically differently than they are today. Most organizations employed a form of forced labor, including slavery, serfdom, and apprenticeships. As the Industrial Revolution took shape, organizations began to pay their workers through a *piece rate system*, where the organization paid employees by the items produced, rather than the hours worked. This system was notoriously uneven in terms of both production and employee pay. Into this organizational stew came a new form of organizing that was supposed to even out the workflow, and in theory, was supposed to be more humane than previous forms of organization. What is now known as classical theory was based on some common principles. Classical theory was founded on what was possibly the most successful organizational structure of its time—the Catholic Church. The Catholic Church is rigidly hierarchical, with the Pope at the top and congregants at the bottom. In addition, church leaders were selected based on God-given talents to lead their less able and less skilled congregants, who are called flocks, metaphorically comparing the individual members to sheep who need to be tended. Similarly, classical theorists argued that workplace organizations needed to be rigidly hierarchical, with those better suited to management placed higher up the hierarchy and those better suited to physical labor placed at the bottom.

In classical organizations, communication is top down. Leaders tell the workers what to do. Workers then unquestioningly do what they are told. Upward communication is discouraged. After all, the thinking went, workers are not very bright, so there would be no purpose in listening to workers speak. Not only is communication downward, but it is focused exclusively on tasks. For classical theorists, the very idea of sexual harassment or other unauthorized behavior is unthinkable—its existence does not fit into the neatly sanitized vision of classical organizing. When management does acknowledge sexual harassment as a problem, their communication would be top down and directive—"Stay focused on your work. Do not talk to your coworkers. Do not sexually harass your coworkers." You might be surprised by the number of organizations that base their response to sexual harassment on classical assumptions of organizing. This simplistic response to a complex problem provides some clues as to why and how sexual harassment persists in these organizations.

Generation 2—Human Relations Theory

In 1920, the Western Electric Company's Hawthorne plant managers hired a group of researchers to conduct something called a *time and motion* study, a classical management technique designed to create the most employee output using the least effort by employees. As part of this study, they wanted to see what level of light would be conducive to creating the most output. What they discovered is that any variation in light when observers were present, with the exception of near darkness, resulted in higher employee productivity. Interestingly, instead of concluding that workers need constant surveillance to work hard (consistent with classical management theory), these researchers decided that employees thrive when given attention. After all, they concluded, everyone needs to be affirmed as worthy contributors. A number of other studies were then conducted at the Hawthorne Plant that the researchers used as the foundation for the human relations movement (Mayo, 1949). Although the movement was based on flawed analysis, human relations became the dominant way of thinking about organizations. There are two important innovations in this movement. First, human relations theorists were the first to recognize the presence of an informal organization. Specifically, these researchers recognized that there is both a formal organization that is best controlled through classical management techniques, and that there is an informal organization in which people do things that are not organizationally sanctioned.

A second innovation of human relations theorizing is the recognition that people need to feel important. Abraham Maslow's (1943) hierarchy of needs is an example of this type of theorizing. According to Maslow, once people's basic needs—such as food and shelter—have been met, then they begin to need to be part of a bigger group, ultimately feeling like an important part of that group. Employee suggestion boxes were a popular way of helping employees feel important by asking for their input on organizational issues. However, that input was rarely taken seriously by leaders. From a human relations perspective, the value was in allowing employees to provide input. There was little value in actually using that input (Think About It 2.4). In some ways, employees in human relations organizations are treated as childlike, with managers filling the parental role.

Think About It 2.4 Suggestion Boxes

Some years ago, when my oldest child was in grade school, I noticed a "suggestion box" attached to a pole outside of the school. I asked the new principal about the box and what type of suggestions they received. She said, "I did not even realize that we had a suggestion box." We went out together and she pried open the box. Inside were suggestions with dates going back more than 10 years. It was the giving of suggestions that was important. These suggestions were not typically taken seriously.

Discussion Questions

1. How do suggestion boxes illustrate the human relations movement?
2. In your opinion, what were these organizations missing in their treatment of employees?

Although communication in human relations organizations is both task and social, and upward communication is encouraged, only downward communication is given any importance when it comes to solving important problems. Human relations communication about sexual harassment would provide information through policies and training. Messages would focus on making organizational members feel like they are important. For example: "Every member of Organization X is valuable. For this reason, we need to treat each other with respect. If you see sexual harassment, you must report it." You don't have to look very far to find an example of this type of sexual harassment response. This is how most organizations communicate about sexual harassment. While more sophisticated than classical management responses, the human relations responses to sexual harassment are primarily top down and fail to recognize the complexity of communication and organizations.

Generation 3—Human Resources Approach

The human resources approach emerged over a period of time as leaders and researchers recognized the limitations of the human relations approach to organizations. Human resource advocates recognized that employees can be active and mostly intelligent agents in the organization. The idea is that if you hire people with the right skills and psychological capacity, they can contribute to the organization in important and unique ways. The two keys to the human relations perspective are skills and personality. An employee obviously needs basic skills required to do a job. However, those skills, according to the human resources approach, will be dependent on personality traits. Because employees with the right combination of skills and personality are viewed as willing resources for the organization, many organizations have undertaken an organizational restructuring that either flattens the organization by eliminating layers of management or moved toward team-driven organizing that reshapes the organization in less hierarchical ways. Like most organizational change (Deline, 2019), restructuring around human resource principles is met with widespread resistance (Larson & Tompkins, 2005). J. Barker (1993) argued that employees are so well trained to traditional hierarchical organizations, that when given the opportunity to organize differently, there is a tendency to revert back to traditional bureaucratic structures.

Communication in the human resources organization is multidirectional and is both task and social focused. My experience with human resource organizations coping with sexual harassment is that management focuses on policy, training, and hiring people with personalities that make them less prone to sexual harassment. There are, of course, some psychological measurements that can be used to sift through potential employees to find those who are not prone to harassment (Bingham & Burlseson, 1996). However, there are problems with these measurements that make them ultimately ineffective as hiring tools. First, the assumption that sexual harassment is a personality problem is highly problematic in organizations, especially since, as discussed in Chapter 1 of this book, research has repeatedly confirmed that organizational climate and culture are the primary propagators of sexual harassment. Second, it is unlikely that people will admit to personality quirks such as misogyny when applying for jobs, making the results of these measurements less accurate than would be desired. I could be wrong, of course, but I doubt it.

> In organizations, research repeatedly demonstrates that sexual harassment is not a personality problem. It is a product of an organizational culture.

Generation 4—Communication Constitutes Organizing (CCO)

Recently there has been a revisioning of organizations. Instead of viewing communication as something that happens *in* organizations, we now view organizations *as* communication. From the CCO perspective, we don't just work *in* an organization. We *ARE* the organization. Instead of thinking of organizations as things, and stuff, it is critical to shift your thinking to organizations as people communicating. You will find it helpful at this point in the chapter to do the activity in Think About It 2.5.

Think About It 2.5 Short Video on Communication Constitutes Organizing

At this point, I would like you to take a minute to watch Matt Koschmann's (2012) YouTube video describing CCO. The video is not only informative, but also creative and interesting. Here is the link:

https://www.youtube.com/watch?v=e5oXygLGMuY

Well, go on, watch it.

Did you watch it? Good job.

Discussion Questions

1. What is CCO?
2. How is it different from other ways of thinking about organizations?
3. From a CCO perspective, what is communication?
4. How can a CCO perspective help us think differently about sexual harassment?

The CCO perspective can roughly be divided into two different orientations toward communication. CCO that assumes *communication as enactment* represents the more popular orientation (Schoeneborn et al., 2014). CCO that centers *communication as meaning making* is less well understood, but is the core focus of my own work.

CCO as Enactment

The best known CCO theorizing centers on communication as enactment. This perspective has a clear lineage to speech act theorizing (Taylor, 2006), and focuses on how interactions create and recreate the organization. To illustrate, I discuss the Montreal School of CCO because I have found it particularly instructive in my own thinking about how sexual harassment happens in organizations.

At its core, the Montreal School CCO is about how organizations are communicatively developed from idea to institution. A central feature of this theory is **co-orientation**, or the ways that people and objects are "caught up in ongoing interactions" (Taylor, 2006, p. 150). Here is how it works. It begins with a conversation—people talk. Two or more people get together and engage in conversation to communicate an idea. *Text* represents the ways in which that conversation is converted into some form, usually a written form. At its most basic level, conversation converted to text would look something like this, based on a real conversation:

> **Myke:** I have a great idea for a nonprofit. What if we made a school for kids whose parents can't afford a quality preschool? We would make sure they have quality food and a learning space that is built on their developmental needs.
>
> **Debbie:** Myke, I love it! Can you send me an email outlining your idea? I have a class full of students who could develop this idea for their senior project.
>
> **Myke:** Sure thing. [Myke spends 24 hours writing down his idea and then sends it to Debbie.]

In this example, Myke and Debbie have a conversation. That conversation is then converted into a text. In CCO, text is then converted back to conversation. In this case, Debbie had her students read Myke's email. She then engaged in a conversation with her class about what Myke's nonprofit would look like. This conversation/text/conversation exchange illustrates distanciation and scaling up. In **distanciation**, the original conversation becomes distant from its source. Take a sexual harassment policy as an example. Originally, some person said, "We probably need a sexual harassment policy." Someone else said, "Good idea. Let's write a policy and send it to Manager X." Manager X read the policy, maybe made changes, and sent it to Manager Y, who presented it at a meeting. The CEO at the meeting likely formed a committee, that again edited the policy. The policy is then sent out with an email saying, "Here is the organization's sexual harassment policy." By this point, no one remembers the name of the person who created the policy. In fact, over time, it will seem as if the policy has always existed and it is simply a part of the organization and how it operates. In distanciation, the idea has become distanced from its originator and now belongs to the organization.

Scaling up describes the way that an organization moves from conversation between two people to an institution involving many people. Scaling up demonstrates the ways in which organizations form, starting with conversation and moving to a textualized institution through the process of distanciation. Eventually, the origination of the organization is forgotten through the scaling up process, to the point that the organization seems naturally occurring. To illustrate, the preschool organization that Myke and Debbie created started with a conversation, was scaled up into an organization, was scaled up to involve a board, and so on. Through distanciation, Myke and Debbie moved on, and their role in forming the organization was soon forgotten as both the vision and mission of the organization became distanced from the originators. Interestingly, the very strengths of CCO also form the core of its limitations. Specifically, it was designed to understand organizing as enactment. There is no pathway for understanding organizing as a meaning-making activity.

Matthew A. Koschmann (2013) published an excellent study illustrating the co-orientation, distanciation, and scaling up processes. I strongly recommend that you read it.

CCO as Meaning Making

In this book, I make the case for understanding CCO from an enacted meaning-making perspective, which I refer to as *meaning-CCO*. Here I join a less well-known group of CCO theorists who are committed to the idea that organizations can best be understood as networks of meanings. Essentially, from a ***CCO networks of meaning perspective***, organizations do not exist outside of our communication.

Instead, they are constituted, or created, through coordinated meaning making that occurs over time.

To give a sense of what meaning-CCO might look like, let's consider how sexual harassment becomes woven into the fabric of the organizational culture. As an organization develops, so does the communication that either encourages or discourages predatory sexual behavior. I can think of at least three ways in which sexual harassment can develop within an organization. First is the *predatory founder*, in which the founder of the organization engages in predatory sexual behavior. Think Harvey Weinstein and the Weinstein Corporation. This is a guy who carefully and deliberately preyed on women who were trying to get into the movie business. This predatory behavior was then scaled up with the rest of the organization. Second, *misogynistic beliefs and values* can be built into the organization such that people who perpetrate sexual harassment are hired and promoted over more qualified leaders. Take Uber for example. This organization was built on the odd ideal of "bro culture" and valued hiring "bros" over more qualified applicants. This bro culture is weird, yet continues to emerge as an important form of homonormative masculinity. Third is the *cultural embedding of sexual harassment through neglect*, in which sexual harassment and other socially problematic behaviors are ignored and therefore allowed to worm their way into the organization, very similar to the ways in which weeds emerge in my garden every year, shaping the outcome in unintentional but meaningful ways. Essentially, in the startup phase, organizations fail to consider what it wants to value and to implement the behaviors that would scale up those values over time. Sexual harassment becomes problematic because the organization failed to prevent it from becoming a problem. Regardless of the way in which sexual harassment becomes woven into the culture of an organization, the ideal time to prevent sexual harassment is during the startup phase.

One of my friend's teenage sons wanted to cancel a date with a woman to hang out with a group of male friends. When his father questioned him about it, the son said, "You know, Dad, bros before hos." This young man's mother turned to him and said, "So who counts as a ho? Am I a ho?"

"No, I did not mean you."

"How about your sister? Is she a ho?"

"It is just a saying, Mom. It does not mean anything."

"Yes it does mean something. It means everything any woman needs to know about who you are and what you value."

Meaning-CCO closely ties meaningful communication and organization together, suggesting that they are inseparable. You cannot have an organization without enacting meaningful communication. The failure to recognize this reality means that many organizations simultaneously fail to manage the communication that produces their organization. Think about the implications of this perspective for understanding and solving organizational problems. Instead of thinking of sexual harassment as something that individuals do in the organization, meaning-CCO suggests that sexual harassment becomes woven into the very fabric of the organization through patterned behaviors that produce and reproduce organizational meanings of predatory sexual behavior. This type of thinking represents a profound shift in how we think about, and how we resolve, predatory sexual behavior.

Recap and Looking Forward

In this chapter, I provided a model of communication as information, messaging, enactment, and meaning making. I suggested ways in which communication is treated in organizations. I then proposed meaning-CCO as a way to understand the relationship between enactment and meaning making in creating an organization in which sexual harassment is a meaningful part of the organization.

For organizational members wishing to understand how problems become entrenched in organizations, a meaning-CCO perspective provides the most useful mental model. However, the real question is, once the problems become patterned parts of the organization, with the weight of habit and meaning over time, how do we change those patterns in productive ways? The great news is that, with the right mental models and a lot of effort, those patterns that form the basis of organizational problems can be changed. The unfortunate news is that, when problems have become woven into an organizational culture, there is no quick and easy solution. It will take a large amount of smart and dedicated hard work. The next chapter introduces organizational culture, the perspective that I use to help my clients manage predatory sexual behavior.

Chapter 3

Organizational Culture

By the end of this chapter you should be able to do the following:

1. Recognize major theories of organizational culture, including the strengths and limitations of each.
2. Understand the myths and legends about organizational culture.
3. Conceptualize organizational culture as a complex communication process.

When I get a call from a new client, they are reaching out to me because they have come to recognize that sexual harassment is a cultural phenomenon. One of the first questions I ask them is, "What does organizational culture mean to you?" I get a variety of responses:

> Organizational culture is created through policy.
>
> Organizational culture is directed by management.
>
> We don't have an organizational culture.
>
> We need a survey so we can change our culture.
>
> We have a strong culture.
>
> We have a weak culture.

> Organizational culture is imposed by the national culture.
>
> I don't know.

What strikes me as most interesting about these responses is that these people understand that their cultures are problematic, but they have a limited idea as to what constitutes organizational culture. I don't blame them. The academic and practitioner guidance on this issue is scattered. Some theorizing suggests that organizational culture is a managerial tool that can be easily manipulated, while in contrast, other perspectives view culture as fixed and unchanging (Alvesson, 2002). In reality, organizational cultures cannot be easily placed in binary categories of change/no change. As I tell my clients, organizational cultures are resistant to change, but they can evolve over time. As such, managing culture is more like a marathon than a sprint. I define **organizational culture** as the shared communicative process through which meanings are constantly employed, negotiated, and contested to create a stable communication environment within which organizational life becomes patterned and persistent over time. Organizational cultures are always power laden and are functional for the reproduction of organizational values and outcomes. I will discuss this definition in more detail in the next chapter, but understand that organizational cultures are not things. They are processes that are constantly being reproduced.

Organizational cultures are not "things." They are processes that are constantly being reproduced.

In this chapter, I'll take you on the journey that I went through as I developed my definition and my model of organizational culture, both of which appear more prominently in the next chapter. To begin, let's discuss three prominent organizational culture theories, followed by a discussion of the myths and legends that surround organizational culture.

Three Theories of Organizational Culture

Learning is a journey. Knowledge does not just appear. It is cultivated overtime. For me, the journey I went through in developing my model of organizational culture began many years ago, when I first read Edger Schein's theorizing on this topic. His work was exciting, and yet imperfect. Later I read Joanne Martin's theorizing on the three ways in which organizational cultures are conceptualized. Her work helped me to think more broadly about organizational culture and how it operates. Finally, I read Joanne Keyton's book on communication and culture. The theorizing in her book helped me envision the ways in which communication is central to organizational culture. The combination of these theories, my own research on organizational culture, and the applied work I have been doing for the last number of years are the muse upon which I have developed my work. Each of these theories will be helpful as you think in increasingly complex ways about the relationship between organizational culture and organizational problems.

Edgar Schein's Model of Organizational Culture

Schein's model of culture played a pivotal role in my early consulting and research activities. While I have moved toward a more communication-based model of culture, I owe a debt of gratitude (as do all organizational culture scholars) to the innovative early work done by Schein.

Schein defines organizational culture as

> the accumulated shared learning of [a] group as it solves its problems of external adaptation and internal integration; which has worked well enough to be considered valid and, therefore to be taught to new members as the correct way to perceive, think, feel, and behave in relation to those problems. This accumulated learning is a pattern or system of beliefs, values, and behavioral norms that come to be taken for granted as basic assumptions and eventually drop out of awareness. (Schein & Schein, 2017, p. 35)

This definition translates into Schein's three-layered model of organizational culture. Although his model is often presented as an onion, Schein frames his model as a pyramid, often known as the iceberg model of organizational culture (Figure 3.1). As you can see, there are three layers: artifacts, espoused values, and basic assumptions. The term "iceberg model" came about because only the very tip of the culture—the artifacts—is visible.

Artifacts represent the layer that can be identified with the physical senses. These are the most visible components of culture and include *things and behaviors*. It is important to note that not all artifacts are culturally relevant. The challenge for a change agent is to not only identify those artifacts that are culturally relevant, but to "decipher" (Schein & Schein, 2017, p. 45) how those artifacts are culturally relevant. *Things* roughly translates to

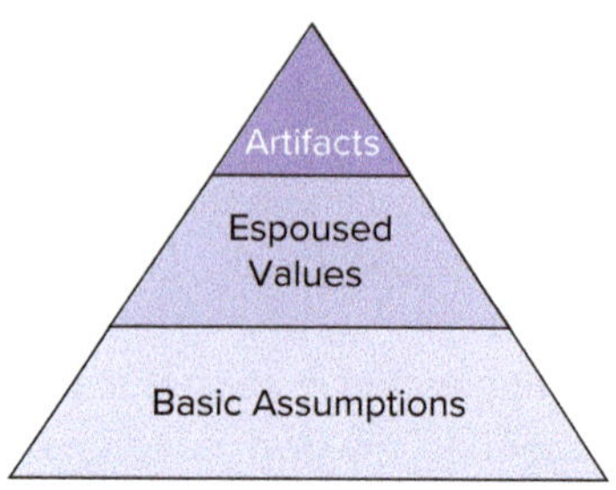

FIGURE 3.1: Schein's Model of Organizational Culture

the material items in the culture. In terms of sexual harassment, examples of things would be policies and sexually suggestive pictures. Behaviors includes the activities in which people are engaged. In terms of sexual harassment, examples include sexually suggestive behavior, hiring rituals and practices, and gender norms. What fascinates me is that communication can be found in both the things (e.g., policies are communicative creations) and behaviors (sexually suggestive behavior is communicative). Although Schein is not explicit about the role of communication in his model, clearly, communication is, in fact, a central feature of cultural artifacts.

Espoused beliefs and values represent the midlevel of Schein's model of culture. This level is characterized by what organizational members believe "ought to be" (Schein & Schein, 2017, p. 47). Specifically, these are the ideals, goals, values, aspirations, and ideologies of the organization. Equally important, this is where people rationalize their actions, although, as Schein notes, espoused values are not always consistent with the cultural artifacts. I admit that I struggle with this aspect of Schein's model. To me, espoused values simply represent another artifact. Espoused values are typically written artifacts that describe what the organization claims to value. That is very different from values that organizations enact. Espoused values may or may not be culturally meaningful, as discussed in Think About It 3.1.

Think About It 3.1 Espoused Values

There comes a point in my training when I ask participants to tell me the values their organization espouses. This is the tale of two organizations:

Organization 1

Debbie: Someone in this room, list your organization's values.

Trainees: [Silence]

Debbie: How about one value?

Trainee A: Do we have values?

Trainee B: We do have values. [Reaches into her back pocket and pulls out a small slip of paper.] These are the ones I was given. [Proceeds to read the values off the card.]

Trainee C: Where did you get the card?

Trainee B: They gave it to me years ago during orientation.

Trainee E: Those values don't even make sense for who we are.

Organization 2

Debbie: What are this organization's values?

Trainees: [Hands shoot up. Debbie points to each in turn.]

Trainee A: Have fun.

Trainee B: Work hard.

Trainee C: Ownership mentality.

[Trainees continue to list values until list is complete.]

Debbie: How do you know these values are important to your organization?

Trainee A: We are trained on the values by the founder.

Trainee B: There are posters everywhere.

Trainee C: We have picnics and contests.

[Trainees continue with list.]

Discussion Questions

1. How can we tell when espoused values are culturally relevant artifacts?
2. Which organization's values will be more useful to a cultural change agent? Why do you say that?
3. What role do espoused values play in organizational culture?

The inner level of Schein's model of culture is called **basic assumptions**. According to Schein's most recent work on this topic (Schein & Schein, 2017), basic assumptions are composed of beliefs, values, and attitudes that have become hardened and unquestioned over time. Schein envisions these assumptions as formed during the initial startup phase of the organization and as relatively fixed and unchanging. One example Schein offers is that it is unthinkable for those organizations formed under assumptions of capitalism to structure themselves so that they do not make a profit. In terms of sexual harassment, for many organizations, sexual aggression is so frequent and expected that when you call it out, organizational members are surprised and offended, excusing their behavior with language such as, "can't take a joke," "victim complex," "this is just who we are," and even "those people just don't get us." Predatory sexual behavior becomes a deeply held assumption that is highly resistant to change. Schein's model would suggest that cultural assumptions are impervious to change. However, with all due respect to Schein, I believe that belief is more a limitation of his model of culture. Specifically, his model fails to address the power of communication to construct and reconstruct our organizational worlds.

Schein's model fails to address the power of communication to construct and reconstruct our social world.

As I said at the beginning of this section, I used to use Schein's model to anchor my training. However, as hinted at earlier, there are problems that I faced as a communication expert and organizational problem solver that this model cannot resolve. For example, how is communication embedded in this model? Schein and colleagues treat communication as an artifact, but it is not at all clear how communication functions at the other two levels. Further, the model focuses on espoused values, but how are values enacted within organizational cultures? For example, one common espoused value is respect. However, when predatory sexual harassment is woven into the culture, is respect really a value? If so, how is it enacted so that it supports the predatory behavior? Finally, how can this model help organizational managers understand how to communicate differently to produce different cultural outcomes? After yet another trainee asked, "How do I use this model?" I began the search for a model that better fit my clients' needs. In my search, I turned next to Martin's three forms of organizational culture.

Joanne Martin's Three Perspectives of Organizational Culture

Martin views organizational cultures as the meanings derived from different symbolic processes, such as rituals, stories, and jargon, all of which are forms of communication. Although she views meaning as *cognitive*, something that is held by an individual, rather than as *communicative*, something that is created between individuals, her focus on meaning moves our understanding of cultures toward a more dynamic system, honoring the central role communication plays in the production of organizational culture.

Martin argues that much of the theorizing on organizational culture is overly simplistic, failing to capture the complexity that comprises these cultures. As a result, many early models of culture created an overly enthusiastic expectation that using specific, well-defined processes would create strong cultures that would function better. What a disappointment that perspective turned out to be for organizations looking to be better versions of themselves. How does this simplistic approach play out in research? Martin demonstrates that researchers conceptualize organizational culture in three ways: integration, differentiation, or fragmentation. The problem, she explains, is that taken alone, each of the perspectives oversimplifies organizational culture. To address this issue, she advocates combining the three perspectives to create a more complex and useful understanding of organizational culture. I describe each of these perspectives next.

Early models of organization were overly simplistic, overpromised positive outcomes, and were a disappointment to organizations.

Integration studies assume that organizational culture is shared. If it is not shared, then it is not culture. Focusing only on the basic assumption component of Schein's model, Martin makes a case for Schein as advocating an integration position. Reading Schein's entire book, I do believe that this is a reductionist take on his argument, but does at least partially capture the nature of his theorizing.

Differentiation studies explore the ways in which subcultures engage differently with organizational cultures. My own research with Maria Dixon illustrates this approach (Dixon & Dougherty, 2010). We discovered that there were two important subcultures in the Residential

Life Department of Rural University, what we called First Borns and Youngests. These subcultures emerged based on the participants' tenure in the organization. Those who had helped form the department had a distinctive "First Born" subculture, while those who came later formed the "Youngest" subculture. While I still really like this study, I acknowledge that it may oversimplify the organizational members' adherence to their subcultural group. I have often wondered how these groups also experienced internal fragmentation.

Fragmentation studies focus on the ambiguities in the culture. This body of research tends to explore the ways in which organizational members have varying and ambiguous meaning systems that make it hard to see and understand culture. In this way, organizational culture is messy, contested, and maybe even transitory. My work on language convergence/meaning divergence provides a useful example of culture, language, and ambiguity (Dougherty et al., 2009). My colleague Michael Kramer and I had been discussing how difficult it was to distinguish between how people talk about sexual harassment and flirting, so we decided to conduct an interview study to see how people defined these two terms. We discovered that, although people used the same words, their meanings for these words varied wildly. Take, for example, excerpts from two women participants who were providing examples of flirting (Think About It 3.2).

Think About It 3.2 Diverging Meanings of Flirting

Flirting Example 1

Zelda:* Well, a friend of mine who doesn't have children was at our house watching *Blues Clues* one day. And she'd never seen it. And she said, "I understand why the kids like this show so much." She said, "He's flirting with them." In a, but that was kind of, in a teasing sort of way. There was nothing inappropriate about it. But it was that kind of back and forth.

Interviewer: Between the character on TV and the people watching?

Zelda: Yeah, you know, there are some aspects of it that can be interactive. You know, and he would say something like, um, uh, "Oh, I'm going to play, uh, that game with the ball and you know, uh, you shoot it through something, and uh, there's a net on it. What do you call that? Oh, right, basketball. You are so smart." You know, that kind of, you know, I mean it's kind of a teasing aspect to it, but like she said, "He's flirting."

* All names are pseudonyms.

Flirting Example 2:

Dierdre: It was a wonderful place to work. They had, just, they did so much for their employees. But they, you know, they had ice cream every Wednesday in the summer, they had bagels and doughnuts every Tuesday and Thursdays. You know, they had huge parties all the time and, you know, just showered you with things.

Interviewer: Wow.

Dierdre: And um, just, almost made it a situation where it was too good to ever leave. Paid real well. You know, real flexible with hours. Good vacation.

Interviewer: Well, tell me the flirting story.

Dierdre: It was just a constant. You know, the men were always just making inappropriate comments to the girls. Um, we had one manager in particular ... his sales name was Cloud. Huge um, I don't know maybe a 350-pound Black guy.[†] He was a very, he was an intimidating kind of guy and definitely used that to his power. There was an incident where we were all out at a, it wasn't at work, but it was a work function. ... And he um, you know came up and grabbed my butt and said, "have you ever had chocolate love?"

Interviewer: You're kidding me.

Dierdre: No no. I said "no." He goes, "well, do you want some?" kind of thing.

Interviewer: Wow, and he was your boss?

Dierdre: Yeah. Directly reported to him.

Interviewer: Wow. Tell me, you tell me this as a flirting story. Tell me what makes this flirting. Why do you recount this as a flirting story?

Dierdre: Um, well, just cause the, the actions were more sexual harassment. But the flirting was just their everyday. That's how they talked to you. That's how they did it.

Interviewer: So, they just flirted constantly?

Dierdre: Constantly. It was constant. And if you ever gave them any attitude back, it was a sales organization. So it was competitive. It was commission based. And so every time, you know, you, you know, if anyone talked back or if anyone didn't like it they were punished for it, and they [male managers] didn't give them the good accounts. And those girls, I mean, everyone left.

---

† Although Cloud was a Black man, Black men are no more likely to perpetrate sexual harassment than men from any other race. It is important to state this here due to the stereotypes and stigmas surrounding Blackness in the workplace.

Discussion Questions

1. What were the key differences in how each woman defined flirting?
2. What are the similarities between these women's definitions of flirting?
3. What role does sexuality play in each example?
4. How is power enacted in each example?
5. Write a script of what you imagine a conversation between these two women would sound like.

The definitions of flirting used by the participants in this study varied widely. For some, flirting was a nonsexual way of engaging with children. For others, graphic and disturbing sexual behavior was labeled as flirting because it occurred frequently. In all likelihood, if these folks had a conversation about sexual harassment, they would likely think they agree, when in actuality, they do not. This is called the **illusion of agreement**. Consistent with Martin's notion of culture as fragmented, the language of flirting and sexual harassment can create the illusion of an integrated culture, when in fact, the meanings circulating in the culture may be fragmented.

Which of these is a superior way of thinking about organizational culture? Is it integrated such that all members share the same culture? Is it differentiated between different subcultures? Is it fragmented and ambiguous? The answer is yes. Organizational culture is *all these things*. There is a core set of shared meanings that are remarkably resistant to change. There are subcultures that both challenge and reinforce the dominant organizational meanings. Finally, organizational culture is ambiguous and fragmented and messy. Martin argues that the best work will utilize a multiperspective approach that accounts for all three of these cultural perspectives.

Organizational culture is integrated, differentiated, and fragmented, all at the same time!

Despite the genius of Martin's work, I still struggle to use her theorizing to help organizations solve their cultural problems. There are at least two reasons for this limitation. First, Martin's work is designed for researchers. It is not designed to help organizations solve problems. No surprise, then, that it does not do that work. Second, although Martin hints at the relationship between organizational culture and communication, her cognitive focus limits her theorizing on this relationship. Recall that the fourth form of communication identified in Chapter 2 is the creation of meaning, so from my perspective, culture at its most fundamental level should be understood as intertwined with communication. However, Martin views meaning as cognitive, rather than as communicative. In other words, she conceptualizes meaning as something that happens *within* people rather than as something that happens *between* people. This limits our ability to understand culture as something that people do together.

Joann Keyton: Culture as Communication

Communication scholar Joann Keyton (2011) utilizes the previous two scholars' work to move the study of organizational culture to a new and powerful plane. She uses Schein's notion of artifacts, values, and assumptions to ground her project. One notable difference is that she exchanges the language of "espoused values" with "values," addressing one of the most important limitations of Schein's work. Keyton's greatest innovation is recognizing that organizational culture is a communication phenomenon. Specifically, she explains that communication creates, sustains, and evolves culture over time. Using a communication constitutes organizing (CCO) perspective, she demonstrates that organizations are constituted through patterned communication. As a result, organizational culture is both the process and product of communication. Other scholars have also utilized a CCO perspective of organizational culture (Pacanowsky & O'Donnell-Trujillo, 1982), which Keyton uses to develop her own theoretical terrain.

Keyton (2011) identifies five characteristics that are linked to organizational culture. First, organizational cultures are

1. **"Inextricably linked to organizational members"** (p. 35). This means that all organizational members, not just leaders or managers, create and sustain organizational culture. Even new members learn how to recreate culture from other organizational members.
2. **Dynamic, not static.** The great irony is that one reason organizational culture is so resistant to change is because it is in constant motion, with different configurations of communication forming and reforming to regulate and maintain the culture. The good news, however, is that this dynamic quality also means that organizational cultures can be carefully managed to evolve over time.

3. **Composed of competing values and assumptions.** Think of an overlapping Venn diagram with different values in each circle (Figure 3.2). Although the culture is not fully coherent, there is a great deal of overlap that creates a sense of coherence among organizational members.

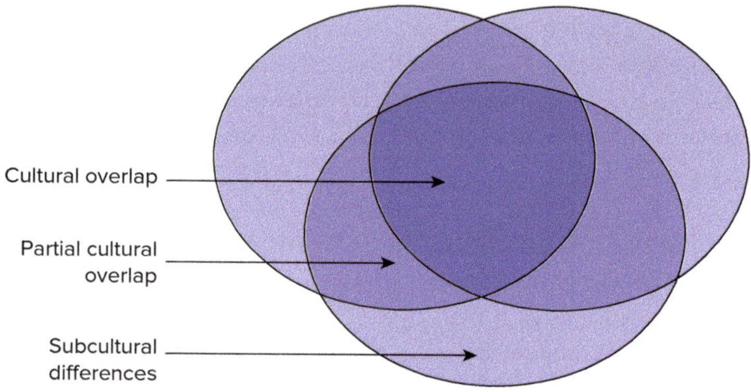

FIGURE 3.2: Organizational Cultures as Both Different and Coherent

4. **Emotionally charged.** Many people believe that good businesses are not emotional. Instead, we like to think of them as clinically rational. My own research (Dougherty & Drumheller, 2006) demonstrates the lengths people will go to claim that they are not emotional at work, even when telling a story about a strong emotion they experienced at work. Yet organizational culture is saturated with emotions. Culture tells us who gets to experience what emotions, when, and for what reasons. These emotion rules (Kramer & Hess, 2002) governing organizational culture are part of the reason why sexual harassment is so hard to report in a way that will trigger action by managers. Consider Think About It 3.3.

Think About It 3.3 Emotions and Reporting Sexual Harassment

There are rules regarding how emotions can be expressed in the workplace. Given the unrealistic demand that business should be stripped of emotions, sometimes emotional events are recounted in nonemotional ways. For example, some years ago, Lyndsey Gilpin, writing for *The Atlantic* (2016), published a series of stories about sexual harassment occurring in the National Park Service. It used a specific instance of sexual harassment from one woman worker named Olivia, who worked as an intern at Death Valley National Park in Southern California. A male coworker had driven her to a housesitting job. Instead of leaving, he entered the home. The internal labels are mine.

Excerpts from The Atlantic, *December 15, 2016*

The Incident

Uncomfortable being alone with him, she said she was sleepy and feigned a yawn. He ... suddenly started tickling her. She tried to wriggle free, pushing him several times, but he grabbed her and wouldn't let go. Then, to her horror, he shoved her to the floor and pinned her down.

Olivia yelled, kicked, screamed, but his knees pushed down harder and his tight grip held her wrists above her head. Tears in her eyes, Olivia pleaded with the man. "You're hurting me," she said.

[...]

After approximately 20 minutes, Olivia's attacker allowed her to stand up. According to The Atlantic*:*

He followed, trying to kiss her and pull her on top of him. She was sure he would rape her, but eventually, after more struggle, he left. The moment the door banged shut, Olivia fell to the floor, sobbing. She walked to the bathroom and stared in the mirror, brushed her teeth harder than she ever had, as if to erase something.

The Report

[...] She went to the park's chief ranger and described the incident in detail. He jotted down notes and told her that she had a choice: She could either press charges, or let the park handle it internally.

Unaware that there was a formal complaint process, Olivia said that the park could handle it and left. Two days later, her supervisor, her alleged assailant's supervisor, and the park's chief of interpretation—another high-level employee—asked her to recount the incident for the third time. Afterward, the chief of interpretation told her they had talked to her alleged assailant. It was all just a "misunderstanding," he said, and he would not move forward with her case.

The Outcome

Ultimately, the park supervisors transferred the perpetrator to another dorm right across the parking lot. The article continued:

Days later ... Olivia's supervisor emailed the chief of interpretation to tell him another intern had concerns about the same young man. He responded: "Thanks for ... trying to keep the rumors from really taking off. I'm glad to hear (Olivia) is getting back into a better frame of mind, but I hope (she) is not creating an uncomfortable environment for (him) if it is not warranted. Something to watch out for."

Lyndsey Gilpin, "The National Park Service Has a Big Sexual Harassment Problem," *The Atlantic*.

Discussion Questions

1. Take a moment and write down word for word how you would have reported this incident if you had been Olivia.
2. What are the emotion rules you used to write this report?
3. What emotions are the managers likely to read into your report?
4. How do emotion rules likely shape the way that targets report predatory sexual behavior?

5. **Both the *foreground and the background* of organization life.** Specifically, people's patterns of meaning making reinforce organizational culture. Personally, I like a fabric or web metaphor. To me, organizational culture is woven into everyday life through communication.

The key limitation for me of Keyton's theorizing is that although she articulates organizational communication as intertwined with culture, her continued focus on artifacts, values, and assumptions limits our ability to theorize about the ways in which communication constitutes organizational culture. As a result, there is not a mental model that both practitioners and scholars can use to think about organizational culture as a pathway to solving important social problems—problems like predatory sexual behavior. Unfortunately, there are a number of myths and legends about organizational culture that serve as a barrier to creating a mental model that can address problems in organizational culture. In the next section, I address these myths and legends that surround organizational culture.

Myths and Legends About Organizational Culture

There are lots of unfortunate notions as to what constitutes organizational culture. There are some folks who believe that organizational culture is the same as organizational policy. There are some who believe that organizational culture can be easily manipulated, and others who believe organizational culture is an unchanging monolith. I want to address these myths because they get in the way of organizations trying to use culture to solve important problems. To address these issues, let us visit the mythical society of What-the-Heck, where cultural myths and legends were roughly divided into two warring factions, each led by a well-known cultural leader:

Mary Poppins and Darth Vader. Let us begin with Mary Poppins's version of organizational culture.

Dear Readers, I hope you are willing to get playful with me. It makes learning so much more interesting, don't you think?

Mary Poppins's Version of Organizational Culture

Do you remember Mary Poppins? She is best known as the nanny who saves families from working too hard. Her skill sets include using an umbrella to fly, talking to animals, defying gravity, and singing happy songs with lyrics like "Just a spoon full of sugar helps the medicine go down." Not only does she have strong opinions about the positive power of organizational culture, but she has a powerful fan club dedicated to her viewpoints. In essence, Mary Poppins believes that, with just a spoon full of **S.U.G.A.R.**, organizational culture can be shaped in very positive ways. The key points of her opinion are as follows.

Image 3.1

Organizational Culture

- **S**ets organizational norms, rules, and standards/expectations
- **U**nifies by providing a sense of shared identity
- **G**enerates a collective commitment
- **A**llows the organization to differentiate itself from other organizations
- **R**eminds employees to work harder and happier

Ms. Poppins believes with all her heart that with the right kind of positive energy, organizational culture can swoop in on an umbrella and magically save the day. This is a delightful version of organizational culture, bound to give hope for a new tomorrow to organizational leaders everywhere. Unfortunately, this vision is a bit, well, Mary Poppins for the real world. As most organizational members can attest, there is also a dark side to organizational culture. Our next cultural leader, Darth Vader, is a huge advocate for the dark side of the force and has serious points of disagreement with Ms. Poppins.

Darth Vader's Version of Organizational Culture

It is time to introduce you to Darth Vader, the evil Jedi master who was persuaded to go to the dark side. He is best known for killing underperforming employees by simply clenching his fist, destroying planets with a single laser beam, and crushing rebellions. While he does not sing, his movements are preceded with an ominous "Da Da Da, da te da, da te da." He and his minions believe that with intensive control over organizational culture, organizational members can be subdued into producing at near maximum capacity. After all, how can you create an **E.M.P.I.R.E.** without practicing exquisite control over your people? The key points of his philosophy are as follows.

Organizational culture is created and enforced through:

- **E**motional control of employees
- **M**anagerial control, with communication downward only
- **P**ower, both formal and informal, employed to prevent resistance
- **I**ndividuals are valued over the collective
- **R**igid rules and structures are utilized to enforce work process
- **E**nvironments of fear and abuse through formal punishments and informal punitive processes

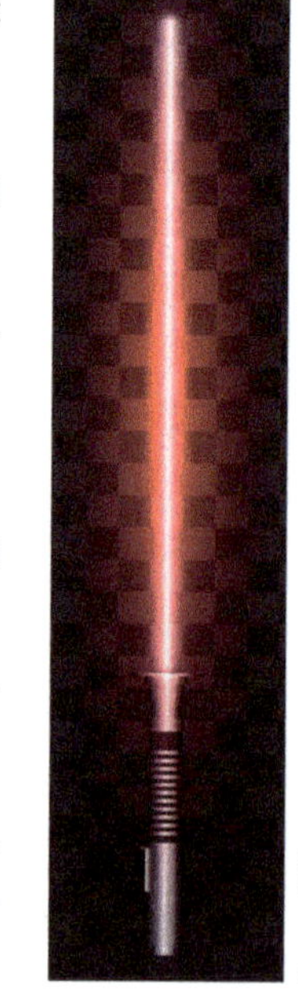
Image 3.2

Mr. Vader is a believer in the capacity of organizational culture created through tight control and punitive outcomes. He believes that fear is the primary emotion that underpins his version of culture, because after all, nothing is more fun than fear. Mr. Vader views organizational culture as a club that can be used to force employees to be productive. So what if the employees burn out? They are easily replaced.

The Battle for Organizational Culture as Good Versus Evil

Mary Poppins's fan club and Darth Vader's minions were in a big snit about what constitutes organizational culture. There was, of course, a major debate on Twitter about which version is right and which is wrong, with all kinds of meaningless name calling and, gasp, memes with pictures of cats saying horrible things. Finally, this whole thing erupted into a pitched battle at the annual academic conference of What-the-Heck. Fortunately, on the way to the conference to duke it out, Mary Poppins and Darth Vader by chance hopped into the same cab, which then became stuck in rush-hour traffic. They decided to walk to the conference. As they walked, they moved from hostile silence, to arguing about culture, to sharing personal stories and laughing about magical moments. The rest is, well, mythical history. They fell in love, got married, and had a baby called Mary Vader.

Mary Vader's Version of Organizational Culture

Mary Vader grew up learning how to create an empire with a spoon full of sugar. Although her parents often tried to bring her into their debates and outrageous verbal and magical battles (imagine the magical umbrella against the light saber!), she declined to participate. When she became a teenager, she did what all good teenagers do. She became disdainful of her parents, frequently slammed doors, and developed her own ideas about organizational culture. Using a combination of her parents' names (**Pop-Der**) for her acronym, Mary articulates the key points of her approach as follows.

Real organizational cultures are

- **P**aradoxical
- **O**rganizationally dynamic
- **P**roductive
- **D**estructive
- **E**volve over time
- **R**esistant to change

Ms. Mary Vader's complexity perspective on organizational culture is pragmatic without the moral baggage accompanying her parents' visions of organizational culture. Her perspective recognizes that organizations are not particularly rational, nor are they irrational. Instead, she recognizes that organizations are paradoxical, inhabiting competing possibilities simultaneously. Organizational cultures are neither good nor bad, right nor wrong, productive nor destructive. Instead, organizational cultures are both good and bad, right and wrong, productive and destructive. She also acknowledges that organizational cultures are resistant to change. Organizational cultures evolve over time to address organizational needs, and that carefully evolved culture does not accept change easily. However, Mary Vader argues, with some careful planning and thoughtful implementation, cultures can evolve into a better—or worse—version of themselves.

In case you were wondering, as the author of this book, I am a serious adherent of Mary Vader's perspective on organizational culture. In fact, in the next chapter I present a problem-solving model of organizational culture that is built on these ideas.

Recap and Looking Forward

It is clear that predatory sexual behavior is woven into organizational cultures. But what is organizational culture? In this chapter, I explored three important theories on organizational culture that have shaped my journey as a scholar practitioner. It is understandable why many practitioners want organizational culture to be a managerial tool that can be easily manipulated to improve certain preidentified outcomes. Wouldn't it be nifty if you could change culture by changing seating arrangements, or by creating a policy and then declaring, "There is no place for sexual harassment in Organization XYZ?" Of course, as most of your savvier organizational leaders and change agents will tell you, organizational culture is not a "thing" that can be easily manipulated. It is not a tool that managers can pick up and use, at least not in the traditional sense. Organizational culture is a process. It is complicated. It is communication in action. It is this reality that has led me to create the transformational model of organizational culture that I present in Chapter 4.

Credits

Chapter 4

Communicating Organizational Culture

A Transformational Model

By the end of this chapter you should be able to do the following:

1. Understand how problems can be hidden in organizational cultures.
2. Be able to define and conceptualize organizational culture.
3. Understand the fundamentals of the problem-solving model of organizational culture.

"If organizational cultures are so resistant to change, why even bother trying?"

So far in this book, you have discovered that predatory sexual harassment is far more complex and messy than current remediation efforts can address. You have learned that current sexual harassment management processes are overly simplistic and doomed to failure, in large part because they fail to recognize the complexity of both communication and organizational communication. You have learned that communication is not just the simple transmission of information. Communication is also the creation of messages, it is enacted, and it is the production and reproduction of meaning. You understand that organizations are not just their structures and tasks. Organizations are not just places where people communicate. Organizations ARE communication. It is at this juncture, where we come to understand that organizations are created through meaningful communication, that the value of organizational culture becomes apparent.

The training participant quoted earlier speaks to the weaknesses and limitations of previous research and training. Typically, organizational culture is assumed to be easily changed through managerial control, or it is assumed to be so fixed that it is unchangeable. Part of the problem is that, to my knowledge, there are no research-based, coherent models that can be used to help organizations manage their cultures. Later in this chapter, I present the **transformational model of organizational culture (Trans-MOC)** that I have developed to help organizations think about their cultures in more productive ways. First, however, it is important to lay the groundwork upon which that model rests.

Hidden Problems in Organizational Culture

Important organizational problems tend to be woven into an organization's culture. This is a critically important point to understand. Typically, we think of problems as a discrete thing, event, or behavior. However, taking an organizational culture perspective, we can begin to understand that the roots of organizational problems are established during everyday communication, long before they grow into a big problem. The hidden nature of organizational problems is analogous to weeds in a garden: The seeds and roots from which weeds emerge are hidden under the dirt and soil of the organization, only becoming apparent after they emerge. Another way to think about this phenomenon is through Gestalt theory, more colloquially referred to as *figure and ground* (Köhler, 1930; Wallace, 1982). **Gestalt** is a German word that means form or figure. This theory was developed to describe the ways in which people focus on the figure in images, ignoring or deemphasizing the background that shapes and frames the figure. The perceived figure becomes accented or marked and the unperceived background or landscape of the imagery becomes unmarked (Koffka, 1922). This theory continues to be used by contemporary scholars to explain how certain forms of communication are accented while others fade into the background (e.g., Dougherty et al., 2018). Consider Think About It 4.1 for an example.

Think About It 4.1 Figure and Ground

What do you see in this picture from the Pittsburg Zoo and PPG Aquarium?

FIGURE 4.1: Looking at the Ground

The first thing I saw was a tree. Upon further examination, I saw animals, specifically a gorilla and a tiger. Interesting to me, these animals are predators that are hidden among the trees. When I chatted with training participants and asked them what they saw first, one individual said that he saw fish. I said, "What fish?" He responded, "Right there. Don't you see them?"

Discussion Questions

1. What was the figure for you?
2. What did you do so you could see other parts of the picture?
3. What was hidden in the background?
4. Why is it important to see the background when it comes to predatory sexual behavior?

Let's consider the Gestalt process in predatory sexual harassment. When you read the words "sexual harassment," what is the first thing that you think about? If you are like most people, the first thing you think about is the target. For people who have had some training in managing predatory sexual behavior, you might first think about the perpetrator. For the more experienced person, you might think about the predatory behavior. Those are what we call the **figure**—the part of the "picture" that we pay attention to. What is in the **ground**, the part of the picture we do not notice but makes the picture visible? For predatory sexual behavior in organizations, the organizational culture is the ground. It is the part of the picture we ignore when we think about and talk about sexual harassment. Yet that culture shapes the nature of predatory sexual behavior and needs our attention.

Here is the point: We are trained to see certain parts of a problem. As a result, we miss the larger part of the picture, the ground. Yet it is in the background that organizational problems lurk. In terms of sexual harassment, predators hide in the background. They are normalized within the larger culture, even imbued with heroic qualities. Most important, they are hidden in plain sight. Targets of predatory behavior, akin to the fish in the image shown earlier, also can be lost in the background of an organization. For these reasons, it is important to consider the larger culture within which these problems are situated. In this way, you can train yourself to see the figure and the ground, and to understand the relationship between the two.

Predators hide in the background. They are normalized, even imbued with heroic qualities. Most important, they are hidden in plain sight.

Defining Organizational Culture

It is time to return to the definition of organizational culture that I presented in Chapter 3. My journey as a scholar and practitioner has led me to believe that organizational culture is not a "thing" to be picked up and examined. Organizational culture is best understood as an active process that is constantly woven and rewoven to shape organizations. Specifically, I define **organizational culture** as the shared communicative process through which meanings are constantly employed, negotiated, and contested to create a stable communication environment within which organizational life becomes patterned and persistent over time. Organizational cultures are always power laden and function to reproduce organizational values and outcomes. Let us take this definition one piece at a time.

Organizational Culture as Process

First, organizational culture is not a thing. It is a *process*. This conceptualization is a serious challenge for those people who need certainty in their lives. You cannot point to a thing and call it organizational culture. Yet, this is precisely what many people do. For example, they point to policies and declare those policies to be the organizational culture. The hope here, I am guessing, is that if you change policy, then you can change the culture. As organizational managers from all over the world can tell you, this is wishful thinking. Organizations are in constant motion and cannot be pinned down with simple fixes. It is far more productive to think of organizational culture as constant, yet patterned, movement.

Contrary to popular belief, organizational culture is not built on shared meanings. Instead it is built on processes of shared meaning making. It is the shared process of making meaning that makes all the difference.

Organizational Culture as a Shared Process

Second, organizational cultures are a *shared* process. This definition is fundamentally different from other definitions of culture because *I do not* define culture as *shared* meaning. People have too many varying and unique experiences to have exactly the same meanings. There are always differences. For example, in one study of an organization that resisted sexual harassment, my colleague, M. J. Smythe, and I discovered that the men in the organization defined sexual harassment differently than the women (Dougherty & Smythe, 2004). Yet despite these differences, the women coworkers who were sexually harassed by an organizational donor felt supported by their male coworkers. Why? Because it was the enacted communication of support, not the shared meaning, that ultimately mattered. It was the shared experience of talking about the harasser in disparaging ways that made the difference for these organizational members. Their meanings may have diverged, but they communicated solidarity with each other. Meanings still matter, but it is not necessary for those meanings to be fully shared (Think About It 4.2).

Think About It 4.2 Multiple Meanings of Sexual Harassment

One of the unique qualities of my research design is that I let participants define the meaning of sexual harassment. This has led me to the realization that sexual harassment means different things to different people. This exercise works best if you can compare results with another person.

Write down what sexual harassment means to you. Be sure to include your worries and fears. Describe the typical sexual harassment predator. Describe the typical sexual harassment target. Now, compare your answers with another person. Using a Venn diagram, identify the areas of meaning overlap (shared meaning). Meanings that are not shared should go into the nonoverlapping circles.

Discussion Questions

1. What meanings do you share, and how did you come to share those meanings? Perhaps reading this book helped create shared meanings, or maybe the organizational training you have received has been helpful.
2. What meanings are different? Talk about how you came to have diverging meanings.
3. How do you talk about shared and different meanings? This talk is where culture happens, so pay close attention to details such as arguments, pretending to agree, head nodding/shaking, storytelling, and so on.
4. What did you find compelling about the other person's meanings?
5. Did your meanings change as you talked to the other person? Why or why not?

Organizational Culture and Communication

Third, organizational cultures are a shared *communication* process. Recall that there are different forms of communication. There is information sharing, message production, enactment, and meaning making. Although all four of these are important to how organizations function, the key to understanding organizational culture is the interplay between communication as enacted and communication as the production of meaning. Those meanings do not need to be shared, although there is usually some overlap. Instead, it is the *shared process of meaning making* that is at the core of organizational culture.

Organizational Culture Is a System of Meanings

Fourth, organizational culture is a *system of meanings* that are constantly employed, negotiated, and contested. Although these meanings may not be universally shared, they are interwoven in powerful ways. Visually, it may be helpful to think about systems of meanings as a spider web that is constantly being woven and rewoven. These interlocking meanings are mutually supporting and make the web very difficult to unweave. As a result, it is not possible to point to a single context or action, such as predatory sexual behavior, and trim it from the culture. Why? Because predatory sexual behavior is supported by many strands of meanings that are woven together to support the behavior.

Image 4.1

Organizational Culture Is a Communication Environment

Fifth, not only do we live in a physical environment, but we enact a communication environment. This communication environment supports certain types of communication and discourages others. For example, in environments rich in predatory sexual harassment, it is likely that the communication environment encourages this form of behavior while simultaneously discouraging bystanders from reporting that behavior.

Organizational Culture Is Patterned and Persistent

Organizational cultures are *patterned and persistent* over time. In fact, one way to know if a behavior is woven into the culture is to discover if this type of behavior is predictable given past organizational behavior. One-off instances of sexual harassment may be painful for the target and coworkers, but it is not culturally important until it becomes a persistent part of how the organization operates. A word of caution: Patterned behavior often happens outside of our line of vision. Just because you only know about one incident does not mean that is all that has occurred!

Organizational Culture Is Laden With Power

Organizational cultures are never power neutral. In fact, a key to understanding abusive behavior in organizations is recognizing that organizational

Why is sexual harassment so prone to becoming woven into organizational culture? Organizational cultures are interwoven with power, and as I keep repeating, sexual harassment is about power. It is therefore relatively seamless for sexual harassment to become part of organizational culture processes.

cultures are *laden with power*, and that power is unevenly applied. It is important to understand that power is not just the formal hierarchy, nor is it purely about the economy. **Organizational power** is a social process that, like culture, represents an ongoing struggle for control and autonomy. Power is exercised in many different ways; the most insidious are not visible within formal hierarchical charts. Sexual harassment provides one example of power in process. In fact, sexual harassment is not about sex. It is about power. It therefore is an excellent resource for organizational members in their struggle over organizational meaning.

Organizational Culture Functions

Finally, it is important to understand that organizational culture *functions* in important ways. Culture is not just a random patterned process. It is a purposeful process that functions to accomplish both formal and informal organizational goals. This point becomes particularly important for organizational change agents tasked with evolving their organizational culture. Recall the *M*A*S*H* example from Chapter 2 (Think About It 2.2). My study participant used this movie to illustrate how sexual harassment creates a sense of camaraderie among workers. If you remove sexual harassment from this man's organization, then how will the workers create camaraderie, manage stress, and the myriad other functions accomplished through sexual harassment? These functions must be considered when addressing sexual harassment.

Although it is certainly important to define and conceptualize organizational culture, for organizational problem solvers it is equally important to understand how organizational culture works. Although organizational culture is highly complex and there is no model that can fully capture that complexity, I developed the following model that can be a useful resource for those tasked with managing an organizational culture. Keep in mind the notion of figure and ground as we go through this model. How does this model help you see the background of predatory sexual harassment more clearly?

The Transformational Model of Organizational Culture (Trans-MOC)

As mentioned earlier, organizational culture is not a "thing." It is a communication process. But what does it look like and how does it work? Here is the model I use to help organizational change agents understand their cultures (Figure 4.2).

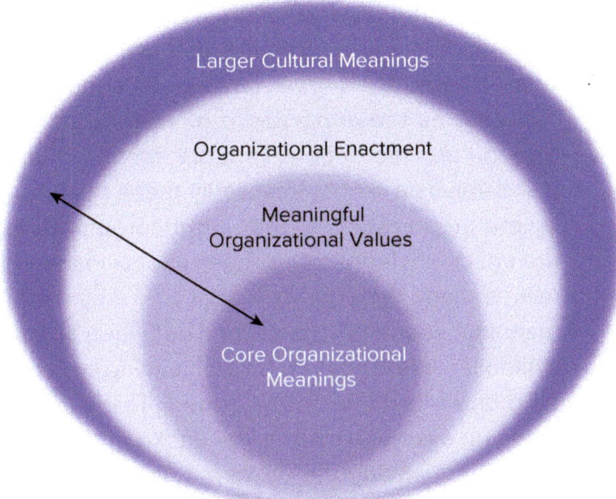

FIGURE 4.2: Transformational Model of Organizational Culture (Trans-MOC)

Trans-MOC is designed to provide a holistic approach to problem solving in organizational settings by exploring the ways in which communication transforms into organization. Of course, not all problems can be analyzed through this model. The focus is on those problems that are woven into the organizational culture—entrenched problems that are wicked and resistant to change. Although this model was developed to address predatory sexual harassment, clients have told me that they find the model helpful in analyzing and addressing other important problems that have become entwined with their cultures, problems such as racism, bullying, sexism, deceit, graft, unearned self-promotion, and even the tyranny of enforced positivity. I am glad that my model has proven useful beyond its foundational purpose, and my clients have made me think in more expansive ways about its functionality. Although this book is focused on addressing predatory sexual harassment, I hope that the processes identified here can be helpful beyond this context.

Trans-MOC is designed to show how organizational cultures form and transform through communication. I provide a brief overview here and then elaborate more fully later in the chapter. Starting from the outside circle, organizational cultures are encased in **larger social cultural meaning systems** that shape people's beliefs before they enter your organization. Those beliefs become transformed into organizational members' **organizational enactments**. Over time, the organizational enactment transforms into **organization values**. Recall that there are two definitions of meanings. The *organizational values* level represents meaning as the *importance or value that is produced through our interactions with our social world.* Organizational values are not necessarily those that are espoused by the organization. In fact, often, organizational values are unacknowledged by organizational leadership. Those values shape the **organizational core meanings**. The core meanings represent the second definition of "meaning" as symbolic representation. Those meaning systems are firmly held and often unacknowledged. These organizational meaning systems reverberate back on the organizational values, enhancing the performative engagement, which can then influence the larger cultural meaning systems. Although cultures are resistant to change, they can evolve through careful and sustained long-term efforts. I will discuss each component of the model.

What makes for a good model? Personally, I look for three qualities. First, it develops from interplay between research and practice. Second, it can be used to advance research. Third, it can be used as a mental model to guide practitioners.

Fuzzy Boundaries

Perhaps the first thing you note about the Trans-MOC model is that the boundaries are fuzzy. Although a bit disorienting to look at visually, these fuzzy boundaries are an intentional attribute of this model. Why? Because cultural boundaries are fuzzy. It can be difficult to know when one component ends and another begins. For example, the larger culture within which an organization is situated helps shape the organizational culture. It is, in fact, this fuzzy border that makes it a challenge to observe organizational culture as distinct from the larger culture within which it is situated. In addition, the boundaries are made even more fuzzy by the varying experiences people bring to organizations, all of which uniquely shape how organizational members engage with the organization and its culture. As a result, although organizational culture is a powerful force, it is not uniformly engaged by its various members and their subcultures, meaning that it is not fully coherent, nor is it easy to identify.

Larger Cultural Meanings

The first layer of organizational culture acknowledges that every organization is situated within a larger cultural milieu. That *larger culture* has its own communicative patterns that function for the cultural members. For example, our larger culture defines gender, creates gender roles, and assigns power differently based on the assumed gender of societal members. Gender roles are enforced, both through physical threat and through social control methods that enable and limit social structures. Sexual harassment is an outgrowth of these social meaning systems that privilege some over others, often in demeaning and humiliating ways. Organizational cultures do not exist in a vacuum. They emerge out of a larger culture and are, therefore, constantly influenced by that culture (Think About It 4.3).

Think About It 4.3 Garden Metaphor

Here is a fun fact about me: I am an avid gardener. In particular, I love to grow a vegetable garden. I have a huge in-ground garden (as opposed to a box garden) that has expanded in scope over the years. Every year, as soon as the ground is soft enough and dry enough, I begin to prep my garden for spring planting. I pull out the old debris and till compost into the soil. Then, just before I plant, I hoe the garden beds to eliminate weeds and to create the right conditions for my seeds. Then I plant my seeds. Planting is the easiest thing that I do every year. As the seeds start to emerge, so do the weeds. I am including a picture of the emerging corn and the weed bed that appeared even as I planted my seeds.

Image 4.2

I did not plant those weeds. I did not ask them to grow in my garden. But there they are. Every year. Every planting. Weeds from the larger environment within which my garden is situated emerge and create havoc among my growing plants. It is incredibly frustrating.

Think of your organizations as a garden. You have carefully prepped your soil, worked for countless hours to create a productive growing season. Weeds are your organizational problems that emerge from the environment within which your organization is situated. You did not invent sexual harassment; you did not invent racism; you did not invent greed—but there it is. If you do not recognize the problem as it takes root in your garden, your problems will grow and your weeds will reduce the productivity that you have worked to create. Let's call the weed bed in my garden "sexual harassment." I did not plant the weeds. I cannot simply rid myself of the weeds by pulling them out one time. They will persist as a problem for as long as I choose to garden and I will need to address that problem if I want to continue to produce my own food.

https://www.debbiedougherty.com/educational-videos

Discussion Questions

1. What weeds are growing in your garden/organization?
2. Can you even see your weeds? Or are you so focused on your seedlings that you have ignored the weeds that strangle your productivity?
3. Use the garden metaphor to discuss the notion of figure and ground. What can you see? What do you not see? How does this impact your garden/organization?

Organizational Enactment

The second layer to the Trans-MOC model is organizational enactment. I use the term *enactment* very deliberately. Organizational culture is best understood as a process in which things, behaviors, and communication become important culturally as they are enacted in patterned and persistent ways. During organizational enactment, patterns of behaviors become physiologically observable. Specifically, enactment is where organizational members physically interact with their cultures. We see, hear, touch, smell, taste, and feel the organization in ways that are patterned and meaningful (Think About It 4.4). Although I will discuss enactment more in Chapter 6, for now I will provide a brief example.

Think About It 4.4 How Do You Weed Your Garden?

Continuing with the garden metaphor, if your organization is a garden, and weeds are problems that emerged from the larger environment, how you manage the weeds becomes part of the cultural enactment. Here are some standard ways people deal with weeds:

- **They create an artificial environment that is mostly detached from the outside culture.** Box gardens, where the soil is brought in in bags and mixed with various ingredients, is probably the most popular technique right now. I tried the box garden technique when I first began to garden. Guess what? Weeds appeared. Some were in that soil I brought into my garden in bags. Some blew in from the plants that surrounded my boxes. Some grew under my box and into my garden. I eventually abandoned the boxes and moved to an in-ground garden.
- **Ignore the weeds.** I have neighbors who plant very elaborate gardens every year. Then the weeds emerge and the gardens appear to be giant weed beds. These are very busy people with children, businesses, and other activities that have pulled their attention from the mundane task of weeding.
- **Pull the weeds one at a time.** Like many gardeners, organizational managers attempt to resolve problems by plucking weeds one at a time. They wait for a sexual harasser to be identified, and then they train, move, or eliminate that person. Unfortunately, using the garden metaphor, if there is one weed, there will be more. It is the nature of weeds to procreate and recreate until the garden is smothered.
- **Weed mats.** I use a lot of fabric, cardboard, and paper to cover the weeds to smother them and block the sunlight. It works pretty well most of the time, but it is imperfect since weeds will grow through the weed fabric, while cardboard and paper degrade over time. Some plants can't tolerate the heat or moisture that comes with this method of weed control. For example, I used weed mats to control weeds around my spinach last spring. I managed to drown all the plants by holding the moisture on the roots for too long. I was disappointed because that spinach looked really tasty the day before it died.

Discussion Questions

1. Let's say that the most damaging weed in your organization is predatory sexual behavior. How does your organization manage that weed?
2. In what ways has this technique been effective?
3. How has this technique failed?
4. The way the organization manages its weeds becomes woven into the culture. What are the cultural enactments for your organization's weed control?

Organizational policy is a primary means through which organizations attempt to stop sexual harassment. Yet, these policies typically fail to achieve their desired outcomes. Why? Because policies are only culturally meaningful when they are enacted by organizational members. Unfortunately, organizational members often enact policy in ways that reinforce the cultural processes already in play. I use a training exercise to illustrate how organizational members enact policy. During a training with organizational managers, I asked participants to read their organization's sexual harassment policy and to comment on this policy. I divided people into different groups. I assigned one group member to be a "social scientist" whose job was to observe the group and to note both content and emotions from group members. I then asked those observers to get together to identify common themes. Interestingly, the primary theme that was discussed by all groups was the vilification of the policy creators. Specifically, all of the groups discussed the policy framers as trying to "cover the organization's butt" and to "protect the organization from lawsuits." Even more telling, every group concluded that the policy creators did not care about the targets of sexual harassment, did not care if the chronic sexual harassment in the organization ended, and concluded that the policy framers were likely perpetrators themselves. To me, this was a masterful performance of policy suspicion. Interestingly, this type of suspicion was very common in this organization, making suspicion a patterned behavior that was communicatively enacted and an underlying component of this organization's culture. These cultural enactments inform us as to what the organization values. Clearly, the way the policy was enacted in these interactions demonstrated the stripping of power from the policy by organizational members.

Contrary to popular belief, not all values are positive. Some values, such as suspicion, are clearly negative. Of course, the organization would never espouse this enacted value!

Meaningful Organizational Values

The third level of organizational culture is *meaningful organizational values*. This is a surprisingly challenging term to define. In fact, before I define organizational values, you might find it instructive to write down your definition of values.

What are values? Please pull out a piece of paper and write down your definition of values.

If you did this exercise, you probably struggled to form a helpful definition of "values." It is a hard concept to pin down. Over time, I have come to define **organizational values** as those things, standards, and ideals through which we evaluate our organizational well-being. Although we typically think of values as a moral compass that dictates what is good and right in our universe, Joe Y. F. Lau (2011) notes that not all values are moral. In fact, according to Lau, there are three types of values. **Personal values** are how individuals determine what is important to them. **Moral values** are used to determine what is right or wrong. **Aesthetic values** are how we determine what is beautiful. To this list, I add a fourth type of value: **Status values** are the ways we determine who gets power and how that power should be deployed. This last type of value is important for two reasons. First, status values are rarely recognized by organizational leaders. Second, these values tend to create hidden problems that are destructive in nature. Because sexual harassment is about power, it is an excellent example of the enactment of status values.

Here is a fun fact for you: Most business and organizational textbooks treat values as universally good. This is what I call the Mary Poppins version of organizational values. In actuality, organizations are often weighed down by toxic values. **Toxic values** can be defined as those values that emerge from repetitive organizational behaviors that are destructive to either the workers or to the organization itself. For example, I have never seen or heard a CEO proudly claim that his organization values unearned power, misogyny, Whiteness, or youth. Yet the patterns of behaviors and communication enacted by the organization clearly demonstrate that these status values are very much present in many organizations. As a result, many of the problems that I am asked to deal with, such as sexual harassment, are reproduced through unacknowledged and toxic organizational values (Think About It 4.5).

Think About It 4.5 What Can Your Garden Tell You About Your Values?

We approach our gardens/organizations with both stated and unstated values. For example, for me, gardens are where we grow food. The first time I heard a person use the term "flower garden," I almost felt hostile, and definitely felt confused. My family has always distinguished between "flower beds" and "vegetable gardens." As you can see from the videos of my garden, it is not exactly beautiful. There is weed fabric, a few tools, usually a dog or cat, and occasionally even a shoe (courtesy of both my youngest child and the puppy, who loves to carry both boxes and shoes around, dropping them in the darndest places). However, my garden is very productive. There are some edible native plants that occasionally grow in my garden. I pluck them like weeds.

Now write a paragraph about how you see your organization. You can use my earlier paragraph as a model if you find it helpful.

Discussion Questions

1. What do you see, hear, smell, touch, taste, or feel when you think about or talk about your garden/organization?
2. What personal, moral, aesthetic, and status values are being expressed in those enactments? Include both preferred and toxic values.
3. What surprises you about your assessment?

Core Organizational Meanings

At the core of Trans-MOC are the *systems of meanings* that are fundamentally important to the organization. Specifically, the *core meanings* are the symbolic representations of the organization. There are at least five types of meanings, all of which can interact in complementary and competing ways.

Cognitive meanings align with dictionary definitions. When I first started conducting research on sexual harassment, one of the critiques I frequently received was that I did not define sexual harassment for my participants. The critique was something along the lines of "how did I know if study participants were talking about the formal definition of sexual harassment that is used in legally binding ways in organizations?" My response was that I wanted to understand how organizational members define sexual harassment. Knowing the *working definitions* people use in the meaning-making process is far more productive than knowing what they think about a legal definition imposed for research purposes.

Emotional meanings shape how we feel about a concept. Emotional meanings are the most intense meanings surrounding sexual harassment. The anger, fear, hostility, disbelief, superiority, hope, frustration, and so on are challenging components of the change process. Why? Because emotional meanings are clearly present, but organizational members will rarely acknowledge that they are experiencing these emotions. Organizations have emotion rules, most of which are designed to suppress the expression of emotions at work. People, especially women, who admit to having emotions at work are treated as bad workers who are irrational. It fascinates me how irrationality has become synonymous with emotionality, even though these concepts are very different, with many emotional experiences being a perfectly rational response to harmful workplace interactions.

Oddly, emotionality is viewed as synonymous with irrationality in organizational contexts. Yet emotions tend to be a rational response to abusive workplace behavior.

Social meanings are constantly being shaped and reshaped by how we communicate together. How we make meaning as an individual is different from how we make meaning in social collectives. Karl Weick (1995) acknowledges this reality in his *sensemaking theory*, where meaning making happens in either social settings or in imagined social settings. Think about how you rehearse potential conversations with other people, imagining how they might respond to your words or actions. This is what Weick means by meaning making in imagined social settings. Recall that organizational cultures are socially produced. We communicate cultures into existence. Social meanings are central to how we organize around organizational cultures.

Identity meanings tell us who we are in relation to a concept. Ronald Jackson (2002a; 2002b), in his **cultural contract theory** of identity, tells us that identity is always formed within and around cultures and relationships. There are typically unstated "contracts" articulating how people can enact their identities based on social meanings surrounding those identities. According to Jackson, "The way we learn to coordinate our cultural identities and perspectives so that they are aligned with

Cultural contract theory was based on Jackson's analysis of race in the United States context. Cultural assumptions about race vary widely from culture to culture. What are the ready-to-sign, quasi-completed, and cocreated contracts regarding race in your organization? I suspect that if you are a member of the majoritized race, you may struggle with this assignment. I also suspect that minoritized people in your organization will more easily accomplish this assignment. Cultural contracts are usually informal and unspoken, making them difficult to articulate but clearly present.

other cultural identities and perspectives is perhaps one of the world's most intricate balancing acts, and everyone who is employed must participate in it" (2002b, p. 50). Jackson articulates three types of cultural contracts. **Ready-to-sign contracts** are based on assumptions of assimilation. Specifically, people are required to take on the physical, behavioral, and mental assumptions of the dominant culture. **Quasi-completed contracts** allow some adaptation to different cultures but retain the primary cultural assumptions. Finally, **cocreated contracts** are based on the mutual valuation of each person. Although Jackson's theorizing does not speak directly to meaning making, it is clear from a cultural contract perspective that we are constantly renegotiating the meaning of organizational cultures and how people should communicatively enact those cultures.

Power meanings shape how power and status is engaged. When I ask people to define power in their organization, most respond by talking about formal power—management, assigned leaders, and the organizational hierarchy. Interestingly, when I ask people to tell me about sexual harassment, most people define it as being "about power," but what power means varies drastically in this context. Specifically, how people define power seems to depend to a large degree on what type of power they have access to (Dougherty, 2006). In one health care organization, where all but one of the high-level managers were men, all the men I talked to described sexual harassment as a hierarchical/managerial power issue. Because sexual harassment was about power, and in these men's view, only managers could have power, they sincerely believed that sexual harassment could only be enacted by managers. This hierarchical definition of power was particularly perplexing given that many of these men engaged in aggressive predatory sexual behavior toward colleagues—especially women colleagues. In contrast, the women I talked to defined power in more social and individual ways. They told me that power was gained through relationships, or through the power to control their own selves. They then described sexual harassment that came from across the organizational hierarchy, from managers to coworkers, from patients to physicians. For most of these women, the most important threat from sexual harassment was social isolation, which would strip these women of their primary sources of power—their relationships with coworkers. Clearly people make meaning of power differently depending on the culture of the organization and their access to power.

Let's put these various types of meanings together into a single example using the core problem of sexual harassment. The term "sexual harassment" has a formal *cognitive* definition in most countries that is used to determine the legal status of the behavior. As previously noted, definitions can vary between countries. Even within a country, the definition of sexual harassment can vary significantly from person to person (Dougherty et al., 2009). Sexual harassment also has *emotional* content. Just saying the words "sexual harassment" can trigger anger, fear, disgust, and so on, both from those who fear being targeted and from those who believe that sexual harassment is a made-up problem designed to damage men in the workplace. Interestingly, both cognitive and emotional meanings can evolve during *social* interactions. In my own research I have seen this many times because of how I design my studies. I listen to the same person talking in different configurations. For example, in one study I listened to the same people talk about sexual harassment on four different occasions (Dougherty, 2001a). Although some meanings were persistent across interactions, some meanings of sexual harassment shifted depending on who the individual was talking to. For example, one woman participant in an all-women's group identified herself as a feminist who hated the misogyny that pervaded her organization. When she spoke in a mixed-gender group, she declared that women always want to play the victim and were likely to make things up just to get ahead. These are very different meanings that change across social engagement partners. These different social meanings are closely tied to *identity* meanings. In one group, this woman's identity as a feminist was very important to how she interpreted sexual harassment in her workplace. In the second group, her identity as a strong (not victim) worker became key to her interpretation of sexual harassment, causing her to shift her focus from predator blaming to victim blaming. Finally, meanings also shape the ways in which *power* is enacted. For this woman, being a feminist may have given her more status and social power in the all-women's group, but being perceived as a strong woman (not a victim) gave her more status

Please pardon my use of the biological gender binary in this and other examples. Sexual harassment is still a binary practice, even when it is used to target nonbinary and trans people.

and social power in the mixed-gender group. As you can see, meanings are rarely as simple as a cognitive definition. In fact, it is far more accurate to talk about *systems of meanings* made up of interwoven components than it is to talk about any formal definition of sexual harassment (Think About It 4.6).

Think About It 4.6 Women Talking

Below you will find a conversation from a women's focus group where they provide their definitions of sexual harassment. Before you read it, note that these excerpts can be challenging to read and process because spoken language does not translate well into written language. I have lightly edited this conversation to help with the translation.

> **Interviewer:** Well, what is your definition of sexual harassment? How would you define it?
>
> **Catherine:** You [perpetrator] are making someone uncomfortable. Like you are really stepping over the line. [Sexual harassment is] not kidding around; it's not joking around at the copier. You're infringing on someone's rights. Civil rights.
>
> **Amanda:** [Interrupts.] It's a different level than just normal camaraderie between comrades.
>
> **Catherine:** And you [the perpetrator] are not bright enough to pick up on the cues that you have crossed the line.
>
> **Betty:** [Earlier] we were talking about personal distance, and sometimes it's [sexual harassment is] an indifference to someone's feelings. To me it's overt. It's lecherous. It's obscene to the point [unfinished sentence]. I had to tell someone once: "Uh, today you just crossed the line. That was just, that was just obscene." And that person, he stepped back and he said, "Yeah, sometimes I just get going. And I don't [unfinished sentence]." You know, his jokes and things, the words that he was using [were problematic]. Some people get into a weird area before you know it. All of a sudden you're talking about things and you didn't even realize you went there. And it gets into a personal place where they think you're okay with that.
>
> **Amanda:** But did he stop?
>
> **Catherine:** Yeah.

Amanda: Stop after you told him that?

Donna: [Did he say] "Sorry about that. Won't happen again"?

Betty: Then it was fine. Yeah, for me [sexual harassment is], I don't know any other word. It's just, lecherous. You know? Their behavior, everything about it is offensive. They're asking patronizing or, um, leading questions like well "how did you get your job?" [The innuendo is that a woman slept her way into a job.]

Amanda: Oh. Yeah.

Catherine: I think anybody saying that to you is unwelcome.

Betty: I mean that's pretty easy to deal with. "I don't appreciate that. Do that again and we're going to have a problem."

Discussion Questions

Search for clues in this conversation to help you answer the following questions. This is a challenging task. Do your best.

1. What clues can you find in this language that suggest shared meanings? Diverging meanings?
2. What are the cognitive meanings? What makes you think that?
3. Emotional meanings?
4. Identity meanings?
5. Social meanings?
6. Power meanings?

Subcultures

One comment that I have received in every training I have done is that cultural enactments, values, and meanings are dependent on the subgroup. This is absolutely correct. Not only is there a larger organizational culture, but there are also subcultures. These subcultures vary based on how much they intersect with the larger culture and based on how influential the subculture is in the larger cultural reproduction. Joann Keyton (2011) provides a number of possible demarcations for subcultures, including by profession, by geography, mergers, generation, and placement in the hierarchy. I would add gender identification, sexuality, and race as demographic differences that can produce subcultures in organizations. Martin and Siehl (1983) describe three kinds of organizational subcultures that function differently within the larger organizational culture. **Enhancing subcultures** are those which are more fervent than the larger culture in upholding the organizational values. An **orthogonal subculture** would adhere to the dominant culture and have different, but not competing, beliefs and values. Finally, a **counterculture** is where some of the core values of the subculture directly contradict the core values of the larger organization. In Figure 4.3, the importance of subcultures is represented by the overlapping circles.

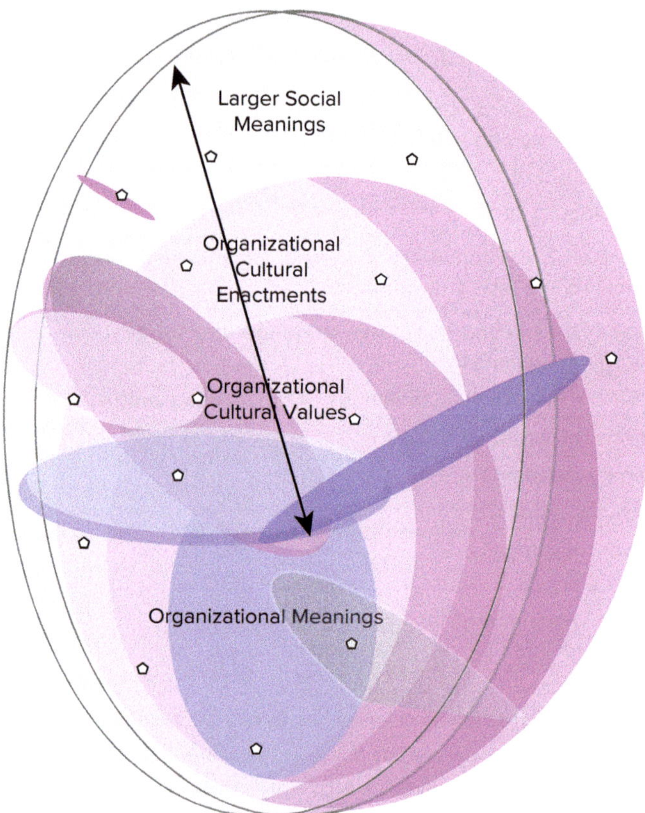

FIGURE 4.3: Trans-MOC With Subcultures and Individuals

Individual Differences

Organizational cultures are not giant amorphous globs. They are comprised of individuals acting together in patterned ways. Of course, individuals are not universally the same. We are shaped by our personalities, religious beliefs, larger cultural systems, and unique experiences. Not everything that an organizational member does is consistent with the patterns that make up an organizational culture. There are constant deviations that are persistent and important. For example, as discussed throughout this book, sexual harassment can become patterned and persistent in an organizational culture. However, there are also always organizational members who do not engage in that type of behavior. Equally important, there are those who push back against predatory sexual behaviors, making them important counterpoints in an otherwise destructive culture. In Figure 4.3, the importance of individual differences is represented by the stars that overlay the larger model.

Recap and Looking Forward

While it would be easy to focus on only one component of the model, TransMOC is intended as a process model, with all of the components working as a whole. Indeed, if organizational managers focused only on the larger social meanings without considering the ways in which those meanings are shaped by communicative enactment, which translate into organizational values, which produce and reproduce core organizational meanings, then those managers would have failed to understand the means through which intervention can happen.

Hyperfocusing on a single component of this model may also induce the false belief that organizational cultures are either immutable or easy to change. For example, focusing only on the larger cultural meanings could give the impression that the organization is at the mercy of the larger culture, with little to no control over what comes into the organization. In contrast, by focusing exclusively on organizational meanings, change agents could view organizations as easy to change. However, by looking at the model as a larger transformational process, change agents should come to understand that organizations don't change quickly. Instead, they evolve slowly, over time. This means that change agents must be patient, long-range thinkers. Those who need immediate gratification will be better off doing other kinds of work.

How does it work as a whole? In the next several chapters, I will break down each component of the model, while keeping in mind the larger process that is organizational culture. As the arrow in the model indicates, influence can go in both directions. Organizational cultures are shaped by the larger culture, but the larger culture can be shaped by organizational culture. I begin from the outside and work inward, using predatory sexual harassment to illustrate. As mentioned in Chapter 1, predatory sexual behavior can be found in most cultures in the world. Rape, misogyny, restrictive clothing requirements for women, and so on make women more prone to being targeted. In addition, trans and nonbinary people are stigmatized because they defy rigid biological gender rules and therefore are at high risk of being targeted by organizational predators (Manning et al., 2020). As we'll see in Chapter 5, these larger cultural meaning systems filter in through the fuzzy borders that permeate organizations. In Chapter 6, we will see how these larger cultural meaning systems are uniquely shaped through communicative enactment. In Chapter 7, we'll discuss the ways in which those enactments tell us what an organization really values. In Chapter 8, we discover how those values impact the larger organizational meaning system, and also how the larger organizational meaning system reverberates back on the organizational values, which can then shape the organizational enactment, which can then reshape the larger culture. As I will say repeatedly: This process is ongoing. Inserting change needs to be careful and deliberate, with change often producing unintended consequences. Chapter 9 will provide insight into how to observe and then evolve your culture using the Trans-MOC model.

Credits

Chapter 5

Predatory Sexual Harassment and Larger Cultural Meaning Systems

By the end of this chapter, you should understand how larger cultural meaning systems infiltrate organizational cultures through the following:

1. Binary logics/binary language and cultural meanings
2. Co-sexuality and cultural meanings
3. Hegemonic masculinity and cultural meanings
4. The paradox of femininity and cultural meanings

In 2020–2022:

- The COVID-19 pandemic emerged, killing millions of people and shuttering the global economy.
- The #MeToo movement resurged, shattering the illusion of gender equality.
- More Black people were senselessly killed, pushing people around the world to remember that Black Lives Matter.
- Global warming continued to threaten the planet, with arctic zones sweltering in 100°F temperatures.

- The gap between the rich and the poor continued to widen around the world, with the poor blamed for their condition.
- Crime continued to plague the world population.
- Recreational drug use continued to destroy communities, reinforce global crime syndicates, and kill millions of people.
- Political polarization continued its global creep, with little movement toward mutual understanding.
- Sexual assault continued to be a global crisis.
- LGBTQ+ people continued to be hunted and criminalized.

Your workplace did not invent these problems. These problems are embedded in the larger culture and they are persistent and devastating, with no clear response. Because they are in the larger culture, and because your organization is also situated in that larger culture, your organization is embedded in these problems. You did not invite the problems in, but you will need to manage these problems for as long as you continue to organize.

FIGURE 5.1: Larger Cultural Meanings

Keep in mind, however, that although your organization may not have invited predatory sexual behavior into your culture, it is very likely that your organization created a warm and welcoming social environment that transformed this problem into a destructive force. In this chapter, I focus on the outer layer of the Trans-MOC model (Figure 5.1) by describing some of the ways in which predatory sexual harassment grows into your organization from the larger culture.

Where Do Problems Come From?

Although some organizational problems are home grown, meaning that they are a creation of the organization itself, large social problems originate in the larger culture within which your organization is situated. As much as you might wish to protect your organization from these external influences by closing the boundaries between your organization and the external culture, this course of action is not recommended. Why? One of the basic principles of systems theory suggests that to thrive, organizations need to have a balance between open and closed boundaries. Organizations that are closed to the outside world tend to experience **entropy**, or the tendency toward decay. As a result, organizations that do not allow information and materials to flow in tend toward decline. Take my garden, for example. Check out the fence that separates my garden from the larger environment. The fence is designed to keep deer and other critters out, while allowing air and water to flow in.

Do you see those plants on the fence line? They are not inside of my garden, but their seeds will be spread throughout it by the very wind and water that I want to enter my garden to prevent system decay. As long as my garden is open to the larger world, I will have to address the problems presented by the larger world. Here is the kicker though: I could have weeded those plants away from my garden by doing some basic landscaping. I would not have stopped weeds from coming in, but I could have limited their entry with just a little bit of care and planning. Similarly, with some effort, you can do some basic pruning and landscaping to limit the way cultural problems enter your organization. So what are the "weeds" that tend to provide the seeds for predatory sexual harassment? Although there are many, in this chapter I focus on the binary nature of language, gender, and sexuality as important cultural weeds that invade your organizational culture and tend to take root as predatory sexual behavior.

Image 5.1

Binary Logics/Binary Language

Language is a primary way in which predatory sexual behavior becomes woven into organizational culture. Martin (2002) identifies binaries as an important building block of organizational culture, especially culture as intertwined with power. For this reason, binary logics provide a useful heuristic for understanding how problems are absorbed into your organization through the larger culture. We typically think about language as the way in which we share information and create meaningful social worlds. However, language does something even more fundamental—it shapes how we think and what we can think about. It structures our social world. **Binary logics** is one significant way in which language structures our social world through oppositional thinking (Cirksena & Cuklanz, 1992). **Binary language**, the primary building blocks of binary logics, is defined as the oppositional pairing between terms that may or may not be opposite. Binary logics is formative in many cultural milieus, meaning it forms the foundation for how we think about and learn about our social worlds. As a result of this oppositional language formation, we learn to think in oppositional ways about the world in which we live.

Take the English language as an example. English is a language that is built around binary logics. The English language is carefully formed around the assumption that both the physical and social worlds are built around opposites. This oppositional language is taught to children from a very early age (Figure 5.2). Oppositional thinking makes some sense when considering the physical world. Oppositional pairs such as in/out, up/down, and small/big provide a particular way of thinking about the relationships between things. Unfortunately, when considering the social world, many oppositional pairs are not opposites at all. Feminists call false opposites false dualities, arguing that this type of binary logic privileges some while relegating others to the social margins of society (Dougherty & Denker, 2015).

Based on the theorizing on binary thinking by French scholars such as Jacques Derrida (1967), it seems that binary language is also a defining feature of French. My friends from Spanish- and Portuguese-speaking cultures assure me that binaries also shape their languages. Although I focus on the English language in this exemplar, the ideas may apply broadly across cultures.

Rationality/emotionality, strong/weak, courage/fear, with us/against us, good/bad, and so on are treated as opposites when they should be treated as related, or even as co-constituting. For example, although we tend to treat emotionality and rationality as opposites, in fact, research is clear that rationality requires emotionality (Bechara et al., 2000). Research has shown that when people have the emotion-centered parts of their brains damaged, they

FIGURE 5.2: Babies Are Taught to Think Using Binary Logics Like Small/Large.

are unable to make decisions, even though the cognition part of their brain remains undamaged (Damasio, 1994). To understand how binaries shape predatory sexual behavior, it is important to first understand the binary logics which shape binary language.

Which of these are true binaries? Which are false binaries? up/down; in/out; inside/outside; boy/girl; male/female; rationality/emotionality; powerful/weak; black/white

There are five components of binary logics that I believe are particularly helpful in understanding how larger cultural meanings shape organizational culture:

1. Binary language shapes meaning.
2. Binary language shapes social structures.
3. Binary language usually privileges one pole over the other.
4. Binaries are woven together such that they are difficult to parse out or eliminate.
5. Binaries are intersectional.

Binary Language Shapes Meaning

Recall that meaning making is one of the key formations of communication. Meaning making is not a free-flowing process that wanders about without restraint. Instead, think of meaning making as a process that is restricted by **cultural rules**—rules that both shape, and are in turn shaped by, language. Binary language is one such cultural rule. Jacques Derrida (1967) is perhaps the best-known scholar who has theorized about binary language, albeit only in its written form. According to Derrida, binary language limits the array of possible meanings that can be produced by making the *presence* of one of the pairs dependent on the *absence* of the other. By this, Derrida means that the written word can only acquire meaning in the silent presence of the oppositional pair. Derrida argues that to regain the meaning that has been made absent, it is necessary to *deconstruct* the oppositional language so that the missing pairing is made present. I recognize that these ideas are challenging, so perhaps an example would be helpful.

In binary language, men and women are typically constructed as opposites. It looks something like this (Figure 5.3):

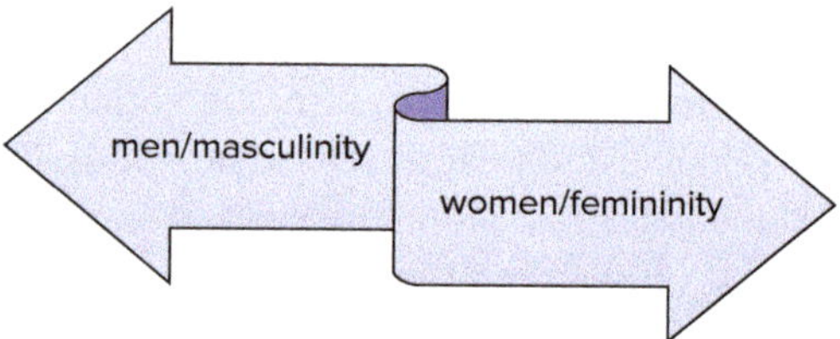

FIGURE 5.3: Men and Women Are Constructed as Opposites.

As you can see, in this pairing, men and masculinity are framed as the opposite of women and femininity. Now, consider the simple statement "he was a real man," a phrase I have heard on multiple occasions. Although the words "not woman" are absent, it has a silent presence because the meaning of the word "man" is formed in the binary man/woman. To claim the label "man" it is necessary for a person to be recognized as opposite of woman. To deconstruct this phrase, Derrida would make present the absent oppositional pairing thusly: He was a real man ~~not woman~~. Using the strikethrough deconstructs the gender binary, making it available for use as part of a chain of deconstruction.

I recognize that Derrida is tough to understand, and that this simple deconstruction process is a bit mind bending. What you need to understand is that many languages are formed around binaries; those binaries are hidden and therefore difficult to discern, yet they shape the very possibility of meaning in our larger cultural milieu.

Binary Language Shapes Social Structure

Binary logics are "powerful because they not only suggest meaning, but also provide a structure by which meaning is created. As a result, it is difficult to use the English language without also using false binaries" (Dougherty & Goldstein Hode, 2016, p. 1750). These binary structures can be seen in various forms of organizing. For example, Facebook originally coded sex and gender binaries into their programing (Bivens, 2017), structuring the platform and the various social relations around binary logics of male/female and heterosexual/homosexual. Although the organization now allows for 58 forms of gender, these gender categories are reformulated into traditional binaries in the organization's deep-level coding, so that advertisers can better market their products along the gender binary (Bivens, 2017).

Sexual harassment policies provide a relevant example of how binary language shapes social structures. Currently, sexual harassment policies tend to avoid obvious gender binary language. However, in our study of cultural interpretations of sexual harassment policies, my colleague Marlo Goldstein Hode and I discovered that when organizational members talked about the policies, they assumed binary differences between men and women, even when those binaries were not written into the actual language of the policy. As a result, the policy was interpreted by organizational members very differently than what appeared to be the policy intent.

Binary Language Privileges One Pole Over the Other

Binaries are not power neutral. In fact, binaries factor into most power relations in countries with binary-driven language. One side of most binaries' pole is typically privileged over the other. Sexual harassment is an excellent illustration of how this privilege operates.

We know that men have more power than women in almost every sphere of influence—politics, economy, labor, education, religion, family, military, leisure. We also know that sexual harassment is not about sex; it is about power. It is, in fact, a way in which masculinized power can be maintained in many of these spheres. So how are gender binaries reinforced in sexual harassment? There are many ways, but the single saddest and most frustrating example is our tendency to believe men over women. I was first introduced to this reality during a women's focus group interview (Dougherty, 2001b). I asked the focus group participants, "What is your greatest fear about being sexually harassed?" They all agreed that it was the possibility that they would not be believed. Then the group spontaneously concluded that women lie and should therefore not be believed. In this example, these women privileged men as more honest than women, and in so doing reinforced the likelihood of their greatest fear related to sexual harassment—that they would not be believed. In this way, these women privileged men over women in their workplace, even though that privilege was not in their best interest.

Can you tell which pole of these binaries is privileged?

- Male/Female
- Rational/Emotional
- White/Black
- Good/Bad

Binaries Are Interwoven

Any single binary is not a particularly powerful force. Why? Because it is a language construct, which means that a single binary can be neutralized through language that identifies it as irrational. However, binaries are never singular. Instead, they are woven together like fabric, pliable and seemingly impenetrable, trapping language users in a system of meanings (Derrida, 1967) that are constantly remaking themselves. Binaries are effective because they are interwoven (Dougherty & Goldstein Hode, 2016). This means they are reinforcing and self-sustaining.

For example, when my oldest daughter, Fionna, was very little, we were often stopped by strangers who wanted to tell me how pretty she was. One example stands out as perhaps the most perplexing. When Fionna was about 2 years old, I took her to a shopping mall. Fionna was wearing a dress and a pair of her mom's sunglasses. A stranger walked up to us and said, "I love your dress. You are so pretty. I bet your Dad will have to beat the boys off with a stick when you get older." Fionna frowned and hid behind me, a perfectly reasonable reaction when confronted by a stranger suggesting that your Dad needed to beat boys with a stick! The stranger said, "Are you being shy? You should smile. I bet you are really pretty when you smile." I said, "My daughter is also really smart." The stranger nodded and walked away.

I wish I had handled this situation more assertively, but I was surprised that a stranger would not only have such strong opinions about my daughter, but that she felt compelled to tell Fionna and me all about her opinions. Further, she seemed to believe that her words would be welcome and would be viewed as a compliment. Instead of responding appropriately, I did what most of us would do in that type of situation: I reverted to politeness norms. When I did come up with a counternarrative (my daughter is smart) the stranger walked away, seemingly fully uninterested in a quality that did not fit the binary string. Had this stranger utilized a simple gender binary, intervention would have been equally simple. However, binaries are woven together, making intervention a challenge. So, what were the binaries in this interaction?

1. **Gender binary:** You are a girl so I will compliment you for not looking like a boy.
2. **Active/passive binary:** Because you are not a boy, obviously you will be a passive observer of your world, needing your Dad to protect you from all those boys who will chase you.
3. **Pursuer/pursued binary:** A boy's role is to pursue. A girl's role is to be pursued. Note the link to the active/passive binary. Because she is passive and pursued, she needs to be protected by her father.
4. **Control/regulation binary:** Girls are regulated by others who are charged with control over girls' bodies. In this case, the stranger acted to control my daughter by regulating her display of emotions (smile so you are pretty), making resistance more difficult. Note the link to the previous three binaries—girls are passive and pursued and must therefore be regulated.

These binaries are interwoven. They are also shockingly difficult to identify. I knew that Fionna was being woven into binary language. I had even written about the insidious nature of binary language in my research, and yet I could not pinpoint those binaries in the moment that they were invoked through the stranger's language.

The interweaving of binaries can be observed in the ways in which sexual harassment policies are framed by organizational members. My colleague and I discovered that the policies can be resisted because of the belief that women who are victims only display one side of interwoven binaries: They are viewed as weak (not strong), emotional (not rational), villains (not victims), and mean (not nice), which causes them to attempt to gain power through false claims of sexual harassment (Dougherty & Goldstein Hode, 2016). Notice how these binaries start to interweave so that they reinforce each other.

Binary Logics Are Intersectional

Scholars have long recognized the ways in which binaries shape race, gender, sexuality, and even age. However, it is premature to stop at the singular level of analysis. Instead of thinking of binaries as about a single demographic characteristic, it is important to understand that binary logics shape and structure meaning at the intersection of difference. Crenshaw (1991) argues that an intersectional approach to social power recognizes the "need to account for multiple grounds of identity when considering how the social world is constructed" (p. 1245). Because binaries are interwoven, it should not require a stretch of the imagination to recognize that these interwoven binaries are shaped by the varying demographic characteristics that are used to ground marginalized status.

Let's consider race as a case in point. Not only is gender an important binary language pairing, but race can also be constructed in binary terms. Because of its traditional oppositional pairing between white and black, people who are coded White/Black are socially constructed in oppositional ways, with Whiteness being the standard by which Blackness is judged (Ferguson & Dougherty, 2021). White person stereotypes are often hidden in the background of research and articles examining stereotypes about Black persons. When I typed in the keywords "stereotypes of Black women" into my library database, thousands of articles popped up exploring the various stereotypes, with a particular emphasis on the angry Black woman stereotype. However, when I typed in the keywords "stereotypes about White women," again, thousands of articles about Black women stereotypes popped up. In other words, rarely are White women stereotypes explored as the central feature of a study. This absence of White women in conversations about stereotypes is an excellent illustration of Derrida's notion of the absent presence. Blackness is defined in opposition to a hidden Whiteness that lurks in the background.

> Blackness is defined in opposition to a hidden Whiteness that lurks in the background.

Yet White women are raced and are therefore subject to stereotypes that matter. Take for example the differing language used to describe Black women versus White women. The stereotype of the angry Black woman is placed in contrast with the stereotype of the nice White lady. Note the binary language dividing these stereotypes: Black/White and angry/nice are concise representations of the intersectional nature of binary language. You can explore these intersecting binaries in Think About It 5.1.

Think About It 5.1 Intersectional Binaries

In the workplace, women, in general, are not allowed to be or appear angry (Smith et al., 2015). Both Black and White women cope with this emotion rule, but for very different reasons. Black women are assumed to be angry and therefore communicate in a way that resists that angry Black woman stereotype, which, according to Snider (2018), is like asking Black women to stand up straight in a crooked room. In contrast, White women who display anger violate the nice White lady stereotype. As a result, White women communicate in a way that will not be perceived as angry to avoid sanctions associated with White women who do not appropriately perform White nice.

Discussion Questions

1. How do binaries shape meanings based on the intersection of race and gender?
2. How do intersecting binaries of race/gender structure social relations?
3. How do intersecting binaries privilege one pole over the other?
4. How are binaries interwoven?

Gender and Sexuality: Illustrating the Binary Incursion

Binaries are the key to understanding how predatory sexual behaviors creep their way into organizational cultures. Gender and sexuality binaries are important foundational cultural meanings, making them an insidious and invasive weed in your organizational garden. In fact, predatory sexual organizational cultures feed off gender and sexual binaries. In this section, I drill down on the ways that these binaries shape gender relations within our larger social culture. I focus on Western cultures here, but research suggests similar patterns play out in other cultures as well. In this section I will discuss co-sexuality, hegemonic masculinity, and the paradox of femininity to demonstrate how gender and sexuality binaries grow into your organization.

Co-Sexuality

Gender and sexuality are different constructs, but both are built on the same set of binary logics and are woven together in the social world through binary language. Sexuality has historically been intertwined with organizing, including the early development of the Catholic Church, which was designed to control and eliminate sex between organizational members (Burrell, 1984). Sexuality continues to be a mechanism of power and control in many contemporary organizations, with member sexuality having a surprising amount of influence on organizational structure and meaning systems (Dixon, 2018).

Some of the newest and perhaps most important theorizing explores the notion of *co-sexuality* (Branton & Compton, 2021; Compton, 2019; Compton & Dougherty, 2017). The language of *co-sexual* was originally created to address the *linguistic inequality* between the dominant heterosexuality and all other sexual groups (Compton & Dougherty, 2017). You can explore linguistic inequality in Think About it 5.2. However, **co-sexuality** has evolved to explore the ways in which all people are both pulled toward and pushed away from heteronormativity. In other words, the binary language that creates the assumption of heterosexual/homosexual oversimplifies the complexity of sexuality. All people, regardless of their sexuality, are *pulled toward* heteronormativity because of the cultural norms and privileges granted to people who perform a heterosexual identity. Of course, not all people perform heteronormativity particularly well, but they are pulled toward it, nonetheless. Heteronormativity has strict cultural and social rules for adherence. Because of the high cost of strict adherence to heteronormativity, including the loss of identity and the limitations of love and pleasure, all people are also *pushed away* from heteronormativity in some way and to some degree. Regardless of a person's sexual identity, we are all in a constant state of flux when it comes to the performance of sexuality. As a result, it is best to think of sexuality as a constant process of becoming rather than as a preexisting thing.

Words matter. They create meaning and that meaning shapes and reshapes human relationships. When language privileges one group of people over other groups of people, it is called **linguistic inequality**.

Think About It 5.2 Sexuality and Linguistic Inequality

Linguistic inequality is by no means a new construct, although it has been explored with greater depth in recent years, particularly in terms of its impact on the lives of people who are socially and culturally marginalized (Hercula, 2020). This type of inequality is prevalent in language surrounding sexuality. Consider the various ways in which sexuality is discussed:

- heterosexual/homosexual
- straight/LGBTQ+
- straight/queer

There are some terms that are less polite, but they all are based on the assumption of heterosexuality as the norm and other sexualities as outside of that norm. The language that we use to discuss sexuality reinforces marginalized groups. As one of my favorite scholars, Mark Orbe (1998), explains, similar privileging can be seen in language surrounding dominant and marginalized cultures. To address this linguistic inequality, Dr. Orbe created the term co-cultures. By using the language of co-cultures, linguistically, all cultures are represented as equal. Dr. Cristin Compton and colleagues' use of the term co-sexuality builds on Orbe's co-cultural theory (Compton & Dougherty, 2017; Branton & Compton, 2021). Here is a link to a YouTube video where Dr. Orbe (2018) describes his theory.

https://www.youtube.com/watch?v=8x87QW8Jybk

Discussion Questions

1. What do you see as the relationship between linguistic inequality and binary logics?
2. What are the strengths of using co-sexual instead of the more common acronym LGBTQ+?
3. What are the limitations of using co-sexual instead of LGBTQ+?
4. In what other ways does linguistic inequality operate?

The push/pull of co-sexuality occurs across the lifespan, with performances first occurring at a very early age. Consider these early childhood examples. When I was in grade school the boys would chase the girls so they could kiss them. As a child, I thought playing keep away from the boys was fun, until the day one of the boys tackled me and they took turns kissing me. This is the pull toward a particular form of heteronormativity. After that day, the girls would not play with the boys, choosing instead to play with each other, a form of homonormativity in which the girls pushed away from the heteronormative assumptions of the male sexual conquest game. In another instance, when one of my daughters was in first grade, a male student passed her a "love" note asking her to go out with him. She said "no" and passed him back the note. He passed it back to her. This sequence occurred about three times before my daughter took the note, tore it up into little pieces and loudly said "no." The boy started to cry. When my daughter explained what happened to the teacher, the teacher told her that she needed to act like a friend to all of her classmates. Note the pull, push, pull of this interaction. The classmate performs toward a particular form of heteronormativity. My daughter pushes away from that form of heteronormativity by saying "no" and ripping up the note. She was chastised for failing to be "a friend," which pulled her back to a heteronormative performance of compliance. In case you were wondering, when she told me about the incident, I explained to my daughter that the boy's behavior was a form of sexual harassment. I congratulated her on her strong stance and told her that she had my permission to get in trouble for failing to be friendly in that type of situation, which pushed her back away from heteronormativity.

Every day from the time we are infants we are pushed and pulled toward and away from heteronormative performances. By the time we get into the workplace we have perfected these performances so that they are hidden and yet persistent. It is within this larger cultural push and pull of co-sexuality that your organization is situated. As a result, you will always need to address the invasive possibilities presented by the fluid movement of co-sexuality.

Hegemonic Masculinity

Have you ever seen the movie *Rescue Heroes*? You should watch it. This movie has been tremendously impactful for emerging men, at least in the United States. Here is the premise: Very large and powerful men with super big feet save the world against impossible odds.

FIGURE 5.4: *Rescue Heroes*

There are a few women in this movie; two skillfully drive rescue helicopters and equipment. One additional woman, who has a lot of courage (but maybe not much common sense), is in constant need of rescue. All men who are not rescue heroes appear to be the size of children next to these powerful male rescue heroes, who easily sling these little men, you know, your typical construction worker and the like, over their shoulders, rescuing them from falling buildings and such. Physically, these rescue heroes are muscular, square jawed, and did I mention the feet? (See Figure 5.4.) My son and I watched this movie repeatedly. I could not figure out why it was so appealing to both of us. Or rather, as a gender scholar, I knew precisely why I loved the movie but could not figure out why my understanding of hegemonic masculinity did not counter my pleasure in watching this film. My son, and many other emerging men who were influenced by this film, are either in or about to enter college. In other words, hegemonic masculinity is alive and well in our many cultures.

What is **hegemonic masculinity**? I define this concept a bit differently from its creator (Connell, 1995), who envisioned this concept as being achievable by some men, but not by others. In contrast, I view hegemonic masculinity as the cultural representation of a mythical ideal male person that imbues men with social power and force. Because it is a mythical representation of an ideal male, it is physiologically unachievable by a human person. However, although no person can achieve the ideal, all men are judged by their proximity to the ideal. Think about the masculine ideal in *Rescue Heroes*. First, note the unnaturally large bodies and muscles. At one time in my life, I frequented a gym where I was the only woman who lifted weights. I made friends with a number of men who struggled to achieve the rescue hero body by constantly working out, by taking anabolic steroids, and

> When I start to talk about hegemonic masculinity, the most common response from men is "I know this guy" who has achieved the idealized muscular body. I suppose it is possible, but I suspect that most of the idealized men have suffered similarly to the men I used to work out with. I also suspect they have body image issues similar to most other men, worrying that they might be physically inadequate.

by "working through the pain." The combination of anabolic steroids and working through the pain meant that many of these men not only had significant personality changes, but that they also were more prone to life-altering injuries. They worked to achieve an ideal body that is physiologically unachievable, often with devastating outcomes. Second, did you notice the enormous feet on the rescue heroes? What do you think those feet are supposed to represent? My best guess is that the feet are a phallic symbol representing sexual virility. Third, although there are both Black and White characters in *Rescue Heroes*, race is not an issue in this idealized world. Everyone communicates the same. All characters have status based only on experience and hierarchy. The idealized culture within which these men are situated is color blind, which is a type of White fantasy about race in America.

Not only is the physicality of these characters unachievable, but the behaviors, such as constant daring and dangerous rescues, are also unachievable—unless you are in a cartoon, of course; then the ideal is possible. Imagine all these little kids, especially little boys, running around pretending to rescue the little people in a race-neutral imaginary in which they embody the ideal. But, of course, they don't embody the ideal. Not even close. And that is the point. As these boys grow into men, they will judge, and be judged, based on an unachievable ideal of what and who they should be—an ideal that can only exist in mediated and cartoon images. Consider the implications of hegemonic masculinity in Think About it 5.3.

Think About It 5.3 Hegemonic Masculinities and Sexual Harassment

Jennifer Scarduzio and colleagues (2018) did a narrative analysis of two men's experiences of being sexually harassed by other men. These scholars discovered that, although there is some overlap between how men and women experience sexual harassment, men targets are expected to take an angry and aggressive stance. For example, when they told others about the harassment, these men were told "don't be a cupcake" and that they should “kick his [the harasser’s] ass.” As one of the men said, reporting the behavior is “kind of like taking your man card away.” Reporting sexual harassment threatened the target’s heterosexual identity and made them appear weak. In this way, their adherence to hegemonic masculinity was threatened by their harassment by other men.

Discussion Questions

1. How does sexual harassment of men threaten hegemonic masculinity?
2. How does sexual harassment of men reinforce hegemonic masculinity?
3. If we were to conceptualize hegemonic masculinity as a process, what processes are suggested when men are targeted by other men?

Nick Trujillo’s (1991) article provides an excellent examination of the ways in which hegemonic masculinity is communicated in the United States. Trujillo uses media images and stories about the famous baseball pitcher Nolan Ryan to provide a clear illustration of five components of hegemonic masculinity.

- **The idealized man is both physically powerful and has exquisite control.** In his early years, the media acknowledged that Ryan was a fast and powerful pitcher, but was excoriated for his lack of control. In his later years, when he was described as both powerful and in control, the media portrayed him as a weapon—such as a cannon.
- **The idealized man works hard and incessantly.** For example, Nolan Ryan was praised for working out on a stationary bike right after a game when the rest of the teammates were preparing to leave the stadium.
- **The idealized man is the family patriarch and a persistent father figure.** For example, Nolan’s role as the family breadwinner was emphasized in the media while his wife, Ruth Ryan, was depicted as a beautiful woman who stood behind her man.
- **The frontiersman is another version of the idealized man.** Nolan was persistently depicted as a cowboy by the media. He also owned three cattle ranches, so the media fixated on his cowboy-related work—castrating cattle, riding a horse, and other seemingly risky behavior. Importantly, Trujillo points out the ways in which his Whiteness was idealized in these images, meaning that the ideal frontiersman is a White male.

- **The ideal male is the ultimate heterosexual.** In Nolan Ryan's case, he was depicted as a virile male who was also safe for women to be around. I was fascinated by Trujillo's description of one advertisement in which Ryan was pictured in front of a spouting oil rig. He was wearing his baseball uniform covered with a long coat, a tall cowboy hat, and gun holsters with a baseball in each, asymmetrically placed so as to resemble testicles. As the author notes, depicting men as phallic symbols has a long history in the media Think About It Box 5.4 provides a recent illustration of the link about heterosexuality and hegemonic masculinity.

Think About It 5.4 Performing Hegemonic Masculinity

Tyler Sorg, currently one of my doctoral students and a frequent collaborator on my applied work, is an avid weightlifter. One day when Tyler was lifting weights at the gym, another White male weightlifter told him that he could bench press more weight than Tyler. The way Tyler tells the story, this man was bragging about his physical strength. They did whatever it is that weightlifters do to demonstrate their superiority, and Tyler was the winner. The other man sat up and started talking about all the women he had sex with. He told Tyler that he had sex with hundreds of women. Tyler was uncomfortable with the conversation, so he told the man that he was hungry and left to get a sandwich.

Discussion Questions

1. How were these men performing hegemonic masculinity?
2. When the White male weightlifter failed to achieve the ideal masculinity in his physical strength, he switched to demonstrating his aggressive heterosexuality, another form of hegemonic masculinity. Was he successful in achieving the ideal?
3. If this man had been Black and declared that he had sex with hundreds of women, how would he have been perceived in this situation?

How is hegemonic masculinity unachievable? Nolan Ryan's achievement of the hegemonic ideal was only possible through the impossible imagery from the media. His representation as a phallic symbol is particularly interesting, because he was essentially represented as a giant penis. By representing Ryan in this way, his humanity was simultaneously diminished. Nolan Ryan was represented as the ideal of masculinity by the media. In so doing, the media stripped away his complexity and humanity, leaving him as a shade of his whole self.

Of course, Nolan Ryan is an American icon and the masculine symbolism is specific to a United States context. According to Connell and Messerschmidt (2005), the complexity of hegemonic masculinity needs to be recognized. Hegemonic masculinity is enacted in culturally distinctive ways and is always subject to the context in which it is performed. In that spirit, I argue that hegemonic masculinity is best understood as an intersectional theory. Take Trujillo's recognition that, in the United States, the ideal man is both White and aggressively heterosexual. How then are Black men perceived in relationship to the hegemonic ideal? According to Katie Harris (2013), White male sexual capital depends on the vilification of Black masculinity. Black men are viewed as inherently criminal, hypersexual, and therefore sexually out of control. Behavior that may be seen as ideal masculinity in White men is viewed as threatening and inappropriate in Black men. As a result, even if a Black man were to achieve the five forms of hegemonic masculinity, they would never be viewed as the ideal for the simple fact that hegemonic masculinity is White and therefore cannot exist in a Black body. Yet, like all men, Black men are judged by their proximity to the hegemonic ideal and are therefore required to perform to that ideal, even though it is categorically unachievable.

Hegemonic masculinity is built on the binary logic that masculinity is the opposite of femininity, and that masculinity is superior to femininity. Power and control goes to those men who can closely perform to the hegemonic ideal, making hegemonic masculinity a core meaning structure in contemporary cultures. The constant need to assert and prove a particular idealized form of masculinity sets the stage for predatory sexual behavior in organizations. Because your organization is situated within a culture that adheres to hegemonic masculinity, this binary construct will constantly threaten your organizational garden, just like weeds threaten to take over my vegetable garden.

The Paradox of Femininity

Like masculinity, femininity is also unachievable. However, instead of an ideal, femininity is best understood as a series of unachievable paradoxes, a phenomenon I call the **paradox of femininity**. A lot of theorists throughout time have recognized that femininity is associated with paradox, yet most of these authors focus on a single paradox. For example, commitment to interpersonal consideration and Cuklanz (1992) demonstrate the ways in which different forms of feminism emerged to resist different binary pairings. Wood and Conrad (1983) articulate the paradox of the professional woman (more on this in the next chapter!), and Wyman and Dionisopoulos (2000) articulate the *virgin/whore* paradox that persists in contemporary media images. When these various paradoxes are combined, it is possible to recognize that the very soul of contemporary femininity is paradoxical and therefore unachievable. Specifically, to be feminine, a person must embody two mutually incompatible traits. They must simultaneously have two characteristics that cannot co-exist: weak/strong, mother/child, tough/delicate, girl/woman, stable/fragile, virgin/whore, helpless/helpful, healthy/anorexic, and so on. There are many ways in which these paradoxes appear in the larger culture and filtrate into organizations.

The oppositional nature of feminine paradoxes is made possible by binary thinking and therefore these paradoxes are shaped by the five components of binary logics (as discussed earlier), with one important caveat. While binary logics create oppositional language, paradoxes go one step further by demanding that both poles of the binary be simultaneously present. Gender paradoxes are therefore both mutually necessary and mutually negating. The virgin/whore pairing provides a useful illustration of the paradox of femininity. According to Wyman and Dionisopoulos (2000), "cultural notions of sexuality often involve fusing sex with power in ways which are perceived as rendering women powerless" (p. 211). Such is the case with the virgin/whore paradox, in which, to be viewed as sexually desirable, women need to simultaneously embody the virgin and the whore. Of course, these roles are mutually exclusive, meaning that women must be, but can never be, ideally sexually desirable because they must be/but can never be simultaneously a virgin and a whore. Women performers provide an example of how women are pressed to perform the virgin and whore pairing simultaneously. Consider Madonna's famous song "Like a Virgin" (Steinberg & Kelly, 1984), in which her heterosexual relationship with a man made her "shiny and new," "like a virgin." Miley Cyrus's transition from child star to adult singer is a case in point (Think About It 5.5).

Hoo, like a virgin
Touched for the very first time
Like a virgin
When your heart beats
Next to mine
(song lyrics from Madonna's "Like a Virgin")

Think About It 5.5 Miley Cyrus

FIGURE 5.5: Miley Cyrus as Hannah Montana

Miley Cyrus is an iconic performer with a versatile and beautiful voice. She exudes talent. Yet her talent was not enough to take her from child star to adult performer. I was first introduced to Miley Cyrus when I watched her hit children's show *Hannah Montana* with my older daughter. In this show, Cyrus's character hid her secret life as a star singer because she wanted to live a normal life while going to a normal school. Watch any episode and you can see Cyrus demonstrating her remarkable talent. When the show was over, Cyrus attempted to transition to an adult career. I clearly remember people mocking her because of her wholesome reputation gained from her Hannah Montana days. My best guess is that Cyrus's reputation as innocent and virginal prevented her adult career from transitioning. In response, she drastically changed her image.

FIGURE 5.6: Miley Cyrus Hosting the MTV Video Music Awards (VMAs)

When Miley Cyrus showed up to host the VMAs, her picture was posted in news and magazine outlets all over the world. This one I took from the August 30, 2015, issue of the *Daily Mail*, with the headline screeching, "Miley Cyrus is a bare-breasted Barbarella as she arrives at MTV VMAs in out of this world outfit that puts her naked ambition on show." She seems to have shocked the world with her sexual imagery, but it also seems likely that taking on the appearance of the whore was necessary for her to be recognized as a serious artist, especially when paired with the virginal Hannah Montana.

Discussion Questions

1. How do women in the workplace attempt to manage the virgin/whore paradox?
2. What are the consequences of women failing to be both poles of the paradox?
3. How do you suspect the paradox of femininity shapes sexual harassment in organizational contexts?

Paradoxical femininity is composed of intertwined and intersectional binary pairings. I strongly recommend that you read Bernadette Calafell's (2012) article exploring the ways in which women of color in the academy are constructed as monsters. Often, they are constructed as monsters that are hypersexualized and dangerous. She describes her own experience in a faculty meeting when her faculty mentor declared the following:

> "If Bernadette wants to stand naked in a cage in front of the building and call that research we should accept that." My face flushes red, my hands sweat, and I avert eye contact. I sit horrified and ashamed. *Am I actually hearing this? Is this really supposed to happen at a faculty meeting?* Suddenly the transformation has begun. *No one will ever take me seriously again.* I will always be marked by this monstrosity; the image of me naked in a cage. I'm trying to process everything all at once. I question everything that is happening to me and my place in it. I feel the weight of everyone's stare. I want to retreat as everything is laid bare and I move from subject to object through his words. I become a "freak" or oddity whose only merit comes in sexual display of my Otherness. The display of women of color as sexual oddities or freaks is not new. Women of colors' bodies are constantly on display because of their constructed Otherness and hypersexuality. (p. 117)

Every time I read Dr. Calafell's story, I feel sick. As a White woman, I am unlikely to experience the weird, caged eroticism expressed by her faculty mentor. That she was expected to calmly accept her treatment is both infuriating yet unsurprising.

I have witnessed the assumptions of monstrosity directed toward Black women. For example, Black women have historically been constructed as sexually out of control, so owning their sexuality is an act of power that simultaneously reinforces stereotypes. Lizzo is currently my favorite performer. She is talented, bold, and powerful (Figure 5.7). She inhabits a healthy body that does not match the stereotype of the healthy White body. A male friend of mine told me that he was appalled that Lizzo was famous because she was teaching young girls that it is okay to be fat and unhealthy. I asked him if he has seen her performing, where she dances vigorously while singing. He had seen videos. The following conversation ensued (Figure 5.7).

How could she be unhealthy if she can do all of those things?

Her body is unhealthy.

You mean she is big, and that makes you uncomfortable because you don't think it is sexy?

What if she was skinny but could not dance and sing, would you consider her healthy?

No

Hm. Don't you listen to male artists who sing about women as whores and treats them as interchangeable objects?

I guess.

You don't like Lizzo because she is a bad role model regarding health, but you like these dudes who denigrate women and are bad role models for how women should be treated?

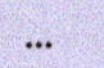

Lizzo is a Black, cisgender woman with lots of curves. How would women who identify with other races and other genders be perceived? For example, a curvy White transwoman? A curvy Asian cisgender woman? Try not to pretend like race does not

FIGURE 5.7: The Performer Lizzo

matter. It does. These women are bound up in different paradoxes and are forced to address those paradoxes in ways that are unique to each. The one commonality that seems to be consistent across women's experiences is that they are constrained, even disabled, by paradoxical expectations that must be simultaneously achieved, yet cannot simultaneously coexist. Your organization is situated in a culture that is embedded in paradoxes of femininity. As I will describe in the next chapter, these gender paradoxes very much shape the production of predatory sexual behavior in contemporary organizations.

Recap and Looking Forward

In this chapter you learned about some of the ways in which your organization is embedded in larger cultural meaning systems. At the larger level, binary logics that undergird binary language shape how people think, how they act, and the meanings that they can communicate. This binary thinking can be seen in processes of co-sexuality, in hegemonic masculinity, and in the paradox of femininity. As long as your organization is situated in a culture that supports these meaning systems, you will constantly be battling the problems that accompany them.

When weeds are small, it can be hard to know if they are weeds or if they are legitimate plants. When I first started gardening, I had to wait for the plants to mature before I could assess their status. I did not know how to tell the difference. Now that I have been a gardener for a number of years, I can pluck the noxious weeds while they are still small. Similarly, organizational change agents may not be able to tell the difference between productive and destructive organizing. In the next chapter, I discuss the ways in which cultural meaning systems are transformed into organizational cultures through communicative enactments. This will put you one step closer to being able to recognize and pluck your weeds before they can do damage.

Credits

Chapter 6

Enacting Predatory Sexual Behavior in the Organizational Culture

By the end of this chapter you should be able to do the following:

1. Recognize organizational cultural enactment.
2. Understand how larger cultural meanings are transformed into the organizational culture.
3. Identify organizational problems through patterns of behavior.

In case you have forgotten the information I provided in Chapter 1, let me remind you of the organizational impacts of sexual harassment.

- Post-traumatic stress
- Depression
- Lowered self-esteem
- Lost personal income
- Increased group/team conflict
- Decreased group/team cohesion
- Lost revenue due to decreased team productivity
- Decreased employee commitment

- Increased employee turnover
- Lawsuits
- Brand damage
- Stakeholder damage

I wanted to remind you of the destruction brought about by predatory sexual behavior for a very particular reason. When I share the information in the previous chapter with my clients, the initial response is invariably, "It is not our fault. We did not invent this problem." My response is twofold. First, you may not have invented predatory sexual behavior, but if you don't fix it in your organization, the cost is almost unimaginable. Second, although your organization did not invent predatory sexual harassment, your organization did invent how it is treated and enacted in your specific culture. You are fully responsible for the way that this behavior has become woven into the fabric of your organizational culture.

In this chapter, I address cultural enactments, which is the second layer of the Trans-MOC model of organizational culture. More specifically, I explore some of the ways in which predatory sexual behavior that comes from the larger social environment can be transformed by the organization such that it is woven into the fabric of the culture. Understand that there are many ways in which this transformation happens. I am going to describe some of the transformation processes that I have observed in the course of my work. To begin, let's review organizational cultural enactments.

Identifying Organizational Cultural Enactments

The second layer to the Trans-MOC model is organizational cultural enactment (Figure 6.1). Recall that this communication formation has many labels (performative, practice, communication constitutes, etc.). I use the term "enactment" because it is more easily understood by my clients. In Chapter 2, we discussed how communication as enactment is both about being and doing. As a result, we create both ourselves and our social worlds through communication in culturally specific ways. Enacted communication is embedded in power and culture and operates to normalize social practices. Organizational culture is enacted through persistent, patterned behavior that both accomplishes the work of the organization and communicates what is normal and natural in this particular organizational space.

FIGURE 6.1: Organizational Cultural Enactment

In fact, according to Yep (2020), a major function of performative communication is to make certain actions seem universal through hardening processes.

Communication as enactment springs from the speech act tradition, which views communication as a practice of being and doing.

Organizational cultural enactment is the point at which culture is physiologically engaged, what contemporary scholars would call the *materializing of communication*. We both do culture and watch culture as it is performed. In this way, organizational members are both performers and audience in a routine that is scripted in impromptu ways. As a result, organizational culture is both routine and evolutionary. To help you understand organizational cultural enactment, I will first discuss the ways that culture is physiologically observable, patterned, and normalized in organizations.

Physiologically Observable

During organizational cultural enactment, patterns of behavior become physiologically observable. Specifically, cultural enactment is where organizational members physically interact with their cultures. We see, hear, touch, smell, taste, and feel the organization in ways that are patterned and meaningful. Notice that I do not end with the standard five senses. Why is this? Because feelings represent an under-appreciated way in which we physiologically engage with our environment.

It is worth taking a moment to consider my articulation of feelings as a sixth sense. Feelings are what practice theorists call **affect**, or the pre-interpretive physiological response to our physical and social environment (Massumi, 2015). In contrast, emotions are the labels that we give feelings. As a result, feelings are enacted—a way of being with and doing our social worlds—while emotions are the meanings that we make of our feelings. I will discuss the relationship between feelings and emotions in Chapter 8, but suffice it to say that I firmly believe that our feelings are as sensorially important as sight, touch, taste, hearing, and smell. It is through these six senses that we engage in the being and the doing of organizational culture (Think About It 6.1).

Are feelings a sixth sense?

Think About It 6.1 Encountering the Enacted Organizational Culture

Here is an exercise that I think you will find helpful. Bring a friend or classmate with you and take a tour of one of your important organizations—be that a workplace, educational institution, church, club, whatever. Whoever you bring should be unfamiliar with the organization.

1. Walk into a familiar space.
2. Close your eyes and breathe in so that you can smell your space. What do you smell?
3. Keep your eyes closed. Listen. What do you hear?
4. Now open your eyes. What do you see? Describe it in detail.
5. Note the textures around you. What are people touching? What do you touch? What do you avoid touching?
6. What can you taste? Some organizations actually have candy or cookies that engage the taste in deliberate ways. However, taste is very closely linked to smell. How do the odors in this organization engage your taste buds?

7. Assess your physiological state. Are you experiencing adrenaline? Are your palms sweating? Are you smiling? Now label your physiological state with emotions.
8. Finally, compare your experiences with your guest's experiences. What do they notice that you do not notice? What do they smell that you can no longer smell? And so on.

These six physiological states are the ways in which your organizational culture is observed. What is interesting here is that many of these physiological experiences become part of the background of the organization. As you become an insider, you are less likely to notice these physiological patterns, even as they play out in front of you every day. This is called **cultural normalizing**, where patterns of behavior come to seem normal and routine, and therefore unworthy of note.

Patterned

Not all behavior is culturally important. Much of daily organizational life is made up of behaviors and communication that have little, if anything, to do with the organizational culture. This reality can be vexing for organizational members tasked with solving organizational problems. Specifically, how can you tell the difference between behavior that is culturally relevant and behavior that is not culturally relevant? There are two ways of knowing:

1. Does the behavior communicate? Specifically, does it tell us something about the organization and what it values?
2. Is the behavior patterned over time? Have you seen similar behaviors play out in the organization across time?

If the behavior communicates and if the behavior is part of a larger pattern, then it is likely woven into the organizational culture.

One of the activities that I ask my students to do when we discuss organizational culture is I have them go out into the building and find the things that they think are culturally important for our department. Students usually bring in an array of items, from flyers to people. One student asked our administrative assistant to come into class as her culturally important "thing." Another student brought in a fire extinguisher. The second part of this activity is for students to explain what these things tell us about the department culture. The student who brought our administrative assistant explained that she symbolized the friendliness of our department. The administrative assistant always greeted the students when they came into the office. In contrast, the student who brought the fire extinguisher could not think of how the item was culturally relevant, although it was always present in a prominent location. One of these "items" is culturally important. One of these items is not culturally important.

The administrative assistant consistently communicated friendliness. Note the patterned behavior (she always greeted the students) and persistent communication (the department is friendly). Her behavior was culturally relevant. In contrast, the fire extinguisher is always present (patterned behavior) but communicates nothing about the department. Why? Because its presence is mandated by government safety regulations. It was not present due to any cultural pattern within the Communication Department.

The administrative assistant or the fire extinguisher—which is culturally relevant and which is not? How do you know?

Here is the thing. It is not always possible to tell if a "thing" or "behavior" is culturally important. The fuzzy nature of organizational culture makes it feel like you need to squint your eyes to recognize what matters and what does not, hence the fuzzy edges of the Trans-MOC model. Many culturally relevant things and behaviors are so deeply woven into the culture that they seem normal, and therefore become invisible to organizational members.

Normalized and Invisible

In Chapter 4 I discussed Gestalt theory, which was developed to describe the ways in which people focus on the figure in images, ignoring or deemphasizing the background that shapes and frames the figure. The perceived figure becomes accented or marked and the unperceived background or landscape of the imagery becomes unmarked (Koffka, 1922). Recall that Gestalt theory argues that for every figure, there is a ground (Figure 6.2). Although many people cannot see the ground, it is every bit as important to the picture as the figure. Similarly, organizational culture can also be represented as a figure and ground. Some

FIGURE 6.2: We tend to focus on one part of the picture, ignoring the background that forms it.

aspects of the culture can be easily observed and recognized. In contrast, there is also a hidden background that shapes the organizational culture in both productive and destructive ways.

How does culture come to be invisible? I suspect that "seeing" the culture can best be represented as a curvilinear relationship. When a person first enters a culture or subculture, the culture is mostly obscured. You simply do not have enough experience to know if a behavior is patterned or meaningful. As you observe the culture, you can begin to see, understand, and even describe the culture. However, as time goes on and you become more integrated into a culture, the less able you are to recognize cultural problems.

Transformed Into the Organizational Culture

Now that you have a sense as to what constitutes organizational enactments, it is time to understand how these enactments weave predatory sexual behavior into the organizational culture. Contemporary organizations did not invent sexism, heterosexism, racism, misogyny, and so on. These are the meaning systems within which organizations are situated. Like weeds in a garden, they come in from the outside environment. If you don't deal with them now, you may not have a harvest later.

2021 was a bad year for my garden. Instead of plucking weeds, I focused on finishing this book, working with Scotti Branton on his dissertation proposal, and accomplishing some essential home maintenance. Next year will be better. I swear it will.

Image 6.1

Although contemporary organizations did not invent sexism, heterosexism, misogyny, and so on, these organizations do transform these meanings in ways that are unique to organizational cultures. For many organizations, these gendered cultural meanings are transformed into the culture through predatory sexual behavior such as sexual harassment. In this section, I am going to discuss three of the ways in which I have observed sexual harassment being woven into the cultural fabric of organizational culture. These processes include the unique working woman syndrome, the paradox of the professional woman, and the idealized male worker. These are not the only ways that predatory sexual behavior is woven into organizational culture, but they should provide a sense for how this weaving happens.

Unique Working Woman Syndrome

At this point, I would like you to take the quiz in Think About It 6.2.

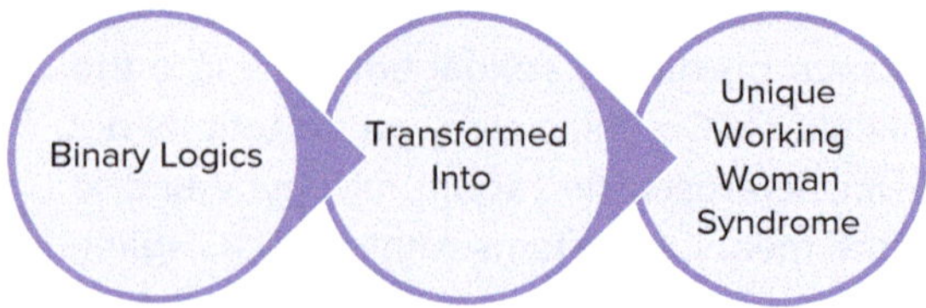

FIGURE 6.3: Transformation of Binary Logics Into the Unique Working Woman Syndrome

Think About It 6.2 The Bem Inventory

Consider your most recent workplace. If you have not yet held a job, think about a volunteer organization or an educational organization you have been part of. Now, on a scale from 1 to 7, with 1 being *not at all*, and 7 being *always*, rate yourself, most women, and most men on each trait.

	Self	Most women	Most men
Acts as a leader			
Aggressive			
Ambitious			
Analytical			
Assertive			
Athletic			
Competitive			
Defends own beliefs			
Dominant			
Forceful			
Has leadership abilities			
Independent			
Makes decisions easily			
Self-reliant			
Self-sufficient			
Strong personality			
Willing to take a stand			
Willing to take risks			
Affectionate			
Cheerful			
Childlike			
Compassionate			
Does not use hard language			
Eager to soothe hurt feelings			
Flatterable			
Gentle			
Gullible			
Loves children			
Loyal			

	Self	Most women	Most men
Sensitive to others' needs			
Shy			
Soft spoken			
Sympathetic			
Tender			
Understanding			
Warm			
Yielding			

Note. From S. L. Bem. (1974). The measurement of psychological androgyny. *Journal of Consulting and Clinical Psychology, 42*(2), 155 (https://doi.org/10.1037/h0036215).

Discussion Questions

1. This inventory is called the Bem Sex Role Inventory (Bem, 1974) and is supposed to measure how much you adhere to positive feminine/masculine stereotypes. Can you draw a line between the stereotypes of femininity and masculinity?
2. Do you perceive these stereotypes of femininity as equally positive as the stereotypes of masculinity?
3. Most women rate themselves as androgynous (highly masculine and feminine); most men rate themselves as masculine, but rate most other women as feminine. How do you compare?
4. Most men rate themselves as highly masculine, most women as highly feminine, and most men as highly masculine. How do you compare?
5. Hold on to this inventory. I am going to come back to it in a minute.

There are a number of human biases that have been identified by scholars from across the social science spectrum. I am personally aware of close to 50 different ways in which we enact biases, some of which I use in my training when I am trying to help clients understand how implicit bias works (Figure 6.4).

To this list of implicit biases, I have identified an additional bias that seems to play out in particularly devastating ways in organizational cultures. I call this implicit bias the **unique working woman syndrome**, which is defined as the assumption by women that they are somehow uniquely exempt from the likelihood, or even the possibility, that they could be targets of sexual harassment. I label this a syndrome because of the destructive impact this bias has on both targets of sexual harassment and the perpetuation of

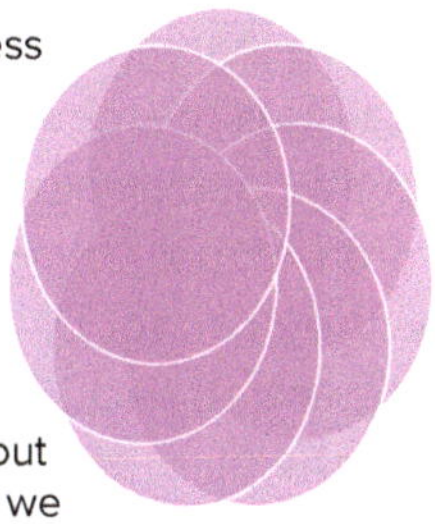

Fundamental Attribution Error: Negative outcomes by other people are attributed to a personality flaw. Negative outcomes by ourselves are attributed to a situational issue.

Bystander Effect: The more people who are present, the less likely we are to intervene.

In Group Favoritism: We have a strong preference for those who we believe are similar to us.

Blindspot Bias: We assume that other people have biases, but that we do not.

Group Think: In order to maintain a harmonious group, we make irrational decisions to avoid conflict.

Confirmation Bias: We seek out information that confirms what we already believe.

Anchoring: We rely heavily on the first piece of information introduced when making decisions.

FIGURE 6.4: Sample of Overlapping Forms of Implicit Bias

sexual harassment in organizational cultures. The unique working woman syndrome actually creates a welcoming environment for predatory sexual behavior.

How does the unique working woman syndrome work, and what does the Bem Sex Role Inventory (Bem, 1974) have to do with it? The Bem Sex Role Inventory was designed to measure how much a person adheres to gender stereotypes. It introduced the notion of androgyny, the idea that people can have both masculine and feminine characteristics. Interestingly, these stereotypes are all supposed to be positive. I think most of us can agree that these stereotypes are not equally positive. In fact, research suggests that the Bem Sex Role Inventory is a better measure of self-esteem than it is of gender. Specifically, people with lower self-esteem rate themselves higher on feminine stereotypes. People with higher self-esteem rate themselves higher on masculine stereotypes (Lamke, 1982).

Of course, this measure was created in 1974, so one would assume that it does not represent contemporary gender stereotypes. Surely not?! Yet, when I ask people to draw a line between masculine and feminine stereotypes in the inventory in Think About It 6.2, almost everyone draws the line in precisely the same place, although a few people do place the affectionate character trait in the masculine

Although I originally identified this as the unique working woman syndrome, research also suggests that this phenomenon plays out as the unique person syndrome. For example, when my coresearchers and I asked employed people to talk about unemployed people, they almost all described how they were uniquely exempt from unemployment because they worked hard, had important skill sets, and were willing to take whatever work was available. What is fascinating is that many of the people making these claims had previously experienced long-term unemployment, meaning they were not so uniquely exempt after all!

category. Here is what fascinates me about this inventory. Most cisgender women rate themselves as androgynous, but believe most other women are highly feminine. Let me frame this for you. Women see themselves as both masculine and feminine—Confident. Rational. Assertive. Acts like a leader. In contrast, women believe that most other women adhere primarily to the feminine stereotypes—gullible, childlike, emotional, and so on. Women believe they are uniquely special in comparison to other women, and therefore believe they are uniquely exempt from discrimination in the workplace. They believe they cannot be harassed because, unlike other women, they are strong and assertive and "would not stand for that behavior." This is similar to the third-person effect (Davison, 1983), in which people believe that they are not influenced by the media, but that other people are.

For example, many women from across my research studies believe if they were harassed, they would enact violence on the perpetrator.

Example 1

Rosemary: I can't imagine like, somebody doing that cause *I'd probably hit them*, like, "listen here!" But like, 'cause I also like, I think it's how you let, 'cause some people let themselves, their personal bubble in closer to people, like to actually touch them and stuff like that so I think there's different things there that I don't deal with 'cause people know that I have a huge personal bubble. Like I don't like, hug people. I don't do stuff like that just 'cause it makes me uncomfortable.

Example 2

Jennifer: And I worked at the [bar] so I got to know everybody. And it was always friendly, it was always very, [slight pause] nobody made it very personal, like made derogatory remarks, it was always. And if you told them "hey that's enough that's getting a little too far," they would stop, they would apologize. *Probably because they know I would slap them otherwise.*

These women seriously believe that they are immune to sexual harassment. What is fascinating is that some of the women who make this claim have experienced egregious sexual harassment that left them afraid and shaken. Yet still, they claim that they would confront a harasser if they were targeted. Why does this matter? Two consequences come to mind.

Consequence 1. To understand the larger issue at play, you need to understand schemas and scripts. A **schema** can be understood as the larger mental frameworks we use to store and process information about our social worlds. Similar to Big D Discourse, we draw on schemas to make sense of who we are and how we should act. Given the historical nature of sexual harassment and the large percentage of women who report being targets of gender and sexual harassment (as described extensively in Chapter 1), our schemas should reflect this reality. However, because women tend to see themselves as uniquely exempt from sexual harassment, our schemas around this phenomenon tend to be that it is "other people's problem." I have found unrealistic schemas surrounding sexual harassment across different types of women, including women from different social classes, races, ages, sexualities, and religion. As a result, women rarely develop realistic schemas around their social position in the workplace.

We use schemas to develop scripts. **Scripts** represent the ways in which we plan and build conversations and interactions based on the assumptions of a predictable social world. Politeness norms, meetings, and informal conversations are all driven, to a greater or lesser degree, by scripts that we create based on our schemas, with schemas allowing us to predict our social world. For scripts to be effective, they need to be based on realistic and probable schemas. If women believe they are uniquely exempt from sexual harassment (schema), they are likely to build unrealistic scripts (I will hit him). The reality is that women rarely hit, kick, or otherwise physically assault a male perpetrator. First, men are usually stronger physically. Second, there are laws restricting us from enacting physical violence. Third, even if the law were on the side of the woman being targeted, her organization would likely fire her for her physical response because, you know, we don't get to hit our coworkers. In addition, sexual harassment is usually enacted in private, or in a way that creates plausible deniability. Once a woman has been targeted and then fails to enact the planned script (direct confrontation), she feels weak, isolated, vulnerable, and embarrassed. As a result, the effects of sexual harassment may reverberate more strongly back on the target who entered the interaction believing she is uniquely exempt.

Shardé M. Davis describes the *Strong Black Woman Collective*, where Black women form and sustain friendships around their strength. How do you suppose this discourse of strength by Black women impacts their schemas and scripts about sexual harassment?

(Davis & Afifi, 2019)

Consequence 2. Women rarely support coworkers who have been targeted. Instead, they view targets as weak, morally questionable, and behaviorally problematic. Take, for example, one group of women talking about women who are targeted (for full analysis, see Dougherty, 2001b):

> **Woman B:** I think what is bad though is that, I'm assuming this too, it, there are so many false accusations [of sexual harassment] that every single one has to be, there has to be proof beyond a doubt. And are you ever at that proof beyond a doubt? Because of the falseness of what people have done because of other people's mistakes?
>
> **Woman A:** It has to be more clearly defined.
>
> **Woman C:** Yeah. Yeah.

I find this type of comment repeatedly in my work. Women constantly ask why other women "don't confront the harasser," claim that "women make false accusations," "women are so emotional," "women don't understand our culture," and so on. As a result, instead of providing pressure against predatory sexual harassment, women workers are as likely as men coworkers to reinforce a culture that welcomes predatory sexual behavior.

Paradox of the Professional Woman

In Chapter 5 we discussed the larger cultural meaning system of the paradox of femininity. Specifically, women are judged and defined by their simultaneous adherence to competing mandates, such as virgin/whore and mother/child. But how does this paradox get transformed in organizational contexts? (See Figure 6.5.) Wood and Conrad's (1983) notion of the paradox of the professional woman provides clues as to how this occurs. Let's begin by considering Think About It 6.3.

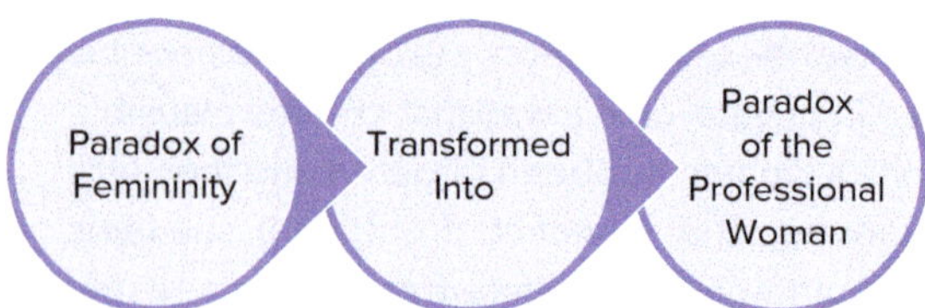

FIGURE 6.5: Transformation From the Paradox of Femininity to the Paradox of the Professional Woman

Think About It 6.3 Gender Stereotypes in Organizational Contexts

Take the Bem Sex Role Inventory back out and look at the gender stereotypes. Now, draw a line between the characteristics that are considered professional and the characteristics that are considered unprofessional. If you are like most people, your line is between *willing to take risks* and *affectionate*. as you may recall from Think About it 6.2, this is precisely where people draw the line between masculinity and femininity.

Discussion Questions

1. Which gender stereotypes are typically associated with professionalism?
2. Which gender stereotypes are typically associated with being unprofessional?
3. If people believe that most men adhere to professional/masculine stereotypes, and most women adhere to unprofessional/feminine stereotypes, how will these beliefs impact the workplace?
4. How might the association between femininity and unprofessional stereotypes perpetuate sexual harassment?

Back in 1983, Wood and Conrad observed that you cannot be considered both professional and a woman. Why? Because the paradox that defines femininity is also at play in organizational contexts. Specifically, as you can see from the previous Bem Sex Role exercise, the characteristics of masculinity align closely with the characteristics of professionalism. If people do not perceive a person as being stereotypically masculine, then they will not perceive that person as being professional. Worse, if a person is perceived to be stereotypically feminine (which is how most women are perceived), they will be perceived as being the opposite of professional, or unprofessional. Yet, to be successful in most contemporary workplaces, it is necessary to be perceived as professional—which is masculine. Do you see the paradox? Women are perceived as feminine, which means that no matter how hard they try to emulate men, they will not be perceived as professionals because professionalism is reserved for masculinity. The numbers play this out, with women making up only 5.8% of CEOs of S&P 500 companies (Catalyst, 2021), making 82.3% of what men make, with these disparities widening based on race (Think About It Box 6.4).

Think About It 6.4 Paradox of the Black Professional

Not only is there a paradox of professional women, but there are also professional paradoxes for other marginalized groups. My colleague, Marcus Ferguson, and I discovered that there is a paradox of the Black professional. This paradox is supported by three interlocking subordinate paradoxes. There is a *discursive paradox* in which there are competing discourses that make it impossible for Black workers to be recognized as professional. These discourses are often experienced as stereotypes and stigmas surrounding working while Black. The paradoxes are also *performative* in that Black workers perform professionalism where the standard script assumes White superiority and Black inferiority. Finally, the paradox of the Black professional is also *embodied.* Specifically, Black professionals must be White while inhabiting a Black body, obviously incompatible directives (Ferguson & Dougherty, 2021).

Discussion Questions

1. How might your behavior or expectations reinforce the paradox of the Black professional?
2. It appears that Black women experience both the paradox of the professional woman and the paradox of the Black professional. How might this double paradox explain the deep disparity they experience in the workplace? Be as specific as possible.

The paradox of the professional woman provides insight into the ways in which external cultural meaning systems infiltrate organizational behaviors. Gender expectations for women demand that they embody mutually exclusive characteristics (e.g., virgin and whore). These expectations are enhanced in organizations because of the paradox posed by the clear association between masculinity and professionalism. Sexual harassment exploits these unachievable expectations by, in some cases, reducing women to the role of professional whore. Take, for example, a conversation between one group of men employed by a large health care organization:

> **Allen:** I think that, sexual harassment, it takes so many ways shapes and forms. Like [Bob] was bringing up about the way people dress. A couple weeks back I was doing some work on the fifth floor, and a woman came out of [room]. It's like she walked out of a catalog. I mean she had a dress on, that was about mid-thigh. And, if it were any tighter, I could have told you whether her belly button went in or out. [Laughter] And, she had her name tag on. If I was at a nice bar downtown, "whoa, she's interesting." But I felt, my thought was at that time, "was that appropriate work clothing?" Because, it was like, she's trolling for something.

Bob: Yeah.

Allen: And that bothered me. You know? It [sexual harassment] can take so many ways, shapes, and forms. Mode of dress. Touching, the words used, hell, even an expression at somebody.

Bob: Yeah, you're going to see somebody walking down the hallway, you know, like you said, it looks like she's trolling. But then all of a sudden you say something to the effect that, "hey nice outfit" or something like that, and she kind of knows that you're checking her out. And all the sudden she gets ticked off because, "what are you trying to do? You're trying to pick me up?" And I said, "what are you dressed that way for then," you know? I mean, it's professional but you know, come on. I've seen secretaries dressed like that, just to get ahead.

Allen: I've seen professional women standing on street corners almost dressed like she was. [B. laughs.]

Let's consider this conversation. There are five points that are most relevant here.

- First, note the hegemonic masculinity at play between Bob and Allen. Neither of these fellows was particularly muscular—not like the rescue heroes at all. Still, these two men talked as if the woman in question owed them her sexual attention. If she did not appreciate their sexual attention, then she was irrational, because, you know, black dress.
- Second, this excerpt combines the paradox of the professional woman with hegemonic masculinity, demonstrating the ways in which gender is interwoven in Western cultures. Specifically, these men believed that a woman was sexually harassing them if she was perceived as attractive. She did not have to say anything, do anything, or look at anyone. If these men viewed her as attractive, they argued that she was harassing them.
- Third, although the story was told by Allen, note the way that Bob takes on the role of storyteller as if he was in the room and was targeted by this woman. In particular, note the way that he shifted from a second-person account to a first-person account: "And I said 'what are you dressed that way for?'" Something else that I have found repeatedly from harassers is the strange use of the phrase "all of a sudden." In this instance, as in most other uses of this term, it is a way to compress time. It allows the teller of a story to skip over

relevant and important details so that the outcome can be seen as an irrational response by the target of the behavior.

- Fourth, in the most obvious illustration of the paradox of the professional woman, note the way that this woman is called a prostitute. Apparently, for these men, the only professional role that a woman can fill is the oldest profession in the world, standing on a street corner, selling her body for sex. Interestingly, despite the description in the story of this woman's clothing as wildly inappropriate for the workplace, Allen did share with me privately that the woman's attire was appropriate for the workplace. I surmise that the description of her attire did not match the actual clothing that she wore.
- Finally, it is noteworthy that there were two other men in this group who did not speak up. When I asked them in follow-up interviews about their silence, one of them said, "That is just guy talk." When I raised my eyebrow, he explained, "This is how guys talk when they get in a group and there are no women around." I surmise from this statement that, at least in this organization, the reduction of women to the status of a troll or a prostitute is not at all unusual. The other silent man said that he was disgusted by the conversation but did not believe it was his role to speak up.

The interplay of gender, in particular the interplay between hegemonic masculinity and the paradox of femininity, is simultaneously horrifying and fascinating. By closely examining this story, it is possible to understand Ashcraft and Mumby's (2004) theorizing of organizational gender as a set of relations rather than as masculinity or femininity.

It is clear that the feminine paradox enters into sexual harassment–prone organizations, and is transformed into the paradox of the professional woman such that women struggle to be respected and to perform their jobs. The framing of women as whores is incredibly distressing. Notably, women of color are likely to be targeted because of the gender stereotypes associated with their race. For example, Black women are more likely to be targeted because of their history of sexual availability to White slave masters (Forbes, 2009), while some women of Asian descent believe they are more likely to targeted because they have been associated with sex work during various wars (Dougherty et al., 2011). The paradox of the professional woman is a cultural enactment, meaning that it is performed in a way that is unique to the organization and utilizes the unique stereotypes of the women who are targeted.

The Idealized Male Worker

As you will recall from Chapter 5, hegemonic masculinity represents the unachievable masculine ideal. The transformation of this cultural meaning system into organizational cultures can appear in the form of what I call **the idealized male worker**, or the tendency for male sexual predators in organizations to be perceived as uniquely important workers (Figure 6.6). As a result, firing these idealized male workers would result in a tragic loss to the organization, or at least, so goes the narrative. This idea of a worker who is too important to fire is a masculine myth that is passed down through generations within a predatory cultural milieu. Although I have numerous examples that illustrate this phenomenon, I have space in this chapter to provide two.

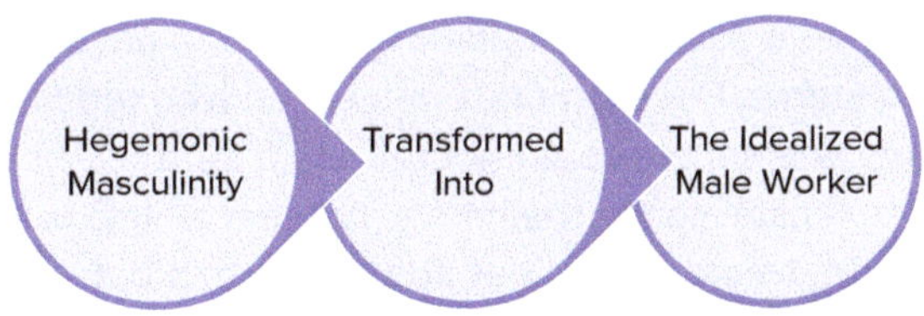

FIGURE 6.6: Transformation of Hegemonic Masculinity Into the Idealized Male Worker

My youngest child asked me when I had cried last. The answer is, I cried when I read Pesta's book. Usually, I can compartmentalize my emotions to a certain degree when doing my work on sexual harassment. Not this time. My heart broke repeatedly as I read the stories of the athletes who were raped by this man. I cried again when the judge who oversaw this case provided healing words to these survivors. It has been a few days since I finished this book, and I still feel raw and angry for these athletes who were trying to live out their dreams in an impossible situation that broke their bodies and their spirits.

Larry Nassar

Larry Nassar is perhaps the best-known organizational sexual predator in contemporary times. He sexually assaulted hundreds of gymnasts and other athletes who were young and vulnerable girls at the time. His predation spanned decades, with the first known instance occurring in the 1990s, while the last known instance was in 2016. How could this happen? I encourage you to read Abigail Pesta's 2019 book called *The Girls* to get a sense of how Nassar was supported in his predation for years. My goal here is to describe one of the many ways in which the predation was supported by the organizational cultures that employed Nassar.

It is important to begin by clearly stating that Nassar was not a good doctor. By this I mean that he did not heal the injuries that these athletes experienced. In fact, according to Pesta, one significant reason why Nassar was allowed to work in gymnastics is because he allowed the athletes under his care to continue training, even when experiencing debilitating injuries. According to Pesta, "many women and girls had reported Larry Nassar over the decades—to coaches, counselors, even the police—but they were dismissed or disbelieved. If anyone had listened and believed, this predator could have been stopped much sooner. Hundreds of girls could have been spared" (Pesta, 2019, p. 15). So, why weren't these athletes believed? There are a number of reasons. One key reason is that he was discursively crafted as a heroic figure with singularly important doctoring skills, despite his obvious inadequacies as a physician.

Despite his ineptitude, Nassar established a reputation as a world-class sports doctor. Many of the athletes came to know him as "a god"-like figure because of his reputation. Trainers, coaches, and family members referred to him as a world-renowned doctor. Because of his reputation, reports of his abuse were treated as a misunderstanding and women athletes were treated as mentally unstable. For example, one woman who reported the behavior was told that she simply could not tell the difference between sexual assault and a legitimate medical treatment. Another athlete, a softball player at Michigan State, asked her trainer about Nassar's behavior and was told that "Nassar was a world-renown [sic] doctor and it was 'legitimate medical treatment'" (CNN, 2016). Over time, according to a lawsuit filed by this athlete and reported by CNN, "Nassar became more bold, having the plaintiff remove her pants, and then inserting his bare, ungloved and unlubricated hand into her vagina." Again, she reported the behavior to a higher-level supervisor, who dismissed the athlete's complaints, treating her as though she was mentally unstable, indicating that "Dr. Nassar used this procedure with many female athletes."

Of note, at least two other sexual predators supported Nassar's capacity as a predator. Dr. William Strampel was dean of the College of Osteopathic Medicine during Nassar's tenure at Michigan State University. When Nassar was required to have a witness present during his medical treatments, and required to have no skin-on-skin contact (he was asked to wear gloves), Strampel did not enforce these restrictions. He later was convicted of misconduct and for sexually harassing women medical students and willful neglect of duty for his complete unwillingness to support the university's protocols after a complaint was filed against Nassar in 2014. Notably, the university had known about Strampel's predatory behavior for at least 15 years, with multiple reports of sexual harassment appearing in his past three 5-year reviews (Michigan State University, 2020). My reading of the university report is that the provost and other officials told him not to do stuff like that. Of course, the report uses more official sounding language like "he was counseled about his behavior," as if telling a predator not to be a predator would end the behavior.

Sorry if I seem a little snarky at this point, but come on! 15 years. Three 5-year reviews. Ample evidence. And Strampel was still considered too important to remove from his position.

The other notable predator was John Geddert, a gymnastics coach who in 2012 was given the honor of being the coach of the U.S. Gymnastics team. By all accounts, he was a bully, exhibited acts of violence, and was a sexual harasser of young girls (see Pesta, 2019). A number of gymnasts described how he would walk into the locker room when the athletes were changing their clothes. He would make commentary about the sexual capacity of the girls he worked with. At one point he asked a gymnast if she knew what "hoo-ha" meant. When the gymnast explained that it was an informal term for vagina, Geddert explained that he already knew that. Some of Nassar's targets claim Geddert knew about Nassar's predation but did nothing to stop it (Banta et al., 2020). Why was Geddert allowed to continue working with child athletes? Because he was a winning coach—too important to fire.

It is not any one of these men that created the conditions for the predatory sexual behavior across multiple organizations. It is not even the combination of these three men who created the conditions. It is the master narrative of the ideal male worker that creates the potential, not only for predatory sexual behavior, but for many of the other destructive behaviors experienced by contemporary organizations, including theft, Ponzi schemes, racism, and bullying. The belief that some men are too important to fire has caused vast and unknowable damage in the contemporary workplace. In the case of USA Gymnastics and Michigan State University, generations of women athletes were devastated by the outcome.

The Perfusionist

The previous example may give the impression that the idealized male worker is an isolated phenomenon, occurring only in extraordinary instances. I do not wish to leave you with that impression. The idealized male worker can be found in any organization, and even among the most common of positions. Take for example this illustration from one of my study focus groups, where a male perfusionist, a medical technician, was idealized by the group participants. To provide context, I had asked the group to provide examples of instances of sexual harassment they had observed or heard about. You have seen this illustration before, but I want you to read it in this new light:

> **Anna:** Another (sexual harassment case) was, I did work with a male surgical tech. If you knew him, he was a very friendly guy. It didn't bother him a bit to give you a hug. And there are guys that I work with that, I can walk up to them and say, "you know, I just need a hug today." And they'll give you a hug. Total friends. My husband knows them. I do it in front of my husband. It's nothing. But, this certain man, he was a, a very touchy-feely kind of person. I never took it as sexual. He knew how far he could go with anybody. That's kind of the way he was. He would feel you out—not literally. He would check you out before and see how far you would let him go. Because he would probably go to the extreme if you would let him. But if you wouldn't let him he would not do it. And, I had told him before, "nope, that's where you stop. You don't mess with me that way. I'm married and I don't take that." But he was fired from an RN [registered nurse] who came down and worked with him and said, "he's doing these things to me and they're wrong." And they brought him to the office and said "look." He was a very good tech. Everybody knew how he was. The manager of the department messed with him the same as everybody else did. I mean it was just, that's how he was. And they told him, "if you deny these claims, we can't fire you because you're saying it didn't happen, she's saying it did, so we have to get into it." And he said "well, it did happen. It did happen. I'm not going to deny it because it did happen. But I didn't think I was doing anything wrong." So he was fired because he didn't deny it. I didn't think that was right. Um, I don't know what you guys feel about that, but.
>
> **Donna:** I think firing is probably inappropriate. If he felt he wasn't doing something wrong, that's probably more of a counseling issue. Obviously he read the person wrong. Or maybe he's got some boundary problems to begin with that need to be addressed.
>
> **Anna:** I totally agree. And that was my problem. He did have issues of his own. His wife works here. I mean, he was married. I don't know, it was kind of an all-around bad situation. I don't think he should have been fired.

Although there are many things that are fascinating about this exchange, the insertion that "he was a very good tech" is at the top of my list. Notice where Anna decided to place this comment. She had spent quite a bit of time building this surgical tech up into an aggressive yet lovable harasser who would go "to the extreme if you let him." She talked about how she used her marriage as a shield against his sexualized behavior, simultaneously claiming that she never saw it as sexual. She could have talked about his excellent work skills at any point during this part of her story. However, his excellence at his job became important only after an RN reported the predatory sexual behavior. I am not exactly sure why his job skills became important at that precise moment, but it is clear that Anna linked the surgical technician's job proficiency, his routine sexual behavior toward colleagues, and the one courageous woman who reported him as justification for why he should be able to retain his job. I also want you to notice how normal this behavior was, as suggested by the language "that is just how he was." In this way, the idealized worker is paired with predatory sexual behavior such that the behavior is viewed as not only acceptable, but also as desirable.

Note how the surgical technician's sexual predation was discursively framed as "friendly," normal, and routine. This type of normalization is one way we can assess if and how sexual harassment is woven into the fabric of an organizational culture.

Clearly, hegemonic masculinity is transformed through enacted communication into the organizational culture, taking the form of the idealized male worker. Think about all the instances of predation that have been allowed to continue because the predator is viewed as too important to fail. Harvey Weinstein, Bill Cosby, Larry Nassar, Governor Andrew Cuomo, the surgical technician, an unknown manager at, perhaps, your organization? The list goes on and on. The known damage from this idealized male worker is the tip of the proverbial iceberg. The hidden costs to the target, the organization, colleagues, work teams, and clients is tremendous, and frankly, horrifying.

Recap and Looking Forward

In this chapter, I described the transformational process by which problems in the external culture are transformed into organizational cultural enactments. Understand that although I focused on three transformation processes, the unique working woman syndrome, the paradox of the professional woman, and the idealized male worker, these do not represent a complete accounting. In addition, remember that each organization transforms problems in ways that are unique to that culture. As a result, sexual predation will look both similar and different across organizations.

My strongly held conviction is that enacted values are key to understanding the similarities and differences between how organizational cultures respond to predatory sexual harassment. In the next chapter, I describe how cultural values are formed through human behavior and how those values are an important meaning-making tool for organizational members and organizational change agents.

Credit

Fig. 6.2: Source: https://commons.wikimedia.org/wiki/File:Duck-Rabbit_illusion.jpg.

Chapter 7

Organizational Values in Action

By the end of this chapter you should understand

1. That values as communicative enactments are complex.
2. How values are culturally embedded through enacted communication.
3. Value orientations are critically important to an ethically reliable organization.

What values drove these organizations?

- Enron imploded due to a Ponzi scheme run by its top employees.
- The CFO of the Trump network of organizations is charged with tax fraud.
- Top talent at Fox News, NBC News, and PBS all were known sexual predators.
- The Red Cross spent 25% of donations for Haiti on internal administrative costs.

It is fascinating that each organization claims (or claimed) to be value based, yet each has committed serious ethical violations. So humor me for a moment and really think about the question above: What values drove these organizations? If your thinking is anything like my own, this question is hard to answer because we are usually asked to think about values as positive and as things. But in each of these instances, values are neither positive nor are they things. Instead, values are better understood as simultaneously constructive and destructive *processes* that have an everyday impact on how organizational members act.

Organizational values represent a central role in the Trans-MOC model because of the profound role values play in both an organization's success and failure. For example, we know that values are critical to achieving an organization's mission (Richardson & Cassop Thompson, 2019), and producing organizational citizenship behavior (Ye, 2012), while the failure to enact organizational values is associated with employee deviance (Biron, 2010). In fact, there is a large body of empirical research demonstrating the relationship between organizational values and organizational outcomes. Trans-MOC helps us understand how values operate as part of a larger cultural system. This complexity approach to organizational values is critical when considering how to solve complex organizational problems.

Because problems are complex, it is important to also think about values as complex. This is necessary from a basic systems theory notion of **requisite variety**, that the system needs to match the complexity of the environment within which it is situated, particularly when it comes to solving complex problems. Therefore, when addressing organizational problems, it is critically important to take a complexity approach to understanding values. In Chapter 4, I defined *organizational values* as "those things, standards, and ideals through which we evaluate our organizational well-being." In this chapter, I will a) explore a complexity approach to organizational values, b) use the Trans-MOC model to show how values are communicatively woven into organizational cultures across time, and c) discuss the ways in which value orientations are key to creating an ethically reliable organization.

Complexity Approaches to Organizational Values

Early research on organizational values tended to focus on **value typologies**, which is a classification system for different types of values. For example, Rokeach's (1973) work documenting a distinction between *terminal values*—your desired outcomes—and *instrumental values*—how you want to achieve

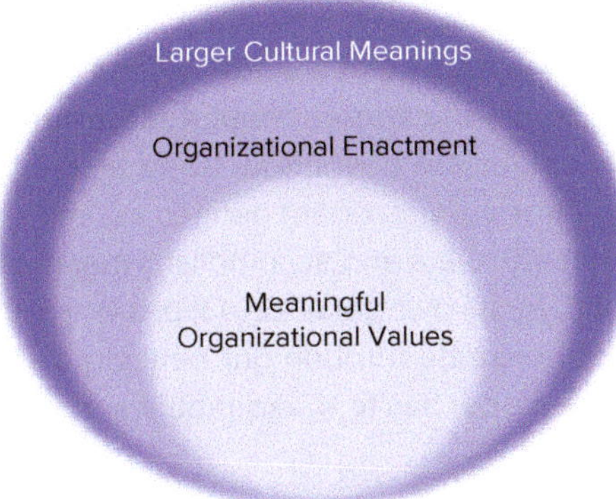

FIGURE 7.1: Organizational Values in the Trans-MOC Model

your desired outcomes—provided a groundbreaking way to characterize organizational values. Schwartz's (1994) 10 value types and related model of values provided new ways of thinking about the relationship between different types of values. In Chapter 4, I added to the value types by suggesting a previously unexplored value type that I call "status values." Recall that status values focus on who gets power and how they are to obtain it. I will come back to status values later in this chapter.

Although valuable, there are some obvious limitations to value typologies. First, they tend to focus on individuals rather than the organizational culture. Yet, as Ryan Bisel, author of an excellent book on organizational moral learning, states, "Our thinking occurs within the context of a group's culture. That idea is important to understanding organizational ethics and strategies for leading organizational ethics" (2017, p. 88). Second, value typologies suggest a relatively simple relationship between human behavior and values. However, moral thinking requires a complexity approach to both organizing and communication. Two emerging models bring clarity to my own thinking about the relationship between organizational values and culturally embedded organizational problems: Gehman et al.'s (2013) **value practice model** and Bourne and Jenkins's (2013) **dynamic perspective model**.

Schwartz's 10 value types

1. Achievement
2. Benevolence
3. Conformity
4. Hedonism
5. Power
6. Security
7. Self-direction
8. Stimulation
9. Tradition
10. Universalism

Value Practice Model

Instead of focusing on values as things that are pre-existing ideals, Gehman and colleagues utilize a communication constitutes organizing (CCO) approach to suggest that values are best understood as practices in an organization. Specifically, **values practices** are defined as "the sayings and doings in organizations that articulate and accomplish what is normatively right or wrong, good or bad, for its own sake" (2013, p. 84). In other words, values are something that we create through our behaviors and communication. The value practice model has four sequential actions.

1. Value practices begin with *pockets of concerns*, which constitute emerging worries about ethical and moral issues in an organization. When various organizational constituents become increasingly concerned about sexual harassment, they have formed pockets of concerns.
2. Second, pockets of concerns become *knotted together into action networks*. In this sequence, social and material concerns are brought together through individual and collective activities. As these individual and collective activities interact, an action network emerges. Because organizational members are not typically able to talk about sexual harassment, it is rare for pockets of concern around this issue to become knotted together into action networks.
3. Third, *performativity* occurs when "values practices do more than simply describe what should be said and done in certain situations. Values practices actively intervene in situations, contributing to the enactment of normative reality" (Gehman et al., 2013, p. 104). In this sequence, values practices are not simply imposed by managers, but instead are in constant motion, being contested and promoted, evolving and sedimenting into the organizational systems and practices.
4. The fourth, and final, sequence is called *circulating discourses*. As the values are performed overtime, they become meaningful—although not coherently so. Because of individual differences, people will have a variety of interpretations of any given value. The larger meanings, sedimented in discourse, circulate in an increasing spiral such that values encompass ever widening swaths of the organization.

The concept of values practices emerged from a case study of a university creating an honor code. As a result, the processes described may be best understood as what happens when values are deliberately crafted and inserted into an organization. Nonetheless, this model contributes two important concepts to the Trans-MOC model. First, values are enacted. We create, shape, and make values meaningful through communicative actions. This linkage can be seen in the relationship between the second (enacted) and third (values) levels of the Trans-MOC model. Second, this model hints at the relationship between organizational values and problem solving. Specifically, the idea that values are in constant motion and are a product/process of ongoing communication between organizational members, strikes me as an important contribution to understanding how values operate in creating, sustaining, and removing organizational problems such as predatory sexual behavior.

Dynamic Perspectives Model

Bourne and Jenkins (2013) make the case for four distinct forms of values that interact in dynamic ways.

- **Espoused values** are similar to those proposed by Edgar Schein. These are the values that the organization claims. Usually, these values can be identified on an organization's website. In my own experience, sometimes organizations train around their values, and sometimes organizations do not. As Bourne and Jenkins note later in their model, this can produce gaps and overlaps between espoused and attributed values.
- **Attributed values** are the values that organizational members believe are "representative of the organization" (p. 499).
- **Shared values** "[position] organizational values as an aggregation of the values of its members" (p. 500). Shared values are acquired through socialization processes and are central to organizational cultures. However, Bourne and Jenkins view shared values as an aggregate of individual values with some variance from the mean.
- **Aspirational values** are those organizational members believe should be the organization's values.

Now, think about these four value types along two dimensions. Dimension 1 is called the level of values and is placed on a continuum between collective/social and aggregated/individual values. Dimension 2 is called the orientation of values and is placed on a continuum between embedded and intended values. Embedded values are conceptualized as those values that emerge through interactions. In contrast, intended values are those imposed by the organization. It looks something like this (Figure 7.2):

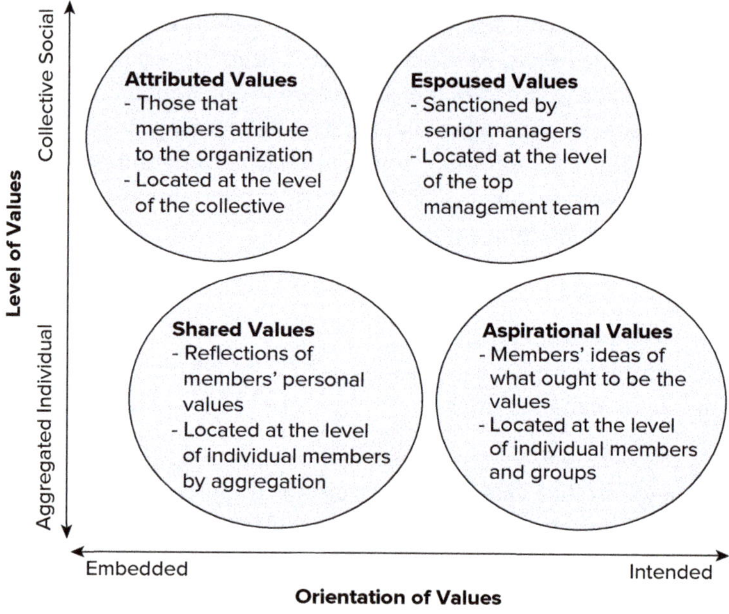

FIGURE 7.2: Bourne and Jenkins's Forms of Organizational Values

Every organization has some degree of gap and some degree of overlap between the different value forms. Ideally, attributed values, shared values, espoused values, and aspirational values would be identical. However, given the value practices that produce and reproduce values, it is not realistic to expect that the value forms would be fully coherent. It is the relationship between value gaps and value overlaps that is of particular importance in understanding the values level of the Trans-MOC model.

Values and the Trans-MOC Model

There are four interrelated values issues that are important to understanding how values become intertwined with organizational culture and how they can be used to address important organizational problems.

Values Emerge From Cultural Enactments

How do we know what an organization values? Is it through the values an organization espouses? The individual values that people bring to their organizations? No. Although espoused values and individual values are important, they are not necessarily culturally important. Instead, we know what an organization values through the repetitive enactments that form the foundation of an organizational culture. To understand values as enacted, it is useful to recall that the current conceptualization of organizational culture utilizes a communication constitutes organizing (CCO) approach.

How do we know what an organization values?

We know what an organization values through the repetitive performances and practices that form the foundation of an organizational culture.

Organizational cultures are created through communication that is patterned, persistent, and scaled up overtime. When patterned behaviors become persistently meaningful across time, that is how you know that a behavior is communicative and that it is culturally meaningful. Consider, again, the Larry Nassar case. Recall that he was the team doctor for women's gymnastics. He targeted hundreds of athletes, mostly little girls, but also college athletes, with predatory sexual behavior. He did not act alone. He was surrounded by many people across multiple organizations who served as his support system. Although some of these people were also sexual predators, many were not. How is it that these people provided Nassar with their unquestioning support? Support suggests values. Support is one way in which we enact particular values, both organizationally endorsed values and hidden values that are toxic and destructive. Values that are not enacted are not culturally important. They are meaningless at the cultural level. Maybe they are useful in positioning the organization from marketing or public relations perspectives, but only values that are enacted are culturally important.

Let's do a quick memory check.

- What is CCO?
- How does it work?
- Why is it important?

Values Can Be Organizationally Sanctioned or Unsanctioned

Starting with Edgar Schien, there has been a remarkable amount of theorizing on organizational espoused values. These are the values that organizations claim.

While espoused values can have a positive impact on organizations (Bourne et al., 2019), as Joann Keyton (2011) points out, there is a clear difference between espoused values and enacted values. Just because an organization claims to adhere to a value does not mean that they enact that organizational value. Often, organizational members do not even know what values its organization espouses. It may be instructive to contrast two trainings in two organizations. In organization one, I asked the leadership team that I was training to tell me the organizational values. At first, no one spoke. Then one person said, "Do we have values?" Finally, one person pulled a small card out of their pocket and read the organizational values to the rest of the group. It is clear that the espoused values of this organization are not enacted. They are not, therefore, culturally important.

Think about an important organization in your life—work, school, church, and so on. What are this organization's espoused values? How do you know that these are the values?

Now consider organization two. This organization brought me in to do an annual training—not because they had a problem but because they wanted to prevent sexual harassment from occurring. When I asked these organizational members to tell me their values, they shouted them out. There were a lot of values, and these organizational members knew them all. This was one of the easiest trainings I have done because I was able to align their values with the organization's behaviors, reminding employees to live their values when it came to observing and stopping sexual harassment. That was a fun training.

Every organization operates within a set of values, just not necessarily values that have been verbally sanctioned by the organization's leadership. In fact, it is likely that organizations in general utilize both sanctioned and unsanctioned values. For example, many organizations value change, not because of the outcome that is produced, but change for its own sake (Zorn et al., 2000). Further, many Western organizations value time, including being on time, time spent at work, and working through lunch. Although most organizations do not officially sanction change or time as organizational values, their repetitive behaviors make it clear that these unsanctioned values are important.

Organizational Values Can Be Both Constructive and Destructive

Most people use positive terms to describe values. I call this the Mary Poppins version of organizational values. However, as mentioned in Chapter 3, Darth Vader teaches us that values can be destructive, with many values sucking the lifeforce from the organization. Neils Van Quaquebeke and colleagues (2014) identify positive values as *ideal values*—those values that motivate organizational members to behave in preferred ways. In contrast, Quaquebeke et al. argue for the presence of *counter ideal values*, those values that motivate people to avoid preferred behaviors. Take for example the value of respect. This ideal value should motivate people to engage in ways that are recognized as respectful. However, my experience has been that when predatory sexual behavior is woven into the fabric of an organization's culture, respect is reserved for predators. The counter ideal value of disrespect is a more prominent motivator for organizational members when confronted with a person who has been targeted by a sexual predator. Take any instance of predatory sexual behavior from any type of organization, and you will observe this pattern. Respect is reserved for a few high-powered (mostly) men. Disrespect is most commonly a hidden value that motivates behavior toward (mostly) women and almost all targets of these highly respected men.

Larry Nassar was highly respected./The women he targeted were disrespected.

Roger Ailes was highly respected./The women he targeted were disrespected.

Harvey Weinstein was highly respected./The women he targeted were disrespected.

Andrew Cuomo was highly respected./The women he targeted were disrespected.

Destructive values can develop independent of constructive values. Consider status values. Status values identify who has power and prestige. All organizations have status values, some of which are formalized in an organizational structure. For example, in most organizations, a supervisor has more formal power than their direct report. However, as most women leaders can attest, that formal power is constantly being contested by unacknowledged sources of power that are derived from hidden values that most organizations don't even admit to enacting (Think About It 7.1). For example, gender is a source of social power that is woven into organizational culture, providing status to certain types of men, and disempowerment for most women. If you need more on this process, consider rereading the last two chapters.

Think About It 7.1 Being God in the U.S. Olympics

I am struck by the repeated reference to Larry Nassar as "God-like" in the various stories told about his status in the gymnastics world.

- "I [Carrie Hogan, college athlete who was targeted by Nassar] was very aware of the signed photographs of the Olympic gymnasts he had treated," she said. "He was the best of the best." Others said he was seen as a "god" in the gymnastics world (BBC News, 2018).
- "Larissa [gymnast who was targeted by Nassar] was participating in a youth gymnastics program at Michigan State, and she remembers that Larry had a 'God-like status,' which he used to his advantage" (Pesta, 2019, p. 52).
- "In gymnastics, young girls do what they are told. They hide their pain, they hide their injuries. These young girls bared all of it. Their bodies were constantly on display and under scrutiny. It takes some kind of sick perversion to not only assault a child but to do so with her parent in the room. To do so while a lineup of eager young gymnasts waited to see the gymnastics god, Larry Nassar" (Michigan Assistant Attorney General Angela Povilaitis, addressing the court at Nassar's sentencing, as reported by CNN, 2018).

The word "God" in reference to Nassar appears repeatedly in many different contexts and by many different people. Of course, the word "God" is about status and power. A person who is designated as God-like has been granted deity-like status in an organization. In this case, it is an excellent example of how predators come to be seen as irreplaceable.

Discussion Questions

1. What does it mean to be "God-like"?
2. What values are implied in this label?
3. Think of a very religious person. How would they react if you told them that their God was not real? Would they believe you? Would they still trust you?
4. Many believe that their religious text is the inerrant word of God, meaning that it is absolutely God's words and God's truth. How might this inerrancy have been granted to Larry Nassar?
5. If your God said he needed to do something unpleasant to you, would you let him do it?

Ugly, toxic values represent the proverbial elephant in the room. Values can all be destructive at times depending on how they are enacted. However, *toxic values* are almost universally destructive in an organization. These values may provide status to key individuals, but for the rest of the organizational members, the outcome is flatly destructive. Equally important, toxic values are destructive to the organization within which they reside. It can be a challenge to identify and label toxic values, mostly because we do not have a language for destructive values. For example, what label do you give to an organization that hurts little girls who have been entrusted to its care? Think about the behaviors of the USA Gymnastics organization.

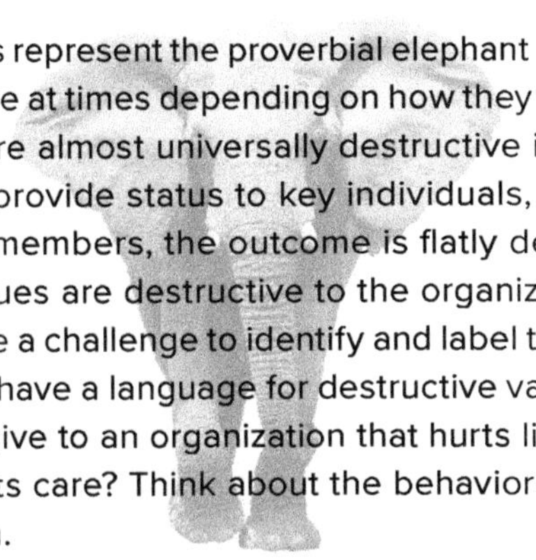

Image 7.1

- **Behavior 1:** According to Pesta (2019), the coach of Twistars Gymnastics berated gymnasts who were injured, claiming that they were lying about their injuries. He would insist that they continue to practice even when obviously injured.
- **Behavior 2:** One reason why Nassar was allowed to be the team doctor was because he made it possible for the gymnasts to practice and compete while seriously injured.
- **Behavior 3:** The gymnastics coaches at the Karolyi ranch, where elite gymnasts were trained for major competitions—such as the Olympics—did not allow parents on the property to advocate for and protect their children. As a result, when these athletes were injured and belittled, they had untenable options. They could either go see Larry Nassar or they could leave in shame.

In each of these examples there are some common behaviors. Gymnasts were only valued for physical success. Injury was considered a failure, as evidenced in the repetitive organizational behaviors. Specifically, gymnasts were not believed when they were injured. Gymnasts were screamed at or ignored when they were injured. Gymnasts were forced to see a sexual predator when they were injured so that they could compete, even when they had life-changing injuries.

Remember, values are not something that we have. Values are something that we do. They are developed through communicative behavior over time. It is clear that the penultimate value of these gymnastics organizations was success. This value makes sense given that athletes also want success. However, this value is also paired with distrust of young women, misogyny, silence, and a casual form of pedophilia. In some of the most interesting research on abusive institutional culture that is pervasive in women's gymnastics, Ryan Bisel and colleagues explore the ways in which one gymnastics gym worked to create a new and more positive culture among its members (Think About It 7.2).

Think About It 7.2 Changing Institutionalized Values in Elite Gymnastics

It seems like it should be easy to establish organizational values when starting your own organization. Unfortunately, as one elite gymnastics organization discovered, institutional pressure is a powerful force in establishing and maintaining organizational culture. Bisel, Kramer, and Banas (2017) describe the ways in which a gymnastics training center had to break the institutional norms and values before they could fully inculcate gymnastics training with new and more positive values. Alexis Reader, the founder of a gymnastics training center that uses positive coaching, had to scale up communication so that the meaning of "success" as a value was more compassionate and was important beyond athletic success.

Bisel and colleagues identified four collections of events that characterize the change process:

- First, Alexis Reader's daughter had been damaged by the abusive training tactics at an elite gymnastics gym, which *triggered resistance to institutional influence on organizational practices*. Having been an elite athlete herself, Reader recognized the coaching behavior as abusive and began to search for a coach who would use life-affirming coaching for her daughter.
- It was shockingly difficult for Reader to find a gymnastics coach who did not ascribe to an abusive coaching model, which triggered the need for her to *lead others to resist institutional influences on local organizational practices*. Eventually, using storytelling that reframed the old style of coaching, she was able to convince an elite coach to shift his values. This shift in values allowed him to engage in coaching that was humanizing, compassionate, and positive.
- This coach talked to people, who talked to other people, and so on. This leadership led to the *acquisition of material and creation of symbolic resources to reinforce organizational practices*. During this series of events, Reader was able to finance her training facility and create a set of practices that embodied new values.

- Eventually, this scaling up process allowed Reader to begin to engage with the larger institution of gymnastics training. This institutional level change continues to be a work in progress that will take many years to complete, showing *the challenges of boundary spanning attempts.*

Discussion Questions

1. How are individual gymnastics organizations influenced by institutional values?
2. What advice would you give Reader as she continues to work toward change?
3. What makes it so hard to change abusive values?
4. What is the relationship between communication and organizational values?

Values Are Learned

Not only are values enacted and performed in organizational cultures, but they are learned by organizational members and then passed down over time. As a result, organizational values come to seem normal and natural within an organizational culture. When an organization's culture is generally productive and healthy, this normalization of values is constructive. However, when the organization's culture is threaded with predatory sexual behaviors, this normalization can set the stage for ongoing destruction. How does this work? The primary way in which organizational values are learned is through socialization. I use Fred **Jablin's model of assimilation** to clarify this process.

Jablin and Krone define **assimilation** as the "ongoing behavioral and cognitive processes by which individuals join, become integrated into, and exit organizations" (Jablin & Krone, 1987, p. 712). In the assimilation process, Jablin distinguishes between socialization and individualization. **Socialization** is defined as the way the organization uses both formal and informal means to influence individuals as they adapt to the organization. **Individualization** is the way in which the individual adapts the organization to meet their own needs. Although individualization is important when considering the ways in which predators create a

Are some organizations more apt to allow employees to utilize *individualization* to adapt the organization to allow their sexual predation? Although I do not have a definitive answer to this question, it does seem to me that organizations that have a culture that supports predation may also be more likely to allow predators to adapt the organization to their behavior.

space for sexual harassment, socialization allows organizational change agents to more carefully consider how values are learned, and therefore to consider how values can be reshaped in preferred ways within the organization.

There are four phases of socialization. First is **anticipatory socialization**, which is defined as how a person learns what it means to work in general, what it means to work in a particular occupation, and what it means to work for a particular organization. Anticipatory socialization occurs through different sources, such as family interactions, media, peers, early work experience, education, and job interviews (Think About It 7.3).

Think About It 7.3 Anticipatory Socialization and the Media

When *CSI* (Crime Scene Investigators) first appeared as a television series, it generated an increased interest in forensics investigations. In my own classes, which have nothing to do with criminal investigations, I continue to have many students who express interest in this field. In fact, when I teach socialization theory to my organizational communication students, I ask them which television shows have most influenced their preferred career; the dominant answer continues to be *CSI*. Consider your favorite show. What does it say about work? Is work done by a team, or is it primarily accomplished alone? What does your show suggest about the ideal worker? In the United States, many television shows situated in a work or career context are centered around some sort of a maverick who beats all the odds to somehow save the day. This anti/heroic figure is often deeply flawed, often is sexually inappropriate to colleagues, and succeeds by violating organizational rules and norms. This storyline socializes viewers into a particular set of beliefs about what it means to work.

Discussion Questions

1. What television series or movie made you consider a possible career path?
2. Who was the lead character? What were that character's strengths? What were their flaws?
3. In what ways are you asked to overlook that character's flaws in order to justify their success?
4. What values are enacted in this show? Provide specific examples.

The second phase of socialization, **encounter**, begins at the point of entry into the organization and continues until the individual has become an insider. This phase is characterized by uncertainty and a long period of learning.

Because of the uncertainty that newcomers experience, they often use less direct means to understand the organization's culture. For example, instead of asking direct questions of leadership, newcomers will often watch the old timers' performances and then emulate those performances. The encounter phase represents a prime opportunity for organizations to teach new members their preferred values, both through training and through careful messaging. Research demonstrates that formal socialization processes can be effective in getting new members to identify with the organization (Pribble, 1990). In contrast, research also suggests that much learning comes through informal means, such as through informal narratives told by organizational members (Gibson & Papa, 2000).

The third phase is **metamorphosis**. Jablin (2001) defines this phase as the time when a person moves from being an outsider in the organization to an insider. There are important caveats to this phase. First, metamorphosis is not fixed. I personally recall the day when I walked out of a faculty meeting thinking that I was finally part of the group, to be confronted by a visitor to campus asking for help finding a building. I had no idea where that building was so I asked another faculty member, who pointed to the building directly adjacent to mine and said, "That is the space you are looking for." I immediately felt uncertainty again and the realization that I had a way to go before I was truly an insider. Second, as my good friend and extraordinary scholar, Michael Kramer, once discovered in a study on transitions (1989), a person who moves to a new area or who changes jobs in an organization is in the precarious position of being both insider and outsider. This person needs to cut ties with the old work unit and create ties with the new work unit, all of which can create the uncertainty of encounter. Finally, not everyone is allowed to achieve metamorphosis. Feminist standpoint theory would call this the outsider within (Collins, 1986). These people are employed by the organization, but because of their precarious social position (gender, race, age, etc.) they are invisible as productive workers, but are hypervisible when it comes to their marginalized position.

Content warning

I had the privilege of meeting Fred Jablin over dinner on a few occasions. He was an incredibly kind and thoughtful person. Shortly after our last meal together, he was murdered, leaving his young children and his scholarly community bereft.

Exit, the final phase of socialization, has always been part of the assimilation model, but was added as a phase toward the end of Jablin's life. Jablin believed that there was much to be learned by how a person left an organization. Much of my own research has been inspired by the belief that organizational exit is one of the most difficult events that a person experiences. In the United States, we have some disdain for people who do not work, creating stigma for those who are unwillingly unemployed (Dougherty et al., 2018) and for men who chose to stay home with their children (Meisenbach, 2010), and anxiety around retirement (Smith & Dougherty, 2012). A person who leaves an organization due to being the target of predatory sexual behavior has to relearn their identity as both a human and as a worker.

Not only can targets be pushed out of an organization, but those who chose not to support or participate in predatory behavior can also find that there is no path to promotion in an unhealthy culture.

In this section I described four interrelated values issues that are important to understanding how values become intertwined with organizational culture:

- Values emerge from organizational enactment.
- Organizational values can be both sanctioned and unsanctioned.
- Organizational values can be both constructive and destructive.
- Organizational values are learned.

Values are the centerpiece of an organization's ethical behaviors. This means that unsanctioned, destructive values may be undergirding the moral behavior of your organization. Those values are passed down through socialization that weaves and reweaves predatory behavior into the fabric of the organizational culture. At this point, you may be asking, "What can I do to gird my organization against unethical predatory behavior?" I am glad you asked. In the next section I will introduce the notion of an ethically reliable organization (ERO) as a way of mindfully engaging ethics in everyday organizational life.

Ethically Reliable Organizing

From an organizational perspective, the question becomes, how do we prevent predatory sexual behavior in a particular organization? If you are thinking, "we don't have a Larry Nassar working here," I have three responses:

- First, good. Let's carefully and deliberately keep it that way.
- Second, how do you know that you don't have a Nassar working for you? None of the organizations Nassar worked for believed that he was a sexual predator. None of them. Not Michigan State. Not Twistars Gymnastics. Not USA Gymnastics. Not the local high school. Not the various other organizations that were proud to have him on staff. What makes you so special that you would know if you had a sexual predator in your organization? It is a real question.
- Third, most sexual predators are not as prolific as Nassar. Many sexual predators are sexual harassers who do not rape or sexually assault their targets. Their behaviors still create damage to targets, coworkers, and the organization. Please reread Chapter 1 for a more detailed accounting of this damage.

To prevent or stop predatory sexual behavior, it is necessary to create what organizational communication scholar Dr. Ryan Bisel (2017) calls an ethically reliable organization (ERO). At the core of an ERO are five value orientations. Enacting these value orientations will lead to what Bisel calls **moral mindfulness**, which is the ongoing, thoughtful vigilance for unethical enactments. Bisel argues that moral mindfulness, as shown in Figure 7.3,

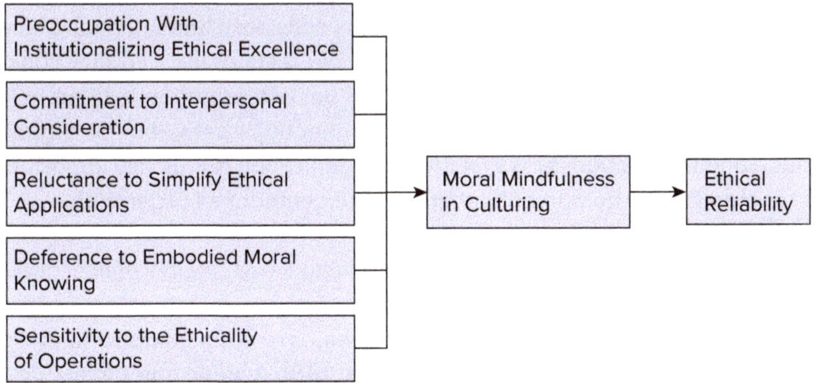

FIGURE 7.3: Bisel's Infrastructure for Encouraging Organizational Members' Moral Mindfulness

will lead to ethical reliability. An ethically reliable organization is one that is constantly thinking ethically in what Bisel calls "the here and now." In other words, in EROs, ethics are always centered in the contextualized moment.

The five value orientations are what I call meta values, or the ways in which organizations approach and engage with their values. As a result, although the moral mindfulness structure does not specifically engage with organizational values, it does provide a nice roadmap for how organizations can become more reliably ethical. Let's unpack each of these value orientations.

1 The first value orientation of an ERO is *enacting a preoccupation with institutionalizing ethical excellence*, which means that "organizational leadership understands the cultural significance organizational routines create and, therefore, the work to ensure such routines are ethically excellent" (Bisel, 2017, p. 245). It seems to me that institutionalizing ethical excellence requires that organizational leaders work on aligning espoused values with enacted values by identifying and linking patterns of behaviors with organizational values. This mindful consideration of how patterned behaviors reflect lived organizational values is critical in the development of applications and interventions designed to help organizations prevent predatory sexual harassment.

2 The second value orientation, *commitment to interpersonal consideration*, means that organizational members not only consider their institutional ethical commitments, but also consider the complexity of ethical considerations in the relationships that shape individuals' connections to the collective. In this way, moral mindfulness considers "the interests of the organization, interests of individuals, and interests of their connections" (p. 247). To wax poetic for a moment, this value orientation is humanely beautiful. Thinking about the fluid interconnections between the organization and the relationships that create organization is critically important in reestablishing the humanity that is at the center of all organizing.

3 The third value orientation is the *reluctance to simplify ethical applications*. "In many organizational settings, organizational ethics is assumed to be static and binary: Organizational members are supposed to avoid the bad in order to remain in the good" (p. 248). A static and binary view of organizational ethics assumes two categories of actors—those who are ethical and those who are not. ERO members view ethics as more fluid and

complex. Asking questions about ethics in what Bisel calls the "here and now" can expand the number of categories for ethical thinking.

4 The fourth value orientation is *deference to embodied moral knowing*. Bisel argues that ethics is not something that happens out there. It is embodied in "feelings, hunches, and the gut" (p. 249). You can feel when something is wrong, even if you cannot explain why or how. I would like to add a couple of caveats to this ethical orientation. First, most people cannot sense, at the gut level, that a person is a sexual predator. However, most people believe that they would know a predator if they saw one. Second, implicit bias is also a gut-level response to perceived threat. Unfortunately, implicit bias is the carrier of much organizational discrimination faced by people who are marginalized. Consequently, I suggest that we need to engage mindfulness *with* embodied knowing if we are to successfully address cultural-level sexual harassment.

5 The final value orientation is the *sensitivity to the ethics of operations*, which means "being attuned to ethical conduct on the front line, where the real work is accomplished" (p. 249). I am concerned with the frontline orientation of this value orientation when considering predatory sexual behavior. Specifically, because predatory sexual harassment can occur at all levels of the organizational hierarchy, it is important to move beyond a frontline mindset when considering ethics. Instead, I suggest that we focus on the ways in which ethics are interwoven throughout the organization, recognizing that no part of the organization is exempt from predatory sexual behavior. Ryan Bisel and I do ultimately agree that ethically reliable organizations must "cultivate trusting interpersonal relationships that allow for employees to discuss their private moral concerns candidly" (249). Courage and trust go hand in hand. If you enact trust as a core value, employees will be more likely to reciprocate with courage as a core value.

Recap and Looking Forward

The goal of this chapter was to help you understand how values fit into organizational culture. Usually we treat values as something that people HAVE. However, when it comes to organizational culture, values are something that organizational members DO. From a cultural perspective, only those values that are enacted in persistent and patterned ways are important. What I want you to understand is that values are communicated. Always. Whether you like it or not, the values that are communicated through actions are far more important than values that are claimed, but not enacted. I cannot emphasize enough the importance of this point. To my way of thinking, enacted values are the linchpin in evolving your culture, so an honest assessment of your organizational enacted values is of critical importance.

In the next chapter, I explain how cultural enactments and enacted values transform into core organizational meaning systems. Once you understand the transformation of culture, you will be ready to think about specific strategies for creating organizational evolution. We will work through some transformational strategies in Chapter 9. See you on the next page!

Credits

Fig. 7.2: Humphrey Bourne and Mark Jenkins, from "Organizational Values: A Dynamic Perspective," *Organization Studies*, vol. 34, no. 4, p. 503. Copyright © 2013 by SAGE Publications.

IMG 7.1: Copyright © 2010 Depositphotos/JohanSwanepoel.

Fig. 7.3: Ryan Bisel, from *Organizational Moral Learning: A Communication Approach*. Copyright © 2017 by Taylor & Francis Group.

Chapter 8

The Cultural Core

Organizational Meaning Systems

By the end of this chapter you should understand

1. How emotions transform enacted values into meanings
2. The sensemaking process that transforms unexpected events into plausible organizational meanings
3. The ways in which language convergence/meaning divergence (LC/MD) creates fractures in organizational meaning systems

> *"What do 'meanings' even mean?"*

In Chapter 4, I identified five types of meanings that form the core of Trans-MOC—cognitive, emotional, social, identity, and power meanings. The Trans-MOC model is, in essence, a model of transformation. It shows the ways in which external meanings are transformed into organizational enactments, which are transformed into organizational values, which are then transformed into organizational meanings. In this chapter, I focus on the ways in which enacted values are transformed into core organizational meanings.

Think about the model I am using in this book as a transformational model in which different sources and forms of communication are transformed into an organizational culture. Figure 8.1 should remind you of what this transformation process looks like. First, external organizational meaning systems are transformed into organizational enactments. Second, organizational enactments are transformed into enacted organizational values. Finally, organizational values are transformed into core organizational meanings. Keep in mind as you work your way through this chapter that this model is multidirectional. As a result, core meanings reverberate back onto organizational values, onto organizational enactments, and even onto the larger culture. As a result, this model is hopeful in that it suggests ways in which transformation can be made to happen.

In the past, researchers have written about the core of organizational culture as immobile and unchanging. In contrast, while I recognize that the organizational core meanings are resistant to change, they are subject to constant processes of transformation. Typically, those transformation processes simply harden the preexisting organizational meaning systems. However, with careful and thoughtful management of internal organizational communication, it is possible to use transformation processes to slowly and carefully evolve a culture into a more humane and thoughtful meaning system. The transformational processes described in this chapter are ones that I have found useful in my own applied work. There are, in fact, many

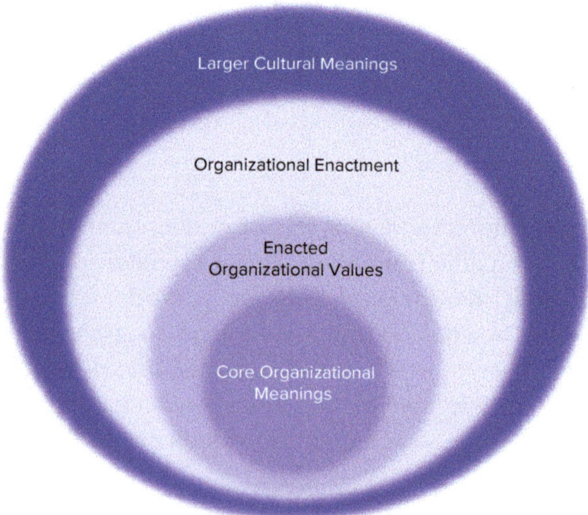

FIGURE 8.1: The Trans-MOC Model and Core Organizational Meanings

transformational processes that I cannot cover in the short space allotted to this issue here. I will discuss emotions, sensemaking, and language convergence/meaning divergence (LC/MD) to explore the various ways in which enacted values are transformed into core meaning systems. My goal is to provide a road map, if you will, of how to use meaning-centered theories to help organizations address significant organizational problems.

Emotions and the Transformation of Meaning

Emotions lie at the heart of core cultural meanings. Emotions are the reason why core meanings are so hard to talk about, and also so hard to change. Why? Because values are laden with emotions, and enacted values are intertwined with core meanings. As a result, emotions are key to understanding how enacted values are woven into the core of an organizational culture. Emotions are also critical to understanding how to reweave the cultural fabric so that a preferred set of values is habitually enacted in an organization.

Emotions are, perhaps, the single most misunderstood phenomenon in organizations. In their now-famous article on bounded emotionality, Dennis Mumby and Linda Putnam (1992) convincingly demonstrate the ways in which emotions have been articulated as the opposite of rationality, the enemy of good decision making, and one demarcation between masculinity and femininity in the workplace. It is likely these types of beliefs that have led to control over emotions as a hallmark of professionalism (Kramer & Hess, 2002), and the flat denial of emotional experiences in the workplace, even when emotions are clearly present (Dougherty & Drumheller, 2006). What is fascinating about this demonizing of emotions in the workplace is the fact that emotions are the centerpiece of good decision making and are a cornerstone of ethical behavior (McManus, 2021). Emotions are essential to meaning making that can ultimately evolve the organizational culture.

To understand what makes emotions central to decision making, it is important to first distinguish between feelings, affect, and emotions (Figure 8.2).

Although humans generally have a common set of physiological responses, the emotions people experience vary based on emotional granularity, context-based emotion rules, and cultural capacity. I will discuss each of these, but before I go further with this explanation, please do the exercise in Think About It 8.1.

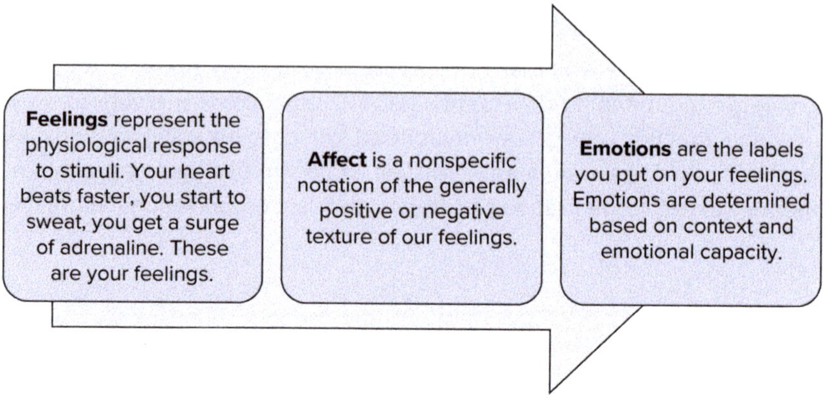

Feelings represent the physiological response to stimuli. Your heart beats faster, you start to sweat, you get a surge of adrenaline. These are your feelings.

Affect is a nonspecific notation of the generally positive or negative texture of our feelings.

Emotions are the labels you put on your feelings. Emotions are determined based on context and emotional capacity.

FIGURE 8.2: Differentiating Among Feelings, Affect, and Emotions

Think About It 8.1 Your Emotional Repertoire

Pull out a piece of paper. Write down all the emotions you have ever experienced.

Yes, I am serious.

Now, don't roll your eyes, shrug your shoulders, and ignore me. This exercise is important to understand the next learning segment.

Go ahead, you have time. Write them down.

No cheating! No Google. Don't borrow emotions from your neighbor. This is your list!

Are you finished?

Discussion Questions

1. How many emotions did you write down?
2. What surprised you about this exercise?
3. What do you think are the average number of emotions that people are able to identify?
4. Closely analyze the emotions you have identified. Do you have more negative than positive emotions? Do you experience much nuance in your emotions? Which emotions are you most likely to experience at work? Why is that?

In my experience using this exercise, on average people identify 11 or 12 emotions. The lowest number of emotions was 2. The highest number was 27. Interestingly, people recall experiencing far fewer emotions at work than they do in everyday life. Why do you think that is?

Hold on to this list. I will come back to it.

Emotional Granularity

The exercise provided in Think About It 8.1 taps into notions of emotional granularity. According to psychologist Lisa Feldman Barrett and her colleagues (e.g., Barrett, 2006; Hoemann et al., 2019; Suvak et al., 2011), people vary based on their **emotional granularity**, the precision with which people can label their feelings. Some people have a common set of emotions that they experience regardless of the context. Other people have a much more refined set of emotional experiences that vary based on the context. For example, a person who only identifies anger in response to negative experiences has little granularity of emotions. In contrast, a person who identifies irritation, annoyance, exasperation, anger, and rage has a much more granular set of emotions.

Emotional granularity is traditionally measured based on affective arousal and valence. *Arousal* is defined as the intensity of the emotions. For example, there is a difference in arousal between being angry and being irritated. Anger is generally more intense than irritation. In contrast, *valence* is the degree to which pleasantness/unpleasantness is represented in an emotion. For example, excitement and fear can have the same high level of arousal but are quite different in their valence, with most people viewing excitement as far more pleasant than fear.

Let's head back to the emotional repertoire activity that you completed earlier in this chapter. The items on this list are not, of course, the sum of all the emotions you have ever experienced. Instead, think of this list as the emotions you were able to access under pressure. These are the emotions that you have available when you experience an unexpected situation with high levels of *equivocality*—where there are multiple possible interpretations. In short, these are the emotions that are available to you, in general, when you are targeted with sexual harassment, or when you hear about sexual harassment from other people.

Interestingly, research has found that those who have a more granular set of emotions have better outcomes overall. First, emotional granularity is associated with better physical and emotional outcomes. The health literature has been particularly useful here. The people who were

In my experience, embarrassment is the most common long-term emotion that comes from being targeted. I suspect that embarrassment is not on your emotional repertoire, making it difficult to give your experience immediate coherent meaning.

Based on the emotions in your emotional repertoire, select the emotion you would likely choose if you were targeted by a sexual predator.

better able to articulate positive granular emotions had better health outcomes than those who were more negative (Tugade et al., 2004). Second, research suggests that emotional granularity is associated with improved functional decision making. In other words, although myths and legends suggest that decision making is impeded by emotions, Myeong-Gu Seo and Lisa Feldman Barrett (2007) discovered that strong emotions paired with granularity actually improved financial decision-making outcomes. Police officers who express positive emotions are more likely to manage the trauma and stress that comes with their jobs (Galatzer-Levy et al., 2013). I don't want to give you the impression that positive emotions are all good and negative emotions are bad. To the contrary, sometimes enforced positive emotions can be both tyrannical and counterproductive. In fact, research suggests that enforced positivity can actually cause moral disengagement and increased incivility (Ilies et al., 2020). Instead, people who are able to articulate granular negative emotions are more likely to engage in ethical decision making (McManus, 2019).

Clearly, emotional granularity is critical to understanding how emotions are transformed into and through organizational meaning systems. However, there are two limitations to this perspective. First, the emotional granularity construct is based fully in psychology, which is the study of the inner world. As a result, it tells us very little about how meaning is transformed culturally and organizationally. Yet, emotions are clearly cultural phenomena. In the next section, we will discuss the ways in which cultures impact emotions.

Cultural Capacity

Emotions are very much bound up in culture. Culture shapes both the emotions that can be experienced as well as the intensity with which emotions are experienced. In this context, culture not only refers to geographical contexts, but to demographic contexts as well. As a result, emotions can be experienced in unique ways depending on a variety of intersecting demographic lived experiences (Figure 8.3).

For those who operate within a Western framework, the notion of emotions as culturally constructed may be a bit jarring. According to Batja Mesquita (2007), a social psychologist who is well known for her research on culture and emotions, the **Western cultural model** assumes that a) emotions take place within the individual, and b) the utility of emotions is best described at the level of the individual rather than the relationship (p. 411). In contrast, a **socio-cultural model** assumes that emotions typically occur in a social context. Why? Because emotions are a driving force in how we engage in our social and cultural environments. As a result, Mesquita views

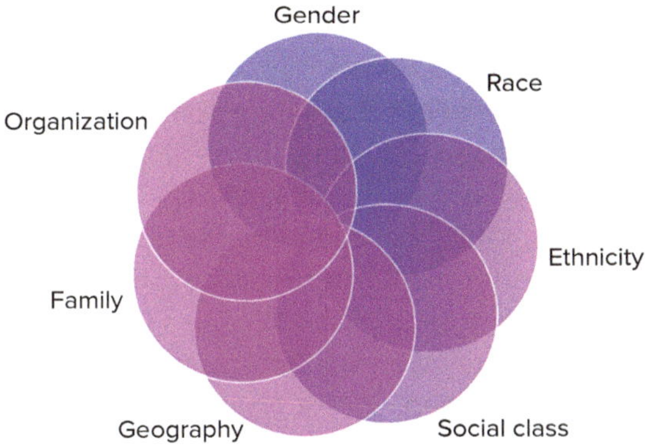

FIGURE 8.3: Emotions Can Vary Based on Intersecting Demographic Experiences.

emotions as "interpersonal events that navigate the social context and are informed by it. All emotional events (perhaps everything more complex than a startle) are intensely meaningful, and meaning is provided by the socio-cultural context" (p. 413).

> "Thinking about emotions as living between people has consequences on how we regulate emotions and how we recognize emotions in ourselves and others" (Batja Mesquita, as cited in *Psychology today*, 2018).

My favorite example of the socio-cultural model of emotions comes from an interview Mesquita did for *Psychology Today* (Pogosyan, 2018). During this interview, Mesquita talked about the cultural experience of shame:

> People in different cultures acquire different emotions. For example, people in many Western contexts may think of shame as a bad emotion. But shame is considered a good emotion in other cultures—it is in one category with modesty and embarrassment and these feelings show that you have propriety, that you know your place in the world.

Having an emotion like shame when you don't behave in ways that fit the cultural norm is considered a good way of doing something about it. In our (Western) cultures, shame is often associated with behaviors that are destructive for the relationship: We withdraw in shame, we don't want to show ourselves. But in other cultures, it's an emotion that comes with reaching out to others—it repairs relationships.

It is through cultural learning that we identify what counts as an emotion, the valence of the emotion, and the intensity of an emotion. Although Mesquita's work focuses primarily on geographical cultural differences, research also demonstrates the ways in which our situated lived experiences that spring from our demographic locations are also culturally formative. For the purposes of this project, I will focus on the interface between culture, gender, and emotions.

There is a large body of literature that addresses the different emotional expectations for women and for men. After reviewing the literature on emotions and gender, Jacqueline Smith and colleagues (2015) concluded that "in sum, the data converge on two expected gender-emotion combinations: angry men and happy women" (p. 116). Not only do women tend to display happiness more than men, but gendered expectation of emotional displays is so strong that people take longer to identify the gender of a person displaying emotions that are inconsistent with those expectations. More specifically, people take longer to identify a happy face as male than to identify an angry face as male. Similarly, it takes longer for people to identify an angry face as female than it takes to identify a happy face as female. Interestingly, when status was added as a variable, the authors found that people only took longer to identify high-status women who were angry. For women, the pressure to conform to happy displays of emotions is strong, even among women who are managers or CEOs. Given that sexual harassment is a highly emotional experience for those who have been targeted, it seems likely that there are serious cultural constraints for how organizational members can display emotions, assign emotions, and therefore use their emotions to meaningfully address this phenomenon.

Culture and emotions help us understand how emotions can transform behaviors into different types of meanings. According to Katie Hoemann and colleagues (2019), culture is a key component of the developmental process children go through in learning to process and apply emotions in context-specific ways. As a result, we learn how to communicate with emotions from infancy, increasing in sophistication over time. Yet organizations come with their own specialized and unique culture, which requires a relearning of emotions for organizational members, both in terms of what emotions mean and how to communicate with them. At the core of this relearning is coming to understand and apply organizational emotion rules.

Organizational Emotion Rules

Organizations are guided by an unspoken, but closely monitored, set of **emotion rules** (Kramer & Hess, 2002). Those rules are used to dictate how people can use emotions as they encounter their organizational culture.

These rules exist at multiple levels, including the larger level of what it means to be a worker, what it means to be in a particular profession, and what it means to be a member of a particular organization.

Perhaps the most important organizational emotion rule is guided by the assumption that emotionality is the opposite of rationality (Mumby & Putnam, 1992). This is a false binary (see Chapter 5 for a refresher on binary logic) that is treated as truth by organizational members. As a result, although emotions a) are key to effective decision making, and b) pervade organizational experience, people will deny experiencing emotions or claim that others who experience emotions are irrational.

There are also emotion rules at the level of a given profession, including for judges (Scarduzio & Tracy, 2015) and border patrol agents (Rivera, 2015). For example, nurses are expected to provide emotional care and technical care when working with patients. For nurses working in a productive organizational culture, they can move back and forth seamlessly between these different types of care. However, when confronted with sexual harassment, these nurses are only able to provide technical care, and that care is only at its most rudimentary level (Mcguire et al., 2006).

My former colleagues, Michael Kramer and Jon Hess (2002), asked a primarily white-collar group of people to identify emotion rules at work. Five general emotion rules emerged:

1. Act professionally, which means maintain control over emotions at all times.
2. Mask negative emotions at work.
3. Avoid emotions that are role inappropriate.
4. Experience and express emotions to support others (not for selfish purposes).
5. Mask self-serving positive emotions.

Emotions and Meaning

It is time to put our knowledge of emotions together to better understand how emotions work to make organizational cultures meaningful. First, emotions themselves are meaning-making labels that we apply to feelings. Some individuals have more emotional granularity than do others, which means they have access to a more sophisticated array of meanings. However, emotions are not "owned" by the individual. Instead, emotions are cultural phenomena. As a result, the emotion-centric meanings we can access, the importance of those emotions, and the valence of those emotions depend to a large extent on the larger cultural meaning system from which you come. Finally, emotions at work are not a simple translation from the larger culture. Instead, there are emotion rules that constrain and enable the expression and application of emotions. These rules are unique to organizational cultures and are premised on the false idea that emotions are unprofessional and lead to bad decision making. As a result, regardless of emotional granularity and cultural norms and expectations, emotions in the workplace are limited, often misinterpreted, and lead to misunderstandings about significant emotional events, such as sexual harassment. For change agents attempting to evolve their culture, one of your biggest challenges will be addressing the emotional boundaries and limitations imposed by employee emotional granularity, cultural milieu, and emotion rules imposed by the organization (Think About It 8.2). Given that emotions and values are interwoven, in order to expand the enacted values of your organization, you will need to also expand emotional capacity.

Think About It 8.2 Sexual Harassment and Emotions

The following is based on the case of sexual harassment presented in *The Atlantic* (Gilpin, 2016, December 15). Recall that Olivia was sexually assaulted by a male coworker while visiting a friend's house. Given what you know about emotion rules in organizations, how should she report this assault to her boss? Consider the following scenarios:

> *(Crying)* Michael was tickling me and would not stop. Then he started kissing me and would not stop. He laid on top of me and I could not make him stop. I was terrified. I am reporting this behavior to get your advice on what to do.
>
> *(Yelling)* Michael was tickling me and would not stop. Then he started kissing me and would not stop. He laid on top of me and I could not make him stop. I was pissed. I am reporting this behavior to get your advice on what to do.
>
> *(Calmly, without emotional display)* Michael was tickling me and would not stop. Then he started kissing me and would not stop. He laid on top of me and I could not make him stop. I am reporting this behavior to get your advice on what to do.

Sexual harassment targets are caught in a catch-22. If they report the behavior while showing fear, they come across as weak and hysterical. If they show anger, then they are violating gender rules indicating that women are not to show anger. If they approach the situation calmly, then managers assume the behavior was not that bad. In Olivia's case, the manager sent an email to her supervisor, telling them that Olivia needed to get herself under control. He hoped that Olivia was not bothering Michael.

Discussion Questions

1. What advice about emotions would you give Olivia when reporting the sexual harassment?
2. What advice about emotions would you give to managers and supervisors who are tasked with addressing sexual harassment?
3. How do gender rules impact organizational cultures?
4. What do change agents need to know about emotions and meaning making if they are to evolve the culture to prevent sexual harassment?

Emotions are critical to understanding how meaning is created and transformed in organizational cultures.

Sensemaking and the Transformation of Meaning

In this book, I have constantly talked about predatory sexual behavior as woven into organizational cultures. The focus of this weaving is the transformation of various forms of communication (information, messaging, and performative/enactment/practice) into core cultural meanings. Sensemaking theory provides an excellent way to understand how this weaving happens. Sensemaking theory continues to be an important part of my sexual harassment training because of the clarity of Karl Weick's (1995) illustration of the process through which people produce and reproduce meanings in the face of unexpected or equivocal events. As a result, sensemaking can provide insight into the ways in which patterned communication produces and reproduce values, which are ultimately transformed into core organizational meanings. Of course, when sensemaking was first produced, the dominant definition of communication was information. As a result, I have adapted the theory to match the changing understanding of communication as the production of meanings.

Sensemaking Process

Sensemaking was originally defined as "the making of sense" (Weick, 1995, p. 4). This is not a very satisfying definition because it uses its own name to define itself, something that is known as a **tautology**. I define sensemaking as the communicative processes through which organizational members make meaning of a constantly shifting organizational environment. Sensemaking, therefore, is a path to both stability and change in organizational life. It is a means through which organizations can both learn and stagnate. Here is the thing, and it is a big thing. Sensemaking will happen in organizations. As a leader or change agent, you cannot stop sensemaking from occurring. However, with thoughtful and careful communication and management, you can help direct the sensemaking process to more productive ends. How can you direct the sensemaking process? To accomplish this, you need to understand sensemaking as a process and the seven properties of sensemaking.

Sensemaking is central to both organizational learning and organizational stagnation.

Sensemaking begins with the assumption that organizational members operate in two interlocking environments (Figure 8.4).

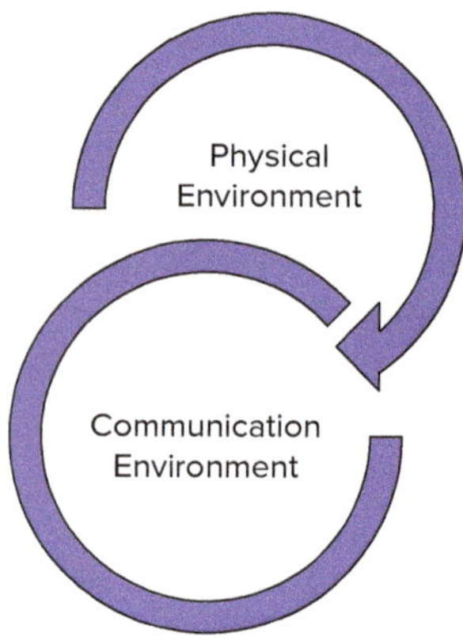

FIGURE 8.4: Sensemaking Occurs in Interlocking Environments.

First, there is the **physical environment** that exists "out there." This environment includes the material features of everyday life. Consider some of the recent unexpected material features of the organizational world: COVID-19, masks, social isolation, Zoom meetings, food insecurity, job insecurity, housing insecurity, and so on. These are part of the physical environment that can trigger sensemaking. Second, there is what Weick calls the information environment. I call it the **communication environment**. It is the environment that is produced and reproduced through the ongoing talk and other communicative behaviors that shape everyday organizational life. It is the interlocking nature of the physical and communication environments within which Weick's theory is situated (Figure 8.5).

This model is the applied version that I have created for organizational change agents. It begins with *people noticing something unexpected*. In Weick's original model, this is called **equivocality**, and it means that there are multiple possible interpretations of an occurrence. Think about it this way: Organizations have a typical flow, a normative set of expectations through which everything operates. Equivocality occurs when something breaks that flow. Interestingly, this break in the flow of everyday routines is not always readily apparent to organizational members.

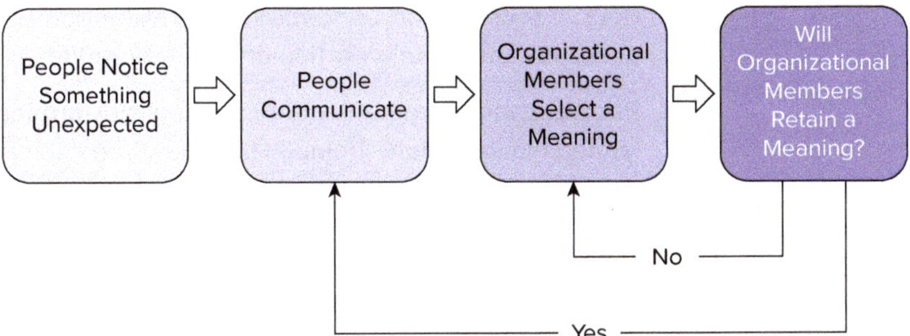

FIGURE 8.5: Applied Sensemaking Model

While unexpected events in the physical environment may be noticed immediately, such as a new virus that creates a need for social distance, other events may not be noticed until the media makes them seem urgent. Sexual harassment usually falls into this latter category.

When organizational members notice that something unexpected has happened, they start an intensified pattern of communication. Weick calls this enactment, but I translate it to *people communicate, a lot*. By communication, I mean the entire spectrum of communication (Figure 8.6), previously described in Chapter 2.

1. When faced with uncertainty, people search for *information* that they can use to make sense of the unexpected. They also supply information, with varying levels of accuracy.

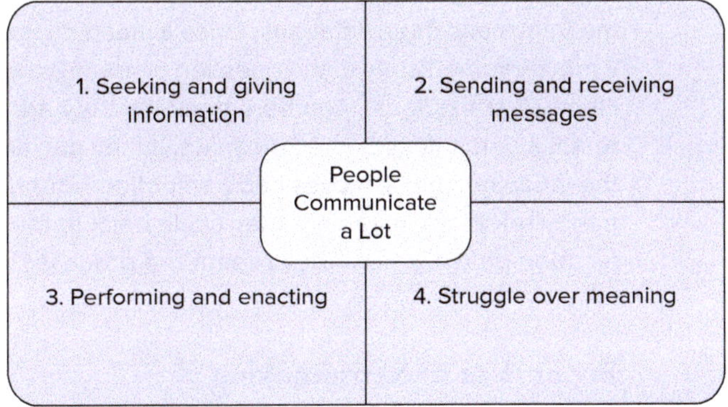

FIGURE 8.6: Sensemaking Utilizes All Forms of Communication.

2. People receive and send *messages* attempting to persuade others to a particular action or belief.
3. People *enact* communication, such as performing leadership, rebellion, "being in the know," and so on.
4. People struggle to make uncertainty *meaningful*.

This is an important point because organizational change agents can become fixated on a single form of communication, which prevents them from managing the larger sensemaking process. Consider an organization I worked with years ago, where their sexual harassment problem was revealed through journalistic reporting. One of their requests when they contacted me was to help them with their communication. They had been sending out all the information that they had to their employees, yet the employees kept demanding more information. The likely problem, I explained to this organization, is that the employees did not need more information. They needed help making sense of the information that was provided. They were seeking information so that they could make meaning out of the predatory behavior that had been uncovered in various media outlets.

Change agents can become fixated on a single form of communication, which prevents them from managing the larger sensemaking process.

As people communicate, they go through a **meaning selection cycle**. Meaning selection is akin to a teenager trying to decide what to wear on a date. "Should I wear this one? How about this one? Or this one?" In meaning selection, organizational members try out different possible meanings and interpretations. Once a meaning is selected, it moves immediately to the question of **meaning retention**. Here, organizational members decide if they are going to retain a particular selected meaning. If they decide to keep the meaning, then it moves into a selection-retention cycle. If they reject the meaning, they cycle back to the communication phase, where they repeat the process.

Properties of Sensemaking

If you just look at the **applied sensemaking model**, you might assume that sensemaking is a rational process through which organizational members identify a problem and then come to understand that problem. However, we are talking about human beings, and humans are not necessarily rational. To the contrary, people can be both rational and irrational, all at the same time. Weick's seven properties of sensemaking demonstrate both the rational and irrational nature of sensemaking. As a result, these properties are important to understanding how sensemaking plays out in the meaning-making process.

Ongoing

Sensemaking occurs as part of an ongoing pattern of organizational life. There is a standard flow in organizations that makes work life sensible. When something unexpected happens, or when equivocality is produced, then sensemaking cycles begin. Consider sexual harassment–prone organizations. In these organizations, predatory sexual behavior is the norm. It is part of the ongoing flow of everyday organizational life. For this reason, it does not often become noticed for sensemaking.

Extracted Cues

Extracted cues are environmental cues that we focus on for sensemaking. Essentially, where do organizational members focus their attention when something unexpected occurs? Recall in Chapter 4 when I discussed Gestalt theory, the notion that people tend to focus on the foreground while ignoring the background.

1. Stop for a moment and look around the room. Find everything that is the color red.

Image 8.1

Extracting cues is a normal part of the human experience. We simply cannot process everything in our environment, so instead we focus on a few cues that we can make sense of. In the previous side box, I asked you to focus on the color red, so it is unlikely you noticed everything that is the color blue, as requested in the next side box. At a cultural level, extracted cues tend to be something that we recognize as fitting into our cultural milieu. In other words, extracted cues are culturally bounded and are often used to reinforce what we already believe to be true. Consider these real-life examples of conversations about sexual harassment.

2. Now, without looking around again, write down everything in the room that is the color blue.

> He was married. *It meant nothing.*
>
> Women tend to lie. *How can we believe them*?
>
> She was wearing a black dress. *She was trolling for something.*

In each of these examples, organizational members were confronted with sexual harassment. In the last case, they even created a sexual harassment narrative where these men became the victim of a trolling woman worker. I want you to notice the two statements paired together. The first statement is the cue that was extracted. The second statement is the meaning that was selected from that cue. These people could have selected cues that would have been supportive of the target and disdainful of the predator. They did not. Instead, the first group dismissed the importance of the predatory sexual behavior reported by a nurse because, after all, the predator was married. In the second example, this group of women concluded that other women lie all the time, so it is reasonable not to believe a woman who claims she was targeted. In the third example, the men concluded that because the woman was wearing a black dress and they found her attractive, that she was asking for predatory sexual attention. Over years of hearing this type of conversation, I have concluded that organizational members in harassment-prone organizations tend to support the behavior by extracting cues that not only excuse the behavior but also encourage predation.

Social

Sensemaking occurs with other people. When other people are not present, sensemaking occurs in imagined interactions with other people. As a result, sensemaking is a *social* process. Obviously, sensemaking is far more efficient when organizational members can communicate rather than imagine communicating. Now consider this. Every organization has what I call "no-go" topics, those topics that cannot be discussed. Often, these no-go topics represent uncomfortable conversations. In my experience, predatory sexual behavior is at the top of the no-go topic list in most organizations. Because sensemaking is social, if people are not allowed to talk about a behavior, they are therefore not able to make sense of it. Although no-go topics may not include formal mandates against speaking, there tend to be culturally enforced mandates that prevent people from communicating. It becomes the elephant in the room. Weick is clear that some sensemaking can happen when we are alone and imagining interactions with others. This is not a particularly useful way to make sense of a culturally embedded problem.

A teacher friend of mine told me about their frustration over three sexual predators that had been identified in their school district. Despite the obvious repetition of the predation, this was a no-go topic for the faculty and staff, outside of a few formal training opportunities. My friend told me they felt they were left trying to solve the problem alone. Of course, no single individual can solve a cultural-level problem.

Enacted

When people engage in sensemaking they are not just contemplating philosophical issues that exist somewhere "out there." Recall that not only do we have a physical environment, we also have a communication environment. That communication environment is created through sensemaking. In other words, sensemaking does not just happen in an environment, it enacts the organizational environment. If an organization makes sense of sexual harassment by assuming the targets are lying, then organizational members will enact an environment of suspicion toward people who report predation. The real question for change agents is how to get organizational members to enact a preferred environment.

Retrospective

Sensemaking is ***retrospective*** because it is based on events that have already occurred. One of Weick's most famous sayings is "how do I know what I mean until I see what I say?" Sensemaking is grounded in history. All that has come before plays out in how we make sense of an unexpected event. However, we are not stuck in the past. Sensemaking is also prospective in that, although we make sense of past events, that meaning making then guides how we respond to future events. Take for example the #MeToo movement, when women were invited first by Tarana Burke and then by Alyssa Milano to acknowledge their experiences with harassment and sexual assault by simply writing "MeToo" in their various social media feeds. And wow did they step forward. All over people's feeds was the simple statement "MeToo." Some women chose to tell their stories for the first time. Others acknowledged the life-changing nature of their experience. This simple phrase served as the unexpected event that triggered massive social sensemaking about predatory sexual behavior. This retrospective sensemaking triggered prospective action. Predatory organizational members were fired, organizations were cancelled, new organizations were formed to stop sexual harassment. While sensemaking may be retrospective, it also reverberates into the future.

Identity

How we make sense of something is very much intertwined with a person's identity. As I sit here writing this, the second impeachment trial of Donald Trump is occurring in the United States Senate. The Democrats almost uniformly believe that Trump was responsible for the insurrection on January 6, 2021, that threatened American democracy. They have presented video evidence of their charges. In contrast, Republicans, who were also present and physically threated during the insurrection, argue that it is unconstitutional to convict a former president. They also remain unconvinced that Trump encouraged the insurrection. Why does this division occur along party lines? Because political identity shapes the meanings that legislators draw from these unexpected and equivocal events. The importance of identity can also be seen in the diverging ways women and men define sexual harassment. As described in Chapter 1 of this book, women define much more behavior as sexual harassment than do men. Men are much more likely to view only the most physically aggressive behavior as sexual harassment. Why? Because women are sexualized differently than men and because they are far more likely to be targeted. Gender identity matters.

Plausible

One reason why organizational problems are reinforced through the sensemaking process is because sensemaking does not have to be accurate.

It only has to seem possible. What makes something seem possible in an organization? Normative behaviors that are woven into the organizational culture. As you have probably surmised by now, when I am doing both research and consulting, I hear the darndest things. Take for example the woman who told the chocolate love story (described in Think About It 3.2). If you will recall, I asked her to tell a story about flirting in the workplace. She responded with a story about her boss grabbing her butt, asking "have you ever had chocolate love." For most people, this story is a clear-cut case of sexual harassment. However, for this woman, the behavior was called flirting. Why? Because sexual harassment cannot possibly be normal. This type of aggressive sexual behavior was normal. Ergo, this type of aggressive sexual behavior could not be sexual harassment. Consider other examples of plausibility in the excerpts I have provided throughout this book.

- The woman wearing a black dress was identified as similar to a prostitute.
- Women are assumed to lie about sexual harassment.
- Men who are targeted by women are assumed to "like it" because it makes them seem more manly.
- Men who are perceived to be doing important work are assumed to be innocent of predatory sexual behavior.

I could go on. None of these statements are accurate. All of these statements seem plausible within their particular organizational culture. As a result, sensemaking often reinforces predatory sexual behavior in organizations.

Sensegiving

If sensemaking tells us how organizational members make sense of the unexpected, then **sensegiving** suggests ways in which change agents can strategically insert meaningful communication into the process so as to shape the trajectory of the sensemaking. Sensegiving is both knowledge intensive and time consuming, but it can be used to shape both organizational and institutional cultures (Scarduzio & Tracy, 2015; Bisel et al., 2017). In the next chapter, application of the model, I will use the notion of sensegiving to help you understand how predatory sexual organizational cultures can learn and evolve.

Language Convergence/Meaning Divergence and the Transformation of Meaning

When discussing core organizational meaning systems, one issue that must be addressed is the expectation that there are coherent meaning systems that are universally accepted within any organizational culture. This is not the case. Although there are overlapping meanings, and organizational cultures tend to have more tightly enforced meaning systems than other cultural spaces, there are as many meaning systems as there are people. This means that people who are organizational change agents need to use complexity thinking when considering how to shape organizational meaning.

Why is it that we tend to think of organizations as having fully sutured meaning systems? According to language convergence/meaning divergence (LC/MD) (Dougherty et al., 2009), it is at least in part because we share the same language and therefore assume that we also share the same meanings. LC/MD emerged from a study exploring the differences between flirting and sexual harassment, making it a particularly rich theory for understanding predatory sexual behaviors in organizational cultures. There are four primary components of LC/MD.

Language Convergence

Language is a hallmark of all human civilizations. Although language was created to communicate, it is not, in and of itself, communication. Instead, language becomes communication when it is used to coordinate activity and to make meaning. It is therefore important to recognize that although meaning and language are closely tied together, they are in fact different constructs. Typically, people from a shared culture use the same language. It is impractical to define every term that we use in every conversation, so we must assume that the other party shares enough meaning to make sense of our words. This is called a *communication shortcut*, and it is critical to accomplishing the tasks of everyday life (Think About It 8.3).

Think About It 8.3 Communication Shortcut

When I was teaching my children to drive, if they were drifting into the wrong lane I would say "watch out." This phrase is a shortcut to the longer explanation: "You are drifting into the lane with oncoming traffic. By lane, I mean the part of the road that is designated for traffic going the opposite direction. If you continue on your current trajectory, and by trajectory I mean the current direction of your automobile, then the oncoming automobile will slam into us, putting our lives in jeopardy. By jeopardy I mean we might die." By the time I finished my explanation, we would have been hit by the oncoming car. Language as a shortcut to meaning is critical to human survival. However, I recall saying "watch out" to one of my inexperienced kid drivers, who then panicked, looked in the rearview mirror, and swerved all over the road, screaming, "What, what?!" We survived, or I would not be here to tell you that story, but the assumption of shared meaning went very wrong that day, illustrating the difference between shared language and shared meaning.

Discussion Questions

1. What do you suppose caused the difference in meanings around the words "watch out"?
2. How do managers use phrases in the workplace that are similar to "watch out" discussed in my narrative?
3. What are ways managers can prevent a "watch out" scenario when communicating with organizational members?

Meaning Divergence

Meaning divergence explores the ways meaning diverges around a common set of symbols (Dougherty et al., 2009). Any symbol has multiple types of meanings. Even the simplest of symbols has a cluster of associated meanings. Not only are there multiple connotative meanings, but there are cognitive, emotional, social, identity, and power meanings as well. All of these meanings comprise a ***meaning cluster***, or a group's or person's holistic meaning for a concept or phenomenon. **Meaning fragments** are smaller meaning bits that, when put together, comprise a meaning cluster.

Meaning divergence occurs when some of the meanings around a shared symbol/language are not the same. This divergence can be subtle, what is called a **subtle cluster divergence** (Figure 8.7). This type of divergence occurs when one or more meaning fragments diverges. A subtle cluster divergence is characterized by small differences in which people espouse similar meaning clusters

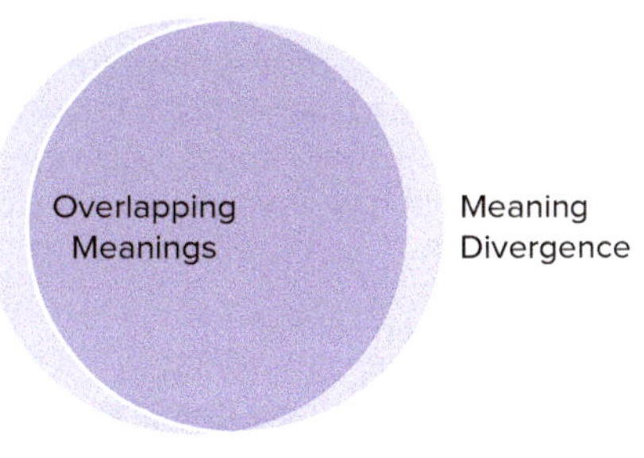

FIGURE 8.7: Subtle Cluster Divergence

with a few different meaning fragments. These differences may be so slight that they are easy to miss or dismiss as unimportant. This divergent meaning may be somewhat subtle, but it may, nevertheless, be important. In fact, it is likely that a large number of interpersonal and social conflicts are products of subtle cluster meaning divergence. A subtle cluster divergence, when it comes to sexual harassment, can be easy to miss. I illustrate this type of difference in Think About It 8.4.

Think About It 8.4 Subtle Cluster Divergence

The following examples are from a study exploring the difference between flirting and sexual harassment. Read these and see if you can identify similarities and differences in definitions of flirting. I highlighted some language to help you out.

Sexual Harassment Example 1

Peter: Our building is either really hot or it is really cold. One day I was sitting there [and said], “you look like you’re really cold.” And her hair was standing up on her arms and one of the other girls perceived that I had something else in mind and went to my boss and said I was talking about some body parts. And I had no defense whatsoever myself. I couldn’t do or say anything. I was guilty. I was written up. BOOM. Right there. Regardless. In the business world now you have no recourse. You don’t even have the recourse now to face your accusers. ...

Interviewer: So it wasn’t her that had a problem with the comment?

Peter: No. It was the other people. It’s such a fine line. What’s sexual harassment to one person may not be to somebody else. But the corporate’s been hit so many times with so many lawsuits, that are, you know—people just getting money or whatever.

Sexual Harassment Example 2

James: But I think that there are sometimes, I mean, there are comments where people will, or there’s instances where people will say, “oh I think you look nice” and you are really honestly just trying to say that you think that person dressed nicely that day or you know, they dress nicely and put their hair up nicely or, you know.

Interviewer: Umhm.

James: And I know there have been instances at work where, there is one person in particular who likes to comment on people’s looks and how he thinks they are looking that day. He does it to both guys and girls and he’s just a really genuinely friendly person. But, people have taken that as sexual harassment sometimes and so, in those cases, I mean, knowing that person. He's been talked to about it, so he tries to make sure people are comfortable with him, now he tries to make sure people are comfortable with him saying, "I think you look nice today" or ...

Interviewer: Umhm.

James: Before he says that, or tries to clarify that he's just meaning it on a purely like you know "I think you did a nice job dressing today" level rather than "I think you look good and want to take you out and, you know, I want to go to bed with you" or something like that. So, I mean, I don't know, people are very sensitive now and you have to be careful what you say.

Discussion Questions

1. What are the similarities/differences in meaning clusters?
2. What role does sexual behavior/language have in each example of flirting?
3. Doing some imaginative play, what would an interaction around a policy on flirting sound like between these two people?
4. What does power look like in each of these exemplars?

In contrast, a *total cluster divergence* (Figure 8.8) occurs when meaning systems around a shared term vary widely with minimal overlap. Given these differences, it is unlikely that these individuals would be able to have a meaningful conversation. I illustrate a total cluster divergence in Think About It 8.5.

FIGURE 8.8: Total Meaning Divergence

Think About It 8.5 Total Cluster Divergence

The following examples are from a study exploring the difference between flirting and sexual harassment. You have seen one of these exemplars before, but now take a closer look and see if you can identify similarities and differences in definitions of flirting. I highlighted some language to help you out.

Flirting Example 1

Zelda: Well, a friend of mine who doesn't have children was at our house watching *Blues Clues* one day. And she'd never seen it. And she said, "I understand why the kids like this show so much." She said, "He's flirting with them." In a, but that was kind of, in a teasing sort of way. There was nothing inappropriate about it. But it was that kind of back and forth.

Interviewer: Between the character on TV and the people watching?

Zelda: Yeah, you know, there are some aspects of it that can be interactive. You know, and he would say something like, um, uh, "Oh, I'm going to play, uh, that game with the ball and you know, uh, you shoot it through something, and uh, there's a net on it. What do you call that? Oh, right, basketball. You are so smart." You know, that kind of, you know, I mean it's kind of a teasing aspect to it, but like she said, "He's flirting."

Flirting Example 2

Anna: Maybe, I think at the time there was, I don't know 50, 60 managers. Maybe three were female. So it was very very male dominated.

Interviewer: Okay.

Anna: Um, well, just 'cause the, the actions were more sexual harassment. But the flirting was just their everyday [behavior]. That's how they talked to you. That's how they did it.

Interviewer: So they just flirted constantly?

Anna: Constantly. It was constant. And if you ever gave them any attitude back—it was a sales organization. So it was competitive. It was commission based. And so every time, you know, you, you know if anyone talked back or if anyone didn't like it they they were punished for it and they didn't give them the good accounts and they didn't do the ... And those girls, I mean everyone left.

Discussion Questions

1. What are the similarities/differences in meaning clusters?
2. What role does sexual behavior/language have in each example of flirting?
3. Doing some imaginative play, what would an interaction around a policy on flirting sound like between these two people?
4. What does power look like in each of these exemplars?

The Illusion of Shared Meaning

The use of shared language and symbols to create communication shortcuts is critically important to accomplishing shared goals. Unfortunately, this communication shortcut can also create an **illusion of shared meaning**, or the perception that all parties agree when they do not. Because language convergence is often a communication shortcut without elaboration, divergent meanings can go largely unnoticed and unchallenged. When the differences are subtle, the meaning divergence is even more likely to go undetected. My experience is that this illusion of shared meaning can impact an organization's ability to address sexual harassment. If you ask most people, they will tell you that sexual harassment is bad. However, given the wide range of meanings of what constitutes sexual harassment, very few organizational members actually agree that the same behaviors are problematic.

Othering

The illusion of shared meaning is never fully complete. At times, any illusion can develop fissures. These fissures in the illusion allow communicators to acknowledge that there are differences. However, most people fail to acknowledge differences in underlying meanings because it simply does not occur to them that their meanings could be different from reasonable others using the same word. As a result, despite the opportunity presented by these fissures to develop an understanding of divergent meanings, previous research suggests that people develop a number of communication strategies to evade this type of understanding (Dougherty et al., 2009). The most common of these strategies is called **othering** (Bach, 2005). Othering is characterized by a highly developed tendency to construct other people in negative ways (Think About It 8.6).

Think About It 8.6 Othering

Below are examples of nurses who were sexually harassed by male patients. In each of these examples, the nurses focused on stereotypes to characterize the perpetrator. Stereotypes are one key way in which othering occurs. See if you can identify the stereotypes used in these examples.

Example 1

Nurse 8: I don't know if that's part of the male, you know, they're very visual creatures. The theory is that they're very visual creatures and, you know, I guess how they would be wanting to get into pornography and how they're very visual and they like a few things that they're in retrospect trying to, you know, display themselves. You know, if they saw someone dressed down they would be completely excited and in awe.

Example 2

Nurse 10: There's the elderly gentleman that's confused and you can't really blame them [sic] for, you know—I mean you can't reproach them for that because they probably won't remember, you know, and they'll do it again. ... And you can't really hold them accountable or responsible I don't think because technically it's not their fault. You know, they can't help it.

Example 3

Nurse 9: I think he was ... he was like, a biker guy. I remember him having lots of tattoos. That was a while ago. But I think he might have been a biker guy. He was rough and tough. And I know they don't have much respect for their women at all.

Example 4

Nurse 22: (When an African-American man grabbed Nurse 22 inappropriately around the neck, she stated) "He was trying to get me to accept him as being black and a lot of times they will ... a lot of times they want to have someone extra ... like a white girl to like them."

Discussion Questions

1. What stereotypes were used to explain the harassment?
2. How is the exact same behavior explained through different stereotypes?
3. Why do nurses use stereotypes when explaining a predator's behavior?
4. How can othering hide or obscure the real nature of sexual predators?

For example, others are often constructed as evil, stereotyped, mentally unstable, insane, or stupid. As a result, the other is rarely understood as a complex human person with both strengths and limitations, just like every other person. Othering causes us to oversimplify a problem or difference, which is never helpful when dealing with complex human issues like predatory sexual behavior.

Recap and Looking Forward

At this point in this book, I hope you are not feeling too overwhelmed with the complexity of solving problems that are woven into organizational cultures. I recognize that it is a lot! Personally, I find it helpful to think in smaller chunks. Take the notion of meaning. There are many theories that can be useful in understanding how enacted communication is transformed into the core meaning system of an organization. While I have discussed the ones I find to be most helpful—emotions, sensemaking, and LC/MD—there are other theories that may be more helpful to you. For example, I have not talked about narrative or narrative sensemaking. Both of these concepts can help you understand how meanings are produced and reproduced in organizational cultures. The key here is to make connections that help you think in complex ways about organizational cultural problems.

At this point in this book, you should be asking yourself, "Now that I have a better sense of how sexual harassment is woven into organizational cultures, how do I go about unweaving this behavior? What are my next steps?" In Chapter 9 I discuss some strategies and processes you can use to evolve your organizational culture.

Credits

Chapter 9

Evolving Organizational Culture

By the end of this chapter you should

1. Understand the basic demands of transforming culture.
2. Be familiar with applied ethnography.
3. Be able to develop activities to engage in cultural evolution.
4. Recognize some of the challenges of culture work.

Training and consulting around sexual harassment has become big business, with lots of organizations, large and small, claiming to have the answer to solve your organization's problems. Yet, as discussed way back in Chapter 1, most training and consulting on sexual harassment fails to accomplish its goals, sometimes even worsening the problem. Why is this?

Myth 1: Sexual harassment is about the harasser/target pair.

Reality: *Sexual harassment is embedded in the larger organizational culture. As a result, all members of an organization participate in the maintenance of predatory sexual harassment.*

Myth 2: Cultures are simple.

Reality: *Cultures are complicated.*

Myth 3: Information-based training will prevent sexual harassment.

Reality: *Training needs to be culture centric and consider all forms of communication.*

Myth 4: Off-the-shelf training can work equally well in all organizations.

Reality: *Although there are patterns and similarities in predatory sexual harassment, there are also unique enactments within each organization. Those unique enactments need to be identified and addressed in training and development activities.*

Because predatory sexual harassment is woven into the fabric of the organizational culture, it is necessary for both the organization and the change agent to take a complexity approach to the change process. Culture evolution work is a long and arduous journey. If you are one of those people who requires instant gratification, this is not the kind of work you will find fulfilling. On the other hand, if you like complexity thinking and long-term goal setting and achieving, you will likely find this work to be engaging and energizing. Doing cultural evolution work can feel like walking up hill, barefoot, through an ice storm, with no sense of when you will arrive at your destination. It can be hard to stay the course, but your persistence and resilience will make a tremendous difference as to whether your organization can successfully evolve into a more comfortable, productive, and safe space.

Although in this chapter I provide some wisdom and tools for your journey, my space here is limited. As a result, I have set three goals that I consider to be realistic for organizational managers and change agents:

Goal 1: I want you to think differently about organizational culture and your role in that culture.

Goal 2: I want you to feel empowered to act differently to create the culture that you envision.

Goal 3: I want you to manage organizational culture in more thoughtful and deliberate ways.

As I have said repeatedly throughout the preceding chapters, organizational culture is resistant to change, but it can evolve over time. I develop my training and organizational work using three overlapping processes (Figure 9.1).

Discovery is the process of learning and understanding an organizational culture. There are two interwoven components of discovery. *Change*

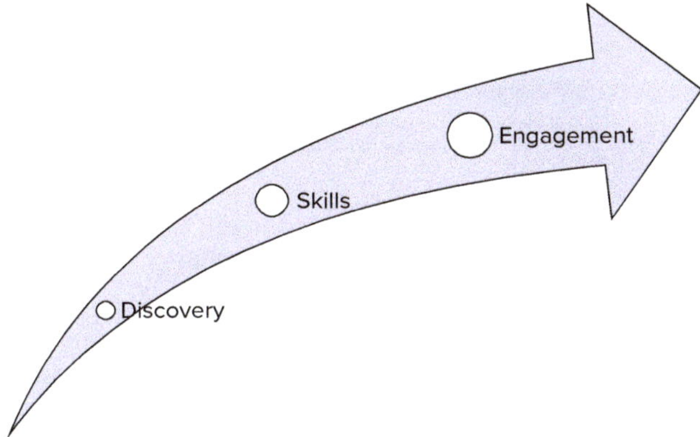

FIGURE 9.1: Overlapping Discovery, Skills, Engagement Process

agent discovery is the process the change agent goes through to learn about the organizational culture. *Organizational member discovery* is the process the change agent leads organizational members through so that they can build a foundation for cultural evolution. **Skills** is the processes of developing capacity to intervene in a culture. **Engagement** is planning and executing processes designed to evolve your organizational culture. Taken as a whole, these processes are designed to help you approach cultural evolution from a systematic and knowledgeable space.

Transforming Culture

Each intervention I do is built around the transformational model of organizational culture (Figure 9.2). I have walked you through the various layers of Trans-MOC, but have not yet discussed the importance of the multidirectional arrows, the subcultural differences, and the fuzzy nature of the model. It is in these parts of the model that you can find cultural fractures and cultural carriers, the two primary ingredients of organizational evolution.

Cultural Fractures

Cultures are powerful, in part because they make human organizing seem normal, natural, and right. The best way to insert change is to find cultural fractures that can be widened and pulled apart to uncover the inconsistencies, tensions, and paradoxes that will reveal that organizations are anything but natural. They are human constructions and are therefore

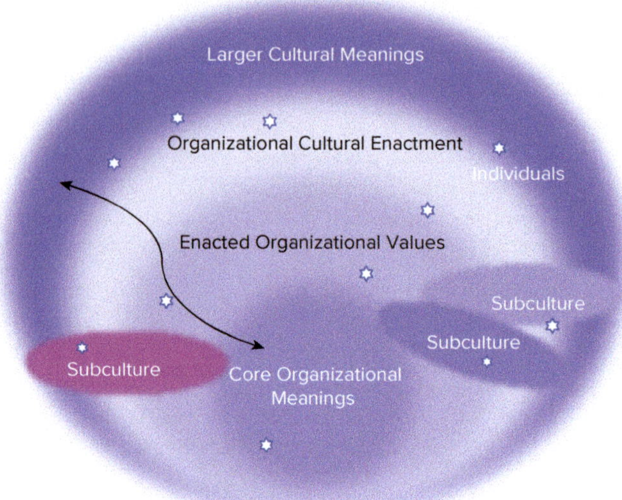

FIGURE 9.2: The Full Trans-MOC Model

subject to human interventions. It is here where we can see the possibilities for what an organization can be. Consider the fault lines made apparent in the Trans-MOC model:

1. Subcultures can be used to reveal fractures in the ways that they are both similar to, and different from, the larger organizational culture.
2. Individual differences, those differences that come from the diversity of experiences and identities, can both produce and reveal cultural fractures.
3. Organizational culture is fuzzy because it is neither fully coherent nor fully complete. Instead, culture is constantly in motion. As Joann Keyton (2011) wisely suggests, it might be more accurate to call it organizational culturing to capture the constant movement that produces and reproduces organizational culture. These fuzzy differences can reveal fractures and cracks in the culture.

There are many kinds of fractures that you can identify. My personal favorite, for intervention purposes, involves organizational values. In particular, I look for espoused values that conflict with enacted values, behaviors that do not match values, or unintended cultural meanings that emerge from toxic values. I will discuss ways to identify cultural fractures later in this chapter. First, it is important to be able to identify cultural carriers.

Cultural Carriers

Cultural carriers communicate culture. They are the primary ways through which culture is created and maintained, and are therefore important for cultural intervention. Pacanowski and O'Donnell-Trujillo (1982) identify cultural carriers in their classic article on organizational culture. Constructs, facts, practices, vocabulary, metaphors, stories, rites, and rituals, and I would add media and technology preferences, are important ways in which organizational culture is communicated. Not all cultural carriers are equally significant in every organization. When I worked with the National Park Service, stories were easy to come by. In contrast, when I worked with the U.S. Army, rituals and symbols were far more prominent in their culture. How can you utilize cultural carriers?

Most models of organizational culture assume that influence goes in one direction—organizational culture is created from the outside in or from the inside out. However, if you look closer at the multidirectional arrows in Trans-MOC, you can see that culture is produced and reproduced from multiple directions. Influence goes both ways. Usually, this mutual influence is mindless. We just let it happen. However, with a more mindful vision of organizational culture, you can at least direct the ways in which this mutual influence occurs. In the next section, I provide an overview of how you can observe, understand, and engage with an organizational culture.

Applied Ethnography

Ethnography, the study of culture as it is lived and enacted by cultural members, is one of the oldest systematic ways of knowing a cultural world. This methodology has been used by scholars in diverse fields, such as education, psychology, anthropology, management, social work, and communication. Ethnography has had a profound influence on how we understand our social worlds. An ethnography can take years to conduct properly, and the outcomes are fully unknown when the process begins.

Organizational change agents dealing with a serious cultural problem, such as predatory sexual behavior, do not have unlimited amounts of time to spend on a project that is unlikely to help manage this devastating problem. I have created what I call **applied organizational ethnography**, in which change agents observe the organization to understand how a particular problem is woven into the organizational culture. This form of observation tends to be more focused than traditional ethnography and can be accomplished in a comparatively short period of time. Applied ethnography involves five overlapping steps: problem, observe, describe, interpret, manage (PODIM). I will discuss each step.

Problem

The first step in applied ethnography is to identify the problem you need to address. Although this seems like a straightforward issue, it is surprisingly complex. Very often change agents misdiagnose the problem when it comes to predatory sexual harassment. It is time to put on your humility hat and really consider the problem. Start by asking yourself these questions:

1. How did I first notice this problem? (Observations? Talking with others? Leadership informed? Media attention?)
2. How does the organization define the problem?
3. What is/may be missing from this definition?
4. What am I noticing (figure), and what am I missing (ground)?

You should struggle to answer these questions. The intent is to sharpen your awareness and to orient you around the complexity of the problem. In fact, if all goes as intended, after contemplating these questions, you should have generated even more questions about the nature of the problem. Write down these emerging questions. They are an important part of keeping your mind open to alternative problems. It is necessary to be humble! You may think you know the problem, but I guarantee that you don't.

Caution: The problem you initially identify is unlikely to be the real problem. In fact, without mind-opening exercises, you risk missing the larger, more complex problem.

Observe

Observation is the systematic examination of your organizational culture. To this point, you have spent a considerable amount of energy and time contemplating the nature of your problem. You have read this book, so you are likely seriously invested in managing the problem. Now it is time to really drill down on understanding how the problem fits into the cultural dynamics of your organization. We understand our cultural problems by physiologically engaging our senses in a deliberate observation of patterned, meaningful behaviors in our organization.

It is important to consider what is worthy of observation. A good observer will look for patterns within and between cultural carriers, such as myths and legends, stories, policies, talk about policies, water cooler conversations, mundane everyday interactions, rituals, special events, and meaningful symbols within the environment (Figure 9.3). You will be observing a lot of stuff. You can expect to feel overwhelmed in the beginning as you struggle to make sense of the culture. As patterns begin to emerge, you will begin to feel increasingly confident in your observations.

Most people cannot observe their own organizational cultures, for two reasons. First, we become too entrenched in cultural patterns and meaning systems to be able to either recognize or understand them. Second, most internal people do not have the observational skills necessary for seeing culture. Consider bringing in a trained outsider and/or developing observational skills through ethnography and qualitative interviewing classes.

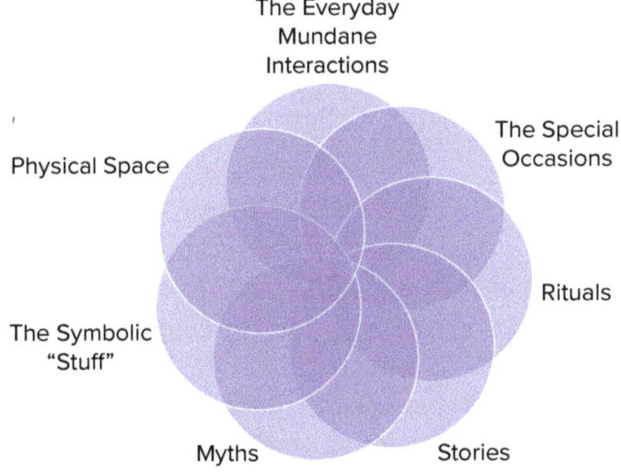

FIGURE 9.3: Observing Organizational Culture

Describe

The describe step of the PODIM process overlaps with the observation step. As you observe, you begin to describe. The longer you observe, the more robust your description. In applied ethnography, all descriptions are considered in relationship to the problem of predatory sexual harassment. Description moves from a very surface level of observation to a deeper level of understanding (Figure 9.4). First, begin by describing *the things*, *behaviors*, *conversations*, *events*, and so on. These are the things you can physically observe.

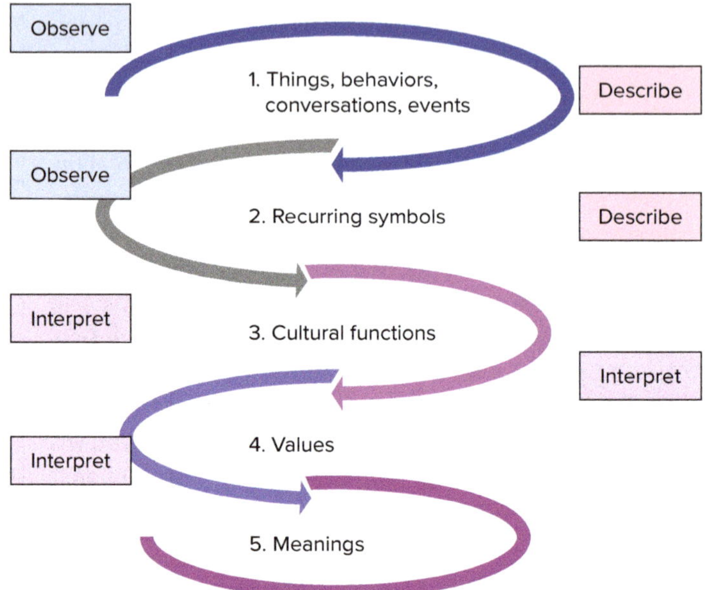

FIGURE 9.4: Overlapping Observe, Describe, Interpret

As you move deeper into description, you can begin to identify *recurring symbols*—those repetitive things and behaviors that are meaningful in an important way. As you identify recurring symbols, you can begin to understand how these symbols *function culturally*. From here you can identify enacted *values*. All of this should lead you toward key *meanings* that underpin predatory sexual harassment.

Interpret

Interpretation is the process by which you come to understand a cultural problem. Interpretation overlaps with description. For me, interpretation involves identifying how predatory sexual harassment functions in the organizational culture, identifying cultural values enacted through predatory sexual harassment, and then understanding how those values are woven together in an ongoing process of meaning making.

Different people will produce different interpretations. That is okay. There are lots of useful ways of thinking about a problem.

As depicted in Figure 9.4, a good place to begin is to ask yourself what predatory sexual harassment accomplishes for the organization. Predatory sexual harassment always *functions* in some way. These functions are not just for sexual predators. Predatory sexual behavior also functions for bystanders. This function analysis should move you toward understanding *cultural values*. This process is difficult. You are unlikely to produce a satisfying answer in your first attempt. Stay with it. To accomplish this analysis, you need to move beyond the obvious. Don't just look at what people say. Look at what their words accomplish. For example, as mentioned previously, I often find women who claim that other women are weak. Does this mean that other women really are weak? Of course not. The words are not speaking The Truth. They are *creating a truth*. During interpretation, you look for patterns that are not immediately obvious. When I see women talking smack about other women, I begin to speculate that in this culture one of the enacted values is hegemonic masculinity.

The culturally meaningful values will point you toward the core *meaning* systems. Although sometimes the meanings are difficult to identify, sometimes they are shockingly easy to articulate. For example, when an organization values hegemonic masculinity, core meanings often include things like, men are best suited for this type of work, men are superior leaders, men are more trustworthy, women are generally incompetent, masculinity is aggressive, masculinity is hypersexual, and so on. You see how this works? Many theorists believe that it is challenging to identify meaning systems. In contrast, I believe that if you do the groundwork, you can come to see enough of the core meanings to begin to actively manage your culture.

Managing Culture

The last component of the PODIM process is managing culture. *Managing* culture is an information-rich way of thinking about and implementing cultural evolution. Although ideally you will have engaged with the culture through some combination of observations, interviews, focus groups, mapping, and so on, the reality is that change agents are often given limited access to the organization. This does make your job more challenging. Luckily for us, understanding culture does not end as you begin your intervention. In fact, some of my best insight comes from the deep-level engagement that happens during training and development activities. The activities identified next comprise a combination of discovery, skill building, and engagement.

Identifying Value Fractures

I mentioned previously that I personally find fractures related to values to be an excellent focus for intervention. To accomplish this, you need to understand the cultural fractures that orient around organizational values, including espoused values, enacted values, and aspirational values. How do you assess the values that undergird an organization's culture? I like to begin with a simple **values orientation model** that I developed to help my clients understand how values interact with behavior (Figure 9.5).

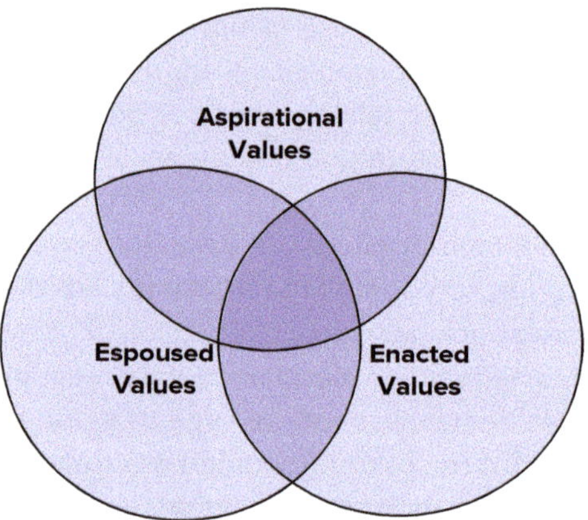

FIGURE 9.5: Values Orientation Model

Getting people to think about values in complex ways is more challenging than it seems like it ought to be. To help organizations solve entrenched organizational problems, it is important to focus their attention on understanding values as communicatively enacted. Communicative enactments not only tell us *what* an organization values but informs us as to *how* organizations engage their values. This process can produce practical insight into how problems and values can be intertwined. This process will take time, 1.5 to 3 days, so make sure you have the organizational commitment to accomplishing this work before you get started.

Discovery

Discovery goal 1: Organizational members will learn about the different kinds of values (espoused, enacted, aspirational, personal).

Discovery goal 2: Organizational members will understand the ways in which their organizational espoused values both converge and diverge with organizational enacted values.

Discovery goal 3: Organizational members will discover shared aspirational values and consider the kinds of behaviors that would communicate those aspirational values.

To begin, get organizational members thinking about values before you interact. Here is what I sent to organizational members 24 hours before our interaction during my most recent engagement (Think About It 9.1):

Think About It 9.1 Values Worksheet

Definitions

1. Espoused values: Values that the organization claims to have.
2. Enacted values: Values that an organization practices—can be acknowledged or unacknowledged. Can be productive or destructive.
3. Aspirational values: Values that organizational members want to practice.
4. Personal values: Values that an individual practices. May or may not overlap with organizational values.

Thought Exercises

1. What are your personal values? How do you know these are your personal values?
2. [Larger organization] has four espoused values.

   (1) ____________ (2) ____________ (3) ____________ (4) ____________

   a. What do these values mean to you?
   b. On a scale from 1–7, how important should each value be to your organizational subunit?
   c. How are these values enacted by [larger organization]?
   d. How are these values enacted by your subunit? Provide an example.
   e. How does you subunit fail to enact these values?
3. Does your subunit have espoused values? If yes, what are they?
4. Every organization has enacted values—those values that are practiced through everyday interactions.
   a. What are the subunit's productive (positive) enacted values? How do you know?
   b. What are the subunit's destructive (negative) enacted values? How do you know?

5. What values should your subunit enact? Think carefully about this. Some personal values are not about the workplace. Think about the work unit. What should your subunit value?

Discussion Questions

1. How does the values worksheet orient around discovery goal 1?
2. How does the values worksheet orient around discovery goal 2?
3. How does the values worksheet orient around discovery goal 3?
4. Why is it important to have clearly defined goals when engaging in cultural management work?

Because values are enacted, it is necessary to get organizational members focused on those enactments. The discovery processes you use will depend on your style and inclinations as a change agent. Some of my students prefer to use case studies, others prefer media clips, while others have signaled a preference for role playing. My personal favorite is through storytelling.

Whichever method you use, the goal is to stimulate conversation around the thought exercises on the values worksheet. Each thought exercise question is oriented around a different type of value—espoused, enacted, aspirational, and personal. Thinking deeply about each type of value will help prepare participants for the skills-building portion of the exercise. As the participants are engaging in the discovery process, I have them write their different values on sticky notes and place them in categories, with some values in overlapping categories. I then have each group share the values they identified.

Some organizations have a storytelling culture, so this task is remarkably easy. When I worked with the National Park Service, I had participants sit around an imaginary campfire, telling stories about their work lives.

Skills Building

Skills goal 1: Organizational members will be able to identify values by observing cultural enactments.

Skills goal 2: Organizational members will be able to identify the values that contribute to predatory sexual behavior.

I begin skills building by asking participants to drill down on how they know what the organization values. In my experience, most people are capable of identifying enacted values, especially when the focus is on positive aspects of the organization. Consider the interaction in Think About It 9.2.

Think About It 9.2 Identifying Enacted Values

Following is my memory of an interaction I had with one group of clients. Although the language is not precise, it is a decent approximation of how I guide clients in skills building around identifying values.

Participant 1: We value respect.

Debbie Dougherty: How do you know?

Participant 1: We are always polite.

Debbie Dougherty: Is politeness the same thing as respect?

Participant 1: I think so.

Debbie Dougherty: Okay. Provide a very specific example of a time when your colleagues were respectful.

Participant 1: My boss always thanks us when we finish a project.

Debbie Dougherty: Tell me about a specific time when the boss thanked you.

Participant 2: [interrupting sequence to challenge Participant 1] I don't think that is respect. Being polite is not being respectful ...

Discussion Questions

1. What is the role of the change agent in skills building?
2. How is identifying enacted values a useful skill?
3. How does this interaction work toward achieving skills goal 1?

Identifying enacted values is a high-level mental skill. Organizational members need to be able and willing to think differently about their organization by considering values that are enacted, and not just those that are espoused. Notice how I ask Participant 1 to become increasingly specific about the enactment of a value. Like most people, the participant starts at a very general level. My job is to move them from general to specific so that they can clearly identify the relationship between enactment and value.

Skills goal 2 is where things get more challenging. How do we get organizational members to carefully consider the patterns of behavior that surround predatory sexual harassment? There are two problems you will face. First, there is often a profound silence protecting predators. Second, when people do talk about sexual harassment, the stories are often shaped to support the predator and to denigrate the target. While this tendency does reveal values, it can also create a face threatening interaction between the change agent and the storyteller. More specifically, it places the change agent in the difficult position of showing participants how their own beliefs and stories reproduce a predatory culture. This can be shaming for many people, an emotion that is sure to create defensiveness in most Western cultures. Defensiveness is the opposite of engagement, and engagement is necessary in cultural evolution.

A useful variation of the social scientist activities is to assign two to three people to discuss the organization's sexual harassment policy. One or two people act as the social scientist. When the social scientists get together, some interesting themes can emerge, creating useful discussion about the relationship between policy, culture, and member interpretations.

I address this issue in two ways. First, I get people in groups. One person is designated as the storyteller, one person is the active listener, and the third person is the social scientist. The social scientist takes notes, makes keen observations, and identifies themes. Then I have all the social scientists get together, talk about the stories they heard, and identify larger themes surrounding the stories. I give the social scientists questions to help guide their analysis. The social scientists then present their "findings" followed by a guided conversation about hidden values that are present in the stories.

Second, I also will give each group a packet of stories about sexual harassment that I have identified either through personal interactions or through the media (Think About It 9.3). I then ask the groups to observe who is the hero, what is the climax of the story, and what patterns the story reveals about organizational performances and practices. From there we can engage with the different forms of values that are present and absent in these stories.

Think About It 9.3 Guided Discussion About Stories

Adapted from a true story:

"Susan" was fresh out of basic training and had been posted to her first military assignment. To get around the base, she needed to purchase an automobile but was in the difficult spot of not having transportation to a car lot to make her purchase. A fellow soldier, let's call him "Tom," a man who was a member of the infantry, offered to drive her if she would meet him at his barracks. When she arrived the other soldiers kept looking at her "funny," which was confusing and made her uncomfortable. Tom drove Susan to the car lot, dropped her off, and that "was the end of that." Or so she thought.

For the next few months, Susan kept getting "funny looks" from male infantry soldiers. She was also propositioned, and some men used suggestive language toward her. Finally, she was told that she had made it into "the book" because of her sexual encounter with Tom. Of course, Susan did not have a sexual encounter with Tom, so whatever he wrote was entirely fictional.

You see, the men in the infantry barracks had a book of all the sexual encounters they claimed to have with women, both soldiers and civilian, who worked on the base. Although the women were all real people, the encounters were apparently fictionalized in order to enhance the male soldiers' hegemonic masculinity. Susan eventually left the military because of this and other predatory sexual behavior that isolated her from the other soldiers.

Discussion Questions

1. What did "the book" accomplish for the male soldiers?
2. What are the values enacted through the book?
3. What makes these values important to these male soldiers?
4. How can this story be used to address skills goal 2?

Engagement

The last step in the process is to help organizational members use their emerging knowledge and skills to deliberately engage with their culture. I have two goals:

Engagement goal 1: Organizational members will develop an aspirational value vision for the organization.

Engagement goal 2: Organizational members will develop a plan for achieving that vision.

Every organization has gaps between the espoused and enacted values. Figure 9.6 is designed to help organizational members work toward increasing the overlap. Values can be (1) espoused but not enacted, (2) enacted and espoused, or (3) enacted but not espoused. When predatory sexual behavior is woven into the fabric of an organizational culture, there is typically very little overlap between enacted and espoused values. The goal of the organization that wishes to eliminate the behavior is to increase

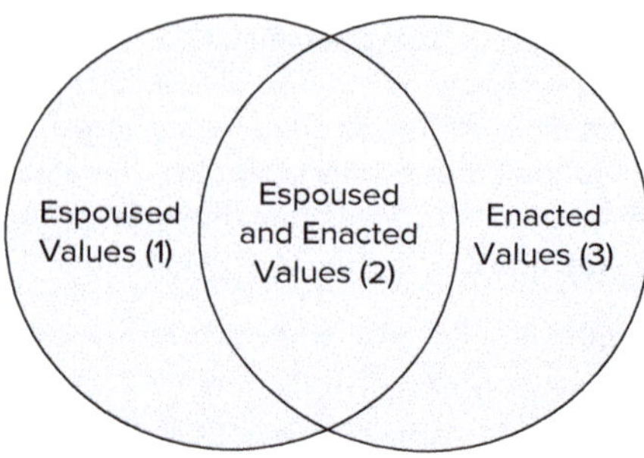

FIGURE 9.6: Value Gaps Model

the overlap so that the values that are espoused are the dominant values driving organizational behavior.

If you worked through this entire process, your clients now have the foundational discovery and skills necessary to engage thoughtfully in the planning process for transforming values. I use four overarching questions to help organizational members plan their best organizational life:

Question 1: What are your organizational values now?

Question 2: What do you want your organization to value in the future?

Question 3: What behaviors do we need to eliminate/change/add to achieve our aspirational values?

Question 4: How can organizational members lead the organization to enact preferred values?

Your training participants should use these foundational questions to struggle with what the organization values and what they want the organization to value. Answering these questions, for me, involves reengaging the sticky notes generated during the values worksheet activity. The sticky notes with different values are placed on a whiteboard in the front of the room. Those sticky notes are moved into different categories by the training participants. This activity engages people both physically and intellectually, which allows for thoughtful conflict and collaboration. For example, you might hear a person say, "I don't think we do this value yet, but I think we should;" or "I think we do this value in (X) way, but not toward (Y) group." In the end, the participants should have negotiated the values they want to achieve, the behaviors and places where enactments of the values need to occur, and a plan for how organizational members can lead the organization to enact their preferred values over time.

Sensemaking/Sensegiving

Recall from Chapter 8 that I define *sensemaking* as the communicative processes through which organizational members make meaning of a constantly shifting organizational environment. Sensemaking, therefore, is a path to both stability and change in organizational life. It is a means through which organizations can both learn and stagnate. Sensemaking is always happening and has an outsized impact on situations with high uncertainty or ambiguity.

As a change agent, you cannot stop people from making sense of their environments. It is a normal part of how we communicatively construct organizations. I have seen organizations attempt to prevent sensemaking by imposing speech moratoriums on administration or on workers. I recall a meeting that I attended as an administrator during campus protests where we were told we would be fired if we spoke publicly about the protests. As a result, workers were met with a wall of silence from administration. I told the organizational leadership at the time that silence is a form of communication. In fact, silence speaks very loudly during social and organizational upheaval. Unfortunately, I was right. Workers used the wall of silence as information during the sensemaking cycle to conclude that the organization was not doing anything to deal with the unrest, that the organizational leaders were racist and privileged, that the organizational leaders did not care. The point is, you cannot stop sensemaking from happening. That does not mean you are helpless in the face of sensemaking. As a knowledgeable change agent who understands how culture is shaped and created through communication, you can provide culturally relevant sensegiving that can shift the trajectory of the culture so that it evolves in more thoughtful ways over time. The following training and consulting activity is considerably different from the value gaps activity above. Nonetheless, it still follows the discovery, skills, and engagement process that I utilize for my training and consulting activities.

Discovery

Discovery goal 1: Organizational members will understand sensemaking and how it impacts organizational culture.

Discovery goal 2: Organizational members will recognize sensemaking habit loops and how they protect a predatory sexual culture.

In Chapter 8 I provided the framework for what I think people need to know to understand the role of sensemaking in organizational culture.

I trust that you can work through discovery goal 1 without further assistance. For that reason, I start with discovery goal 2—habit loops.

Recall that, during sensemaking, something unexpected happens, people start to talk, workers select a meaning, then they either retain the meaning or they select another meaning. A sensemaking habit loop is where workers become caught in a sensemaking routine. No matter what new information they are provided, the employees continue to cycle through the same meaning. Habit loops are one way in which predatory sexual harassment is persistently rewoven into organizational culture.

Habit loops remind me of the "unimind" from Buzz Lightyear. The unimind was a mystical orb that kept the little green people thinking as a single unit. The unimind was a good thing in the Buzz Lightyear movie. In contrast, the unimind represents the reproduction of problems in organizational culture.

Consider this habit loop (Figure 9.7). Sexual harassment occurs → organizational members talk about the target → organizational members decide that sexual harassment targets lie. Repeat. As you can see, in habit loops, people fast-track the selection of meaning and slip right into retention. The possibility of deliberation is abbreviated, and the same meaning is retained. The question becomes, how do you alter a habit loop? What can you do as a change agent to alter a destructive meaning that is woven into the fabric of the culture? As a change agent, you need to engage in sensegiving that inspires bystanders to select and retain new meanings.

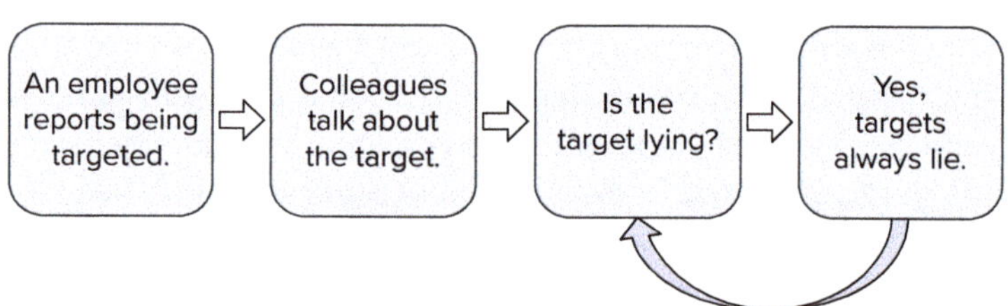

FIGURE 9.7: Sensemaking Habit Loops

Skills

Skills goal: Organizational members will learn how to create sensegiving communication.

We are now ready to talk about creating sensegiving communication. At this point it is important to decide where in the sensemaking process sensegiving will have the best chance of success. The most obvious place to insert meaning is before sexual harassment occurs. Planning for the eventuality of sexual harassment is an excellent choice, but rarely used. If you are in the enviable position of being able to prevent predatory sexual harassment, rather than unweaving it from your culture, then your focus should reasonably be on creating effective policies and training. Planning means not just having a policy and training, but making sure that the policy and training resonate with the organizational culture. For example, a policy that speaks to aspirational organizational values will be more culturally meaningful than a policy that sticks with informational/legal language. Similarly, training on sexual harassment needs to speak to bystanders and needs to resonate with the culture. If you need more on why weaving culture into your policy and training is important, consider rereading Chapter 1 of this book.

If sexual harassment is already woven into an organizational culture, then sensegiving will need to go beyond prevention. You will need to insert sensegiving communication elsewhere in the sensemaking process. Remember, sensemaking occurs constantly. You cannot stop it from happening, but you can shape the direction that it takes. Sometimes sensegiving is profoundly important, and sometimes it is smaller, nudging an organization toward a preferred meaning. Sensegiving communication works to break sensemaking habit loops by allowing members to see a problem in fresh ways. Here is the three-step process I use to help training participants develop sensegiving communication.

First, identify an appropriate cultural fracture. Given that we have already worked through cultural fractures around organizational values, let's begin with a fracture that revolves around a culturally important value. Second, identify an appropriate cultural carrier. Remember, for some cultures, storytelling is a key cultural carrier. In some organizations, informal conversations hold cultural power. For others, cultural symbols are dominant cultural carriers. Of course, all organizations have multiple cultural carriers. The more cultural carriers you can identify, the more powerful your message can be.

Third, identify a culturally resonant rhetorical device. A rhetorical device can tap into a preferred cultural value using important cultural carriers. This rhetorical device provides the core imagery around which a larger message is woven. Consider some of the most important evolutionary rhetorical devices of modern times. Can you fill in the blanks?

- I have a ______________________________.
- Black Lives ______________________________.
- #Me ______________________________.

The most effective rhetorical devices in some way fundamentally shift the sensemaking trajectory. These rhetorical devices tap into a culture, using minimal words and our imaginative understanding of culture. This makes them memorable and powerful. Take the examples above. Martin Luther King Jr.'s "I Have a Dream" speech taps into the American Dream and bootstrap ideals of life in the United States. Its primary cultural carrier is storytelling. Black Lives Matter is a micro story that taps into the American value of equal rights under the law. The primary cultural carrier appears to be social media. However, the women who created the Black Lives Matter organization have successfully used this micro story across multiple cultural carriers. Finally, the #MeToo movement is designed to encourage storytelling by the many people who have been targets of predatory sexual behavior. The primary cultural carrier appears to be the Twitter hashtag, which allows for the sharing and resharing of stories, adding new stories as the hashtag spreads.

"I have a dream"
Black Lives Matter
#MeToo

What counts as an effective rhetorical device depends on the culture. Your communication does not have to be a piece of art, like Martin Luther King Jr.'s "I Have a Dream" speech. It just needs to connect culture with emotion in a way that will help organizational members think differently about their organization. An effective message can be big, or it can be small. Let's consider two prominent values that drive many organizations: respect and time (Think About It 9.4).

Think About It 9.4 Sensegiving and Organizational Values

Respect is a common espoused value that is also often articulated as an aspirational value. The way you shape sensegiving should depend on what respect means in any given culture. Here is a message I created for an organization that espouses and aspires to a value of respect:

> *I have always been proud to be a part of an organization that so clearly values respect. I want you to remember how important respect is to our organization as we continue to make sense of the sexual harassment that has targeted*

our colleagues. We are going to take this situation seriously and we are going to be fair.

Time, in contrast, is a hidden value in many startup organizations. The idea that the company needs to move quickly and with few distractions is often an overriding value. Consider this type of core message:

We do not have time for this shit. Every time one of our team members is harassed, we have to stop everything to correct predatory behavior that should never have crawled its way out of grade school. Grow up. We don't have time for sexual harassers. Either get with the program or get out.

You try it. Pick a cultural value that is disrupted by sexual harassment. Now create a message around that cultural value. When you are finished, share with your teammates, then revise.

Discussion Questions

1. How do the core messages around respect and time tap into a cultural fracture?
2. What type of cultural carrier would be effective in different organizational cultures?
3. How does your message tap into an organizational culture?
4. What is the primary cultural carrier for your message?

Messages do not always have to be big. Sometimes changing a small, seemingly insignificant word can make a tremendous difference. Consider the statement "culture of respect." I hear this statement frequently, and it does make sense to link culture with respect. But what about the word "of." What does this word mean here? Of is a preposition that is supposed to direct attention. Using the word "of" leaves a value phrase without a point of action. In the phrase "culture of respect," the word "of" is a passive filler. How can we change the word "of" to give values greater impact? How about some of these options?

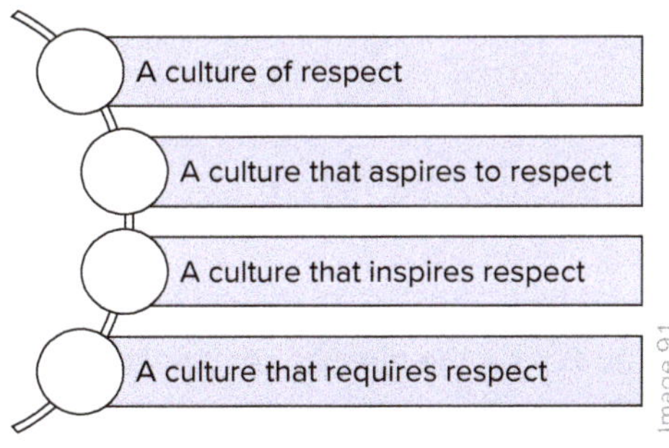

Image 9.1

Each of these small changes can be important in helping organizational members think differently about their actions within the organizational culture. Of course, these changes can only have an impact if they are paired with cultural enactments that reflect the aspirational value of respect. You can't just say it. You also have to do it.

Engagement

> **Engagement goal:** Help organizational members develop communication that will help evolve their culture.

At this point in the training, participants should be ready to consider how to engage with their culture. I start by reminding people that communication is power. Remember that organizations are an ongoing process of people communicating. While organizations seem fixed and solid, that solidity is an optical illusion created through words and communicative actions. If you want to change an organization in fundamentally important ways, change the way organizational members communicate. It is both that simple, and that difficult.

To change how people communicate requires an understanding of the organizational culture, an ability to tap into that culture in meaningful ways, and the drive to sustain your efforts over a long period of time. If sexual harassment is akin to weeds in my garden that are constantly drifting in from the outside environment, then your communication represents the primary tool you use to pluck those weeds so that your garden/organization can become a productive and healthy environment. Communication is the sticky substance that holds it all together (Figure 9.8).

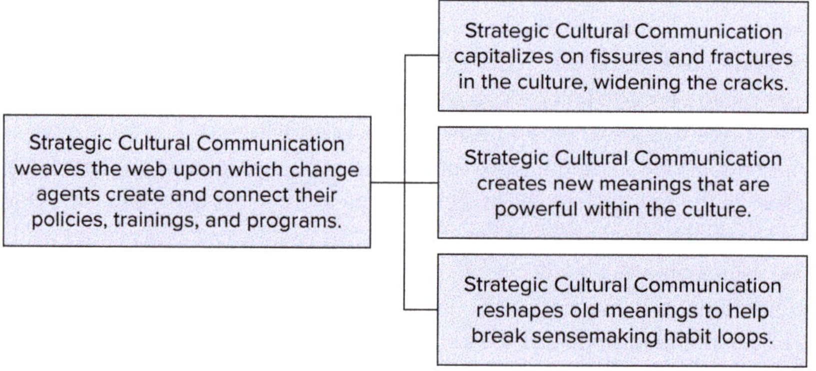

FIGURE 9.8: Strategic Cultural Communication

As you begin to work on your messaging, you need to consider the audience, the messenger, and the message itself. I will begin by discussing the target audience.

Target Audience

When creating messages, people are often stymied by the ridiculously challenging task of creating words that are impactful for all stakeholders. Let me short-circuit that problem by declaring up front that it is not possible, or even necessarily desirable, to appeal to every stakeholder in your organization. There are some people who simply will not be persuaded, no matter what you say or do. For example, you are not going to persuade sexual predators not to target coworkers or other stakeholders. You are not going to be able to persuade core members of their support system that predatory sexual behavior is bad or real or whatever. They have built their careers around their sycophantic support of predators. You can, however, persuade a core group of organizational members. These people are your target audience. You need to decide who you can reach with your messaging. Might I also suggest that you should start promoting those people rather than continuing to support sexual predators and their support system? Just a thought.

So who is your target audience? I have believed for many years that the best opportunity for change is to target messaging toward organizational bystanders. Keeping in mind that communication creates organizations, we need to think of bystanders as people who communicatively create the environment where sexual harassment lives. These are the people who may ignore sexual harassment when it happens because the culture does not allow for them to interpret it appropriately. You need to change how you think about those people in the background of the harassment. Their presence makes the behavior possible.

Messengers

Messengers share sensegiving messages. Although messengers and messages are closely connected, I want to separate them for a moment. I have discovered over time that sometimes the best messenger is not the message creator. I have created a number of culture-centered messages for organizations over the years. I have gotten pretty good at it. However, those messages are only effective when I let go of control and hand them off to someone with enough gravitas in the organization to garner attention and support. For a message to be effective, you must release control.

Imagine that you are on a sandy beach. You reach down and grab a handful of sand. Now, squeeze it tight. What happens to the sand? For those of you who have not walked on a beach or find this type of physical imagining difficult, the tighter you squeeze the sand, the more it slips through your fingers. Now, in your imagining, pick up another handful of sand. This time, hold that sand loosely in your hand. Although some will slip away, more sand will stay in your loosely held hand. This is much like communication. The more you try to control the communication, the more it slips away, and the smaller your impact. Instead, you need to empower as many people as you reasonably can to speak the message into the culture. Remember, with organizational culture, everyone is speaking the culture into being all the time. Everyone who absorbs your message and speaks it back into the culture becomes part of the evolution of the culture. Good messages reverberate throughout the culture, scaling up your ideas into the organization.

The #MeToo movement is an excellent illustration of a sensegiving message that was released into the culture with the invitation to targets of predatory sexual harassment to share their stories. The message was created by Tarana Burke in 2006, but the message went viral in 2017 when Alyssa Milano became the core messenger, tweeting, "If all the women who have been sexually harassed or assaulted wrote 'Me too' as a status, we might give people a sense of the magnitude of the problem." Do you remember when you first saw someone post "Me too"? When I saw it I had a surge of energy accompanied by a desire to participate. My social media was inundated with primarily women chiming in with their own stories. Some people simply posted "Me too." Other people wrote "Me too" followed by their own experience. The beauty of this messaging is that once the right message found the right messenger, who then found the right cultural carrier, the sensegiving message reverberated throughout the larger culture and into organizational cultures around the world. Years later, this message continues to evolve organizational cultures. The goal for organizational managers is to take advantage of cultural fractures and fissures by providing the right information at the right time by the right person, to insert messages into the sensemaking process in meaningful ways. These messages do not always work the way you intend, but they are the key to cultural evolution.

Challenges

I am concerned at this point that I may have given the impression that cultural evolution is a fairly seamless process. That is inaccurate. There are all kinds of pitfalls that can create challenges, and even derail your organizational engagement. Although I have encountered numerous challenges, I have identified three that I find to be most vexing when I am doing consulting and training work.

Challenge 1: Organizational Insiders Who Believe They Are Exempt

All organizational insiders are weavers of culture. No one is exempt from this weaving. This means that if you are an organizational insider, you need to constantly check yourself. Ask yourself how your behavior reproduces the problems you are fighting to eliminate. If you are an external change agent working with organizational members, be aware that many of those organizational members will view themselves as outside of the problem.

For example, in one large organization, I was brought in to do training by the person put in charge of cultural change related to predatory sexual behavior. I did not realize until later that there was a parallel person in charge of structural changes around policy, training, and reporting mechanisms, who was not invited to my training. I asked my contact why the structural change person was not invited. Apparently, my contact did not trust the structural change person and did not want to share their cultural change work with the structural change person. I explained that culture and structure are intertwined in organizations and could she please invite the structural change person. I came to learn that this organization routinely enacted suspicion, especially suspicion toward other units and divisions. Without these two people communicating, change could not be coherent between structure and culture.

This case is not unique. Organizational members may recognize that there is a problem, but they assume that the problem is "out there somewhere." Yet, as I discussed throughout this book, organizational members create their environments through communication. This means that if there is a problem, everyone contributes to the environment that supports that problem. Checking ourselves and teaching organizational members to engage reflexively with their environments are necessary if we are to be agents of change.

Challenge 2: Your Change Efforts Represent a Face Threat

High-level specialists have spent years learning about and working on culturally woven problems. These specialists have been hired to help an organization solve a particularly difficult challenge, presumably because there are no similarly qualified organizational members. Yet, despite your deep knowledge and training, there is almost always one or more key-level personnel for whom it is important to be seen as already knowing what you know. Their lack of knowledge on a particular topic is face threatening, creating some unfortunate behaviors.

Example 1. In one of my early trainings on sexual harassment, I was asked to help the "coms" (communication) people understand how to communicate with internal audiences. This seemed like a reasonable request, since most coms people are trained in public relations, meaning that they focus on external constituencies. In contrast, I am trained in internal organizational communication. I do not even pretend to understand the nuances of public relations. Unfortunately, the lead coms person believed that my training threatened her professional standing and made her look weak. Given that she is a woman in a powerful role, face threat is an important consideration (remember the paradox of the professional woman). Professional women need to be constantly vigilant for threats to their status. Unfortunately, this did make the training more difficult. I had to simultaneously provide strength-supporting messages and knowledge-development messages. It was exhausting. Ultimately, we worked through the issues and had an excellent set of trainings.

Example 2. In one organization I worked with, the office for the Equal Employment Opportunity Commission (EEOC division) was invited to attend a training. Two members of the EEOC division office showed up to the training but engaged in what I perceived to be resistance strategies. It was my impression that my training was face threatening to these people, likely because they were supposed to be the sexual harassment experts in their organization. At one point, the leader of the office declared that women tend to lie about being harassed and that the real victims are the men who are accused of harassment. I was shocked to see this myth of predatory weak woman reproduced by the EEOC people. My job was to train key organizational members in a cultural approach to understanding sexual harassment. As a result, I don't know how sexual harassment remediation efforts played out in this organization over time. However, I suspect that the EEOC people either blocked the change effort or that they were circumvented in the cultural change work.

Challenge 3: Uncertainty Management

Cultural evolution requires an ability to work within an ambiguous and uncertain environment. When you begin your work, you are inundated with uninterpreted information. Your job is to compile that information, search out themes, and then to interpret the information so that you can meaningfully engage with the organization's culture. Maybe the most surprising roadblock I have experienced in my consulting work is the people who cannot work in an uncertain environment. They push back; they get angry and frustrated. They are resistant to discovery, making it challenging to develop skills and to engage with the culture.

For example, when I was working with one large organization, I was asked to bring in information that would help the organization address a second important, culturally woven problem. I cannot give you much context about the information because of privacy concerns, so I will have to be vague. While most of the organizational members eagerly participated in the discovery/skills/engagement activities, two important organizational leaders freaked out. One of the leaders asked, "What does this have to do with sexual harassment?" Another said, "I don't see how this is X organization's problem." One of these participants sat with a grim expression on their face, arms crossed, occasionally making derogatory comments. The only thing that seemed to help was my telling them that I promised the answers to their questions would emerge, that "we will get there." It wasn't until we reached the end of the activity that these leaders gained clarity, their uncertainty was reduced, and they retrospectively appreciated the activity. By then, however, it was too late for them to fully immerse themselves in the discovery/skills/engagement process. I suspect they gained little during this training and development activity.

Since that time, I have found it helpful to warn training participants ahead of time that they will face uncertainty, that they need to embrace it, and to give them strategies for how to manage the uncertainty. I also try to delicately suggest that to be effective cultural change agents, they need to learn how to deal with uncertainty for sustained periods of time. Sometimes this works, and sometimes it does not. If you find more effective strategies for managing participant uncertainty, please feel free to share them with me.

Recap and Looking to the Future

Recall that I started this chapter with three goals:

> **Goal 1:** I want you to think differently about organizational culture and your role in that culture.
>
> **Goal 2:** I want you to feel empowered to act differently to create the culture that you envision.
>
> **Goal 3:** I want you to manage organizational culture in more thoughtful and deliberate ways.

In this chapter, we focused on the less obvious features of the Trans-MOC model to help you envision ways in which you can begin to evolve organizational culture. The fuzzy nature of organizational culture and the multidirectional nature of organizational culture means that there are always fractures and fissures that can be used to influence cultures from the outside in and from the inside out. Unlike other culture scholars, I believe that, although we can't change organizational culture, we can help it evolve in careful and thoughtful ways. This chapter provides insight into how to engage that process.

I believe that with our words and actions, we can create a better world. Although predatory sexual harassment is a truly bizarre and awful feature of many organizational cultures, it does not have to be that way. Communication is a powerful tool in evolving cultures. However, it is not the only tool you need in your toolbox as a change agent. Be interdisciplinary in your research and in your quest to change the world. Discover, build your skills, and then engage with your culture. Thank you for sharing this journey with me.

REFERENCES

ADRP 1: The Army profession. (2015). Department of the Army.

Alvesson, M. (2002). *Understanding organizational culture*. SAGE. https://doi.org/10.4135/9781446280072

American Psychiatric Association. (n.d.). What is posttraumatic stress disorder (PTSD)? Retrieved October 8, 2019, from https://www.psychiatry.org/patients-families/ptsd/what-is-ptsd

Ashcraft, K. L., & Mumby, D. K. (2004). Organizing a critical communicology of gender and work. *International Journal of the Sociology of Language*, *166*, 19–43. https://doi.org/10.1515/ijsl.2004.012

Austin, J. L. (1962). *How to do things with words*. Clarendon Press.

Bach, B. W. (2005). The organizational tension of othering. *Journal of Applied Communication Research*, *33*(3), 258–268. https://doi.org/10.1080/00909880500149478

Banta, M., Lehr, S., & Berg, K. (2020, January 21). Police executed search warrants at Twistars, former U.S. Olympic coach John Geddert's house in Grand Ledge. *Lansing State Journal*. https://www.lansingstatejournal.com/story/news/local/2020/01/21/john-geddert-larry-nassar-michigan-attorney-general-investigation-usa-olympics-womens-gymnastics/4528869002/

Barker, J. R. (1993). Tightening the iron cage: Concertive control in self-managing teams. *Administrative Science Quarterly*, *38*(3), 408–437. https://doi.org/10.2307/2393374

Barrett, L. F. (2006). Solving the emotion paradox: Categorization and the experience of emotion. *Personality and Social Psychology Review*, *10*(1), 20–46.

BBC News. (2018, January 25). Larry Nassar case: The 156 women who confronted a predator. https://www.bbc.com/news/world-us-canada-42725339

Bechara, A., Damasio, H., & Damasio, A. R. (2000). Emotion, decision making and the orbitofrontal cortex. *Cerebral Cortex*, *10*(3), 295–307. https://doi.org/10.1093/cercor/10.3.295

Bem, S. L. (1974). The measurement of psychological androgyny. *Journal of Consulting and Clinical Psychology*, *42*(2), 155. https://doi.org/10.1037/h0036215

Berger, P. L., & Luckmann, T. (1966). *The social construction of reality: A treatise in the sociology of knowledge*. Doubleday.

Bergman, M. E., Langhout, R. D., Palmieri, P. A., Cortina, L. M., & Fitzgerald, L. F. (2002). The (un)reasonableness of reporting: Antecedents and consequences of reporting sexual harassment. *Journal of Applied Psychology*, *87*(2), 230–242. https://doi.org/10.1037/0021-9010.87.2.230

Bingham, S. G., & Burleson, B. R. (1996). The development of a sexual harassment proclivity scale: Construct validation and relationship to communication competence. *Communication Quarterly*, *44*(3), 308–325. https://doi.org/10.1080/01463379609370020

Biron, M. (2010). Negative reciprocity and the association between perceived organizational ethical values and organizational deviance. *Human Relations*, *63*(6), 875–897. https://doi.org/10.1177/0018726709347159

Bisel, R. S. (2017). *Organizational moral learning: A communication approach*. Routledge.

Bisel, R. S., Kramer, M. W., & Banas, J. A. (2017). Scaling up to institutional entrepreneurship: A life history of an elite training gymnastics organization. *Human Relations*, *70*(4), 410–435.

Bivens, R. (2017). The gender binary will not be deprogrammed: Ten years of coding gender on Facebook. *New Media & Society*, *19*(6), 880–898. https://doi.org/10.1177/1461444815621527

Bourne, H., & Jenkins, M. (2013). Organizational values: A dynamic perspective. *Organization Studies*, *34*(4), 495–514.

Bourne, H., Jenkins, M., & Parry, E. (2019). Mapping espoused organizational values. *Journal of Business Ethics*, *159*, 133–148. https://doi.org/10.1007/s10551-017-3734-9

Boushey, H., & Glynn, S. J. (2012). *The effects of paid family and medical leave on employment stability and economic security*. Center for American Progress. Retrieved September 16, 2013. https://www.americanprogress.org/article/the-effects-of-paid-family-and-medical-leave-on-employment-stability-and-economic-security/

Branton, S. E., & Compton, C. A. (2021). There's no such thing as a gay bar: Co-sexuality and the neoliberal branding of queer spaces. *Management Communication Quarterly*, *35*(1), 69–95. https://doi.org/10.1177/0893318920972113

Buchanan, N. T., Settles, I. H., Hall, A. T., & O'Connor, R. C. (2014). A review of organizational strategies for reducing sexual harassment: Insights from the U.S. military. *Journal of Social Issues*, *70*(4), 687.137–151.

Buckner, G. E., Hindman, H. D., Huelsman, T. J., & Bergman, J. Z. (2014). Managing workplace sexual harassment: The role of manager training. *Employee Responsibilities and Rights Journal*, *26*(4), 257–278. https://doi.org/10.1007/s10672-014-9248-z

Burrell, G. (1984). Sex and organizational analysis. *Organization Studies*, *5*(2), 97–118. https://doi.org/10.1177/017084068400500201

Calafell, B. M. (2012). Monstrous femininity: Constructions of women of color in the academy. *Journal of Communication Inquiry*, *36*(2), 111–130. https://doi.org/10.1177/0196859912443382

Catalyst. (2018). Sex discrimination and sexual harassment: Quick take. https://www.catalyst.org/research/sex-discrimination-and-sexual-harassment/

Catalyst. (2021). Women CEOs of the S&P 500. Retrieved March 15, 2021, from https://www.catalyst.org/research/women-ceos-of-the-sp-500/

Chan, D. K., Chow, S. Y., Lam, C. B., & Cheung, S. F. (2008). Examining the job-related, psychological, and physical outcomes of workplace sexual harassment: A meta-analytic review. *Psychology of Women Quarterly*, *32*(4), 362–376. https://doi.org/10.1111/j.1471-6402.2008.00451.x

Chiodo, D., Wolfe, D. A., Crooks, C., Hughes, R., & Jaffe, P. (2009). Impact of sexual harassment victimization by peers on subsequent adolescent victimization and adjustment: A longitudinal study. *Journal of Adolescent Health*, *45*(3), 246–252. https://doi.org/10.1016/j.jadohealth.2009.01.006

Cirksena, K., & Cuklanz, L. (1992). A guided tour of five feminist frameworks for communication studies. In L. F. Rakow (Ed.), *Women making meaning: New feminist directions in communication* (pp. 18–25). Routledge.

Clair, R. P. (1994). Resistance and oppression as a self- contained opposite: An organizational communication analysis of one man's story of sexual harassment. *Western Journal of Communication (Includes Communication Reports)*, *58*(4), 235–262. https://doi.org/10.1080/10570319409374499

CNN. (2016, December 21). SoCal woman becomes 16th accuser to sue former USA Gymnastics team doctor for sexual assault. https://ktla.com/news/local-news/socal-woman-accuses-doctor-of-sexual-assault-files-lawsuit/

CNN. (2018, January 24). Read prosecutor's statement at Larry Nassar sentencing. https://www.cnn.com/2018/01/24/us/nassar-sentencing-prosecutor-full-statement/index.html

Collins, P. H. (1986). Learning from the outsider within: The sociological significance of black feminist thought. *Social Problems*, *33*, 14–32.

Compton, C. A. (2019). Co-sexuality and organizing: The master narrative of "normal" sexuality in the Midwestern workplace. *Journal of Homosexuality*. Advance online publication. https://doi.org/10.1080/00918369.2019.1582220

Compton, C. A., & Dougherty, D. S. (2017). Organizing sexuality: Silencing and the push–pull process of co-sexuality in the workplace. *Journal of Communication*, *67*(6), 874–896. https://psycnet.apa.org/doi/10.1111/jcom.12336

Connell, R. W. (1995). *Masculinities*. Polity Press.

Connell, R. W., & Messerschmidt, J. W. (2005). Hegemonic masculinity rethinking the concept. *Gender & Society*, *19*, 829–859. https://doi.org/10.1177/0891243205278639

Crenshaw, K. (1991). Mapping the margins: Intersectionality, identity politics, and violence against women of color. *Stanford Law Review*, *43*(6), 1241–1299. https://doi.org/10.2307/1229039

Damasio, A. R. (1994). *Descartes' error: Emotion, rationality and the human brain.* Putnam.

Davis, S. M., & Afifi, T. D. (2019). The Strong Black Woman Collective theory: Determining the prosocial functions of strength regulation in groups of black women friends. *Journal of Communication*, *69*(1), 1–25. https://doi.org/10.1093/joc/jqy065

Davison, W. P. (1983). The third-person effect in communication. *Public Opinion Quarterly*, *47*(1), 1–15.

Deline, M. B. (2019). Framing resistance: Identifying frames that guide resistance interpretations at work. *Management Communication Quarterly*, *33*(1), 39–67.

Derrida, J. (1967/1976). *Of grammatology* (1st American ed.). Johns Hopkins University Press.

Dionisi, A. M., & Barling, J. (2018). It hurts me too: Examining the relationship between male gender harassment and observers' well-being, attitudes, and behaviors. *Journal of Occupational Health Psychology*, *23*(3), 303.

Dionisi, A. M., Barling, J., & Dupré, K. E. (2012). Revisiting the comparative outcomes of workplace aggression and sexual harassment. *Journal of Occupational Health Psychology*, *17*(4), 398–408. https://doi.org/10.1037/a0029883

Dixon, J. (2018). Looking out from the family closet: Discourse dependence and queer family identity in workplace conversation. *Management Communication Quarterly*, *32*(2), 271–275. https://doi.org/10.1177%2F0893318917744067

Dixon, M. A., & Dougherty, D. S. (2010). Managing the multiple meanings of organizational culture in interdisciplinary collaboration and consulting. *The Journal of Business Communication (1973)*, *47*(1), 3–19. https://doi.org/10.1177/0021943609355790

Dougherty, D. S. (1999). Dialogue through standpoint: Understanding women's and men's standpoints of sexual harassment. *Management Communication Quarterly*, *12*(3), 436–468. https://doi.org/10.1177/0893318999123003

Dougherty, D. S. (2001a). Sexual harassment as [dys]functional process: A feminist standpoint analysis. *Journal of Applied Communication Research*, *29*(4), 372–402. https://doi.org/10.1080/00909880128116

Dougherty, D. S. (2001b). Women's discursive construction of a sexual harassment paradox. *Qualitative Research Reports in Communication*, *2*(1), 6–13.

Dougherty, D. S. (2006). Gendered constructions of power during discourse about sexual harassment: Negotiating competing meanings. *Sex Roles*, *54*(7), 495–507. https://doi.org/10.1007/s11199-006-9012-4

Dougherty, D. S. (2017, May 31). The omissions that make so many sexual harassment policies ineffective. *Harvard Business Review*. https://hbr.org/2017/05/the-omissions-that-make-so-many-sexual-harassment-policies-ineffective

Dougherty, D. S., Baiocchi-Wagner, E. A., & McGuire, T. (2011). Managing sexual harassment through enacted stereotypes: An intergroup perspective. *Western Journal of Communication*, 5(3), 259–281. https://doi.org/10.1080/10570314.2011.571654

Dougherty, D. S., & Denker, K. J. (2015). Reclaiming connections: Constructing a web-of feminisms. In A. R. Martinez & L. J. Miller (Eds.), *Challenging social norms and gender marginalization in a transitional era* (pp. 229–245). Rowman & Littlefield.

Dougherty, D. S., & Drumheller, K. (2006). Sensemaking and emotions in organizations: Accounting for emotions in a rational(ized) context. *Communication Studies*, 57(2), 215–238. https://doi.org/10.1080/10510970600667030

Dougherty, D. S., & Goldstein Hode, M. (2016). Binary logics and the discursive interpretation of organizational policy: Making meaning of sexual harassment policy. *Human Relations*, *69*(8), 1729–1755. https://doi.org/10.1177/0018726715624956

Dougherty, D. S., Kramer, M. W., Klatzke, S. R., & Rogers, T. K. (2009). Language convergence and meaning divergence: A meaning centered communication theory. *Communication Monographs*, *76*(1), 20–46. https://doi.org/10.1080/03637750802378799

Dougherty, D. S., Schraedley, M. A., Gist-Mackey, A. N., & Wickert, J. (2018). A photovoice study of food (in)security, unemployment, and the discursive-material dialectic. *Communication Monographs*, *85*(4), 443–466. https://doi.org/10.1080/03637751.2018.1500700

Dougherty, D., & Smythe, M. J. (2004). Sensemaking, organizational culture, and sexual harassment. *Journal of Applied Communication Research*, *32*(4), 293–317. https://doi.org/10.1080/0090988042000275998

Dougherty, D. S., & Sorg, T. (2020). Sexual harassment, communication, and the bystander: Setting an applied agenda. In D. O'Hair & M. J. O'Hair (Eds.), *Handbook of applied communication research* (pp. 653–673). Wiley.

EEOC. (n.d.). EEOC policy checklist. Retrieved October 2019 from https://www.eeoc.gov/employers/smallbusiness/checklists/employee_policies.cfm

EEOC. (2009). U.S. Equal Employment Opportunity Commission fact sheet: Sexual harassment. http://www.eeoc.gov/facts/fs-sex.html

Ferguson, M. W., Jr., & Dougherty, D. S. (2021). The paradox of the Black professional. *Management Communication Quarterly*, *36*(1), 3–29. https://doi.org/10.1177%2F08933189211019751

Forbes, D. A. (2009). Commodification and co-modification: Explicating Black female sexuality in organizations. *Management Communication Quarterly*, *22*(4), 577–613. https://doi.org/10.1177/0893318908331322

Ford, J. L., & Ivancic, S. R. (2020). Surviving organizational tolerance of sexual harassment: An exploration of resilience, vulnerability, and harassment fatigue. *Journal of Applied Communication Research*, *48*(2), 186–206. https://doi.org/10.1080/00909882.2020.1739317

Fort Hood AR 15-6 Investigation Executive Summary. (2021). https://www.army.mil/e2/downloads/rv7/forthoodreview/fort_hood_ar_15_6_investigation_executive_summary.pdf

Galatzer-Levy, I. R., Brown, A. D., Henn-Haase, C., Metzler, T. J., Neylan, T. C., & Marmar, C. R. (2013). Positive and negative emotion prospectively predict trajectories of resilience and distress among high-exposure police officers. *Emotion*, *13*(3), 545–553. https://pubmed.ncbi.nlm.nih.gov/23339621/

Gehman, J., Treviño, L. K., & Garud, R. (2013). Values work: A process study of the emergence and performance of organizational values practices. *Academy of Management Journal*, *56*(1), 84–112. https://doi.org/10.5465/amj.2010.0628

Gibson, M. K., & Papa, M. J. (2000). The mud, the blood, and the beer guys: Organizational osmosis in blue-collar work groups. *Journal of Applied Communication Research*, *28*(1), 68. https://doi.org/10.1080/00909880009365554

Gilpin, L. (2016, December 15). The National Park Service has a big sexual harassment problem: The agency tasked with safeguarding America's greatest public lands has neglected to protect its female employees. *The Atlantic*. https://www.theatlantic.com/science/archive/2016/12/park-service-harassment/510680/

Glomb, T. M., Richman, W. L., Hulin, C. L., Drasgow, F., Schneider, K. T., & Fitzgerald, L. F. (1997). Ambient sexual harassment: An integrated model of antecedents and consequences. *Organizational Behavior & Human Decision Processes*, *71*(3), 309–328. https://doi.org/10.1006/obhd.1997.2728

Harris, K. L. (2013). Show them a good time: Organizing the intersections of sexual violence. *Management Communication Quarterly*, *27*(4), 568–595.

Hemel, D., & Lund, D. S. (2018). Sexual harassment and corporate law. *Columbia Law Review*, *118*(6), 1583–1680.

Hercula, S. E. (2020) *Fostering linguistic equality*. Palgrave Macmillan. https://doi.org/10.1007/978-3-030-41690-4_1

Hlavka, H. R. (2014). Normalizing sexual violence: Young women account for harassment and abuse. *Gender & Society*, *28*(3), 337–358. https://doi.org/10.1177/0891243214526468

Hobson, C. J., Szostek, J., & Fitzgerald, L. E. (2015). The development of a content valid tool to assess organizational policies and practices concerning workplace sexual harassment. *The Industrial-Organizational Psychologist*, *52*, 111–119.

Hoemann, K., Xu, F., & Barrett, L. F. (2019). Emotion words, emotion concepts, and emotional development in children: A constructionist hypothesis. *Developmental Psychology*, 55(9), 1830–1849. https://psycnet.apa.org/doi/10.1037/dev0000686

Hogler, R. L., Frame, J. H., & Thornton, G. (2002). Workplace sexual harassment law: An empirical analysis of organizational justice and legal policy. *Journal of Managerial Issues*, *14*(2), 234–250.

Hunt, C. M., Davidson, M. J., Fielden, S. L., & Hoel, H. (2010). Reviewing sexual harassment in the workplace–an intervention model. *Personnel Review*, *39*(5), 655–673. https://doi.org/10.1108/00483481011064190

Ilies, R., Guo, C. Y., Lim, S., Yam, K. C., & Li, X. (2020). Happy but uncivil? Examining when and why positive affect leads to incivility. *Journal of Business Ethics*, *165*(4), 595–614. https://psycnet.apa.org/doi/10.1007/s10551-018-04097-1

Jablin, F. M. (2001). Organizational entry, assimilation and exit. In F. M. Jablin, F. M., & L. Putnam (Eds.), *The new handbook of organizational communication: Advances in theory, research, and methods* (pp. 732–818). SAGE.

Jablin, F. M., & Krone, K. J. (1987). Organizational assimilation. C. R. Berger & S. H. Chaffee (Eds.), *Handbook of communication science*, 711–746. SAGE.

Jackson, R. L. (2002a). Cultural contracts theory: Toward an understanding of identity negotiation. *Communication Quarterly*, *50*(3–4), 359–367. https://doi.org/10.1080/01463370209385672

Jackson, R. L. (2002b). Exploring African American identity negotiation in the academy: Toward a transformative vision of African American communication scholarship. *Howard Journal of Communications*, *13*(1), 43–57. https://doi.org/10.1080/10646170275355 5030

Keyton, J. (2011). *Communication and organizational culture: A key to understanding work experiences* (2nd ed.). SAGE.

Keyton, J., Clair, R., Compton, C. A., Dougherty, D. S., Forbes Berthoud, D., Manning, J., & Scarduzio, J. A. (2018). Addressing sexual harassment in a sexually charged national culture: A *Journal of Applied Communication Research* forum. *Journal of Applied Communication Research*, *46*(6), 665–683. https://doi.org/10.1080/00909882.2018.1546472

Keyton, J., Ferguson, P., & Rhodes, S. C. (2001). Cultural indicators of sexual harassment. *Southern Communication Journal*, *67*(1), 33. https://doi.org/10.1080/10417940109373217

Kirby, E., & Krone, K. (2002). "The policy exists but you can't really use it": Communication and the structuration of work-family policies. *Journal of Applied Communication Research*, *30*(1), 50–77. https://doi.org/10.1080/00909880216577

Knapp, D. E., Hogue, M., & Pierce, C. A. (2019). A gateway theory-based model of the escalation of severity of sexually harassing behavior in organizations. *Journal of Managerial Issues*, *31*(2), 198–118.

Koffka, K. (1922). Perception: An introduction to the Gestalt-Theorie. *Psychological Bulletin*, *19*(10), 531. https://doi.org/10.1037/h0072422

Köhler, W. (1930). Some tasks of Gestalt psychology. In C. Murchison (Ed.), *Psychologies of 1930* (pp. 143–160). Clark University Press. https://doi.org/10.1037/11017-008

Koschmann, M. A. (2012, May 8). *What is organizational communication? (full version)* [Video]. YouTube. https://www.youtube.com/watch?v=e5oXygLGMuY

Koschmann, M. A. (2013). The communicative constitution of collective identity in interorganizational collaboration. *Management Communication Quarterly*, *27*(1), 61–89. https://doi.org/10.1177%2F0893318912449314

Kramer, M. W. (1989). Communication during intraorganization job transfers. *Management Communication Quarterly*, *3*(2), 219. https://doi.org/10.1177%2F0893318989003002004

Kramer, M. W., & Hess, J. A. (2002). Communication rules for the display of emotions in organizational settings. *Management Communication Quarterly*, *16*(1), 66–80. https://doi.org/10.1177/0893318902161003

Lamke, L. K. (1982). The impact of sex-role orientation on self-esteem in early adolescence. *Child Development*, *53*(6), 1530–1535. https://doi.org/10.2307/1130080

Larson, G. S., & Tompkins, P. K. (2005). Ambivalence and resistance: A study of management in a concertive control system. *Communication Monographs*, *72*(1), 1 –21. https://doi.org/10.1080/0363775052000342508

Lau, J. Y. (2011). *An introduction to critical thinking and creativity: Think more, think better*. Wiley.

Lawson, A. K., Wright, C. V., & Fitzgerald, L. F. (2013). The evaluation of sexual harassment litigants: Reducing discrepancies in the diagnosis of posttraumatic stress disorder. *Law and Human Behavior*, *37*(5), 337–347. https://doi.org/10.1037/lhb0000024.supp

MacKinnon, C. A. 1979. *Sexual harassment of working women*. Yale University Press.

Manning, J., Asante, G., Huerta Moreno, L., Johnson, R., LeMaster, B., Li, Y., Rudnick, J. J., Stern, D. M., & Young, S. (2020). Queering communication studies: A *Journal of Applied Communication Research* forum. *Journal of Applied Communication Research*, *48*(4), 413–437. https://doi.org/10.1080/00909882.2020.1789197

Martin, J. (2002). *Organizational culture: Mapping the terrain*. SAGE.

Martin, J., & Siehl, C. (1983). Organizational culture and counterculture: An uneasy symbiosis. *Organizational Dynamics*, *12*(2), 52–64. https://doi.org/10.1016/0090-2616(83)90033-5

Maslow, A. H. (1943). A theory of human motivation. *Psychological Review*, *50*, 370–396.

Massumi, B. (2015). *Politics of affect*. Wiley.

Mayo, E. (1949). *Hawthorne and the Western Electric Company: The social problems of an industrial civilisation*. Routledge.

McDonald, P. (2012). Workplace sexual harassment 30 years on: A review of the literature. *International Journal of Management Reviews*, *14*(1), 1–17. https://doi.org/10.1111/j.1468-232011.00300.x

McDonald, P., Charlesworth, S., & Cerise, S. (2011). Below the "tip of the iceberg": Extra-legal responses to workplace sexual harassment. *Women's Studies International Forum*, *34*(4), 278–289. https://doi.org/10.1016/j.wsif.2011.03.002

McDonald, P., Charlesworth, S., & Graham, T. (2015). Developing a framework of effective prevention and response strategies in workplace sexual harassment. *Asia Pacific Journal of Human Resources*, *53*(1), 41–58. https://doi.org/10.1111/1744-7941.12046

Mcguire, T., Dougherty, D. S., & Atkinson, J. (2006). "Paradoxing the dialectic": The impact of patients' sexual harassment in the discursive construction of nurses' caregiving roles. *Management Communication Quarterly*, *19*(3), 416–450. https://doi.org/10.1177/0893318905280879

McLaughlin, H., Uggen, C., & Blackstone, A. (2017). The economic and career effects of sexual harassment on working women. *Gender & Society*, *31*(3), 333–358. https://doi.org/10.1177/0891243217704631

McManus, J. (2021). Emotions and ethical decision making at work: Organizational norms, emotional dogs, and the rational tales they tell themselves and others. *Journal of Business Ethics*, *169*(1), 153–168. https://psycnet.apa.org/doi/10.1007/s10551-019-04286-6

Meisenbach, R. (2010). The female breadwinner: Phenomenological experience and gendered identity in work/family spaces. *Sex Roles*, *62*(1–2), 2–19.

Mesquita, B. (2007). Emotions are culturally situated. *Social Science Information*, *46*(3), 410–415.

Michigan State University. (2020, September 1). *Report of Employee Review: 2019 Resolution Agreement, Section III*. https://msu.edu/ourcommitment/_assets/documents/nassar-ocr-report-sept-2020

Mumby, D. K., & Putnam, L. L. (1992). The politics of emotion: A feminist reading of bounded rationality. *Academy of Management Review*, *17*(3), 465–486. https://doi.org/10.5465/AMR.1992.4281983

Ohse, D. M., & Stockdale, M. S. (2008). Age comparisons in workplace sexual harassment perceptions. *Sex Roles*, *59*(3–4), 240–253. https://doi.org/10.1007/s11199-008-9438-y

Orbe, M. P. (1998). An outsider within perspective to organizational communication: Explicating the communicative practices of co-cultural group members. *Management Communication Quarterly*, *12*(2), 230. https://doi.org/10.1177%2F0893318998122003

Orbe, M. P. (2018). *Mark Orbe on co-cultural theory, part 1* [Video]. YouTube. https://www.youtube.com/watch?v=8x87QW8Jybk

Pacanowsky, M. E., & O'Donnell-Trujillo, N. (1982). Communication and organizational cultures. *Western Journal of Communication (Includes Communication Reports)*, *46*(2), 115–130. https://doi.org/10.1080/10570318209374072

Palmieri, P. A., & Fitzgerald, L. F. (2005). Confirmatory factor analysis of posttraumatic stress symptoms in sexually harassed women. *Journal of Traumatic Stress*, *18*(6), 657–666. https://doi.org/10.1002/jts.20074

Penrod, C., & Fusilier, M. (2010). Improving sexual harassment protections: An examination of the legal compliance of US university sexual harassment policies. *Journal of Workplace Rights*, *15*(2), 151. https://doi.org/10.2190/wr.15.2.c

Pesta, A. (2019). *The girls: An all-American town, a predatory doctor, and the untold story of the gymnasts who brought him down*. Seal Press.

Pogosyan, M. (2018, September/October). A world of emotions: From a sense of humor to a sense of happiness and from "high-arousal" words to "untranslatables," culture dictates how we speak about and experience the universe, far more than we realize. *Psychology Today*, 54–62.

Preusser, M. K., Bartels, L. K., & Nordstrom, C. R. (2011). Sexual harassment training: Person versus machine. *Public Personnel Management*, *40*(1), 47–62. https://doi.org/10.1177/009102601104000104

Pribble, P. T. (1990). Making an ethical commitment: A rhetorical case study of organizational socialization. *Communication Quarterly*, *38*(3), 255–267. https://doi.org/10.1080/01463379009369762

Raver, J. L., & Gelfand, M. J. (2005). Beyond the individual victim: Linking sexual harassment, team processes, and team performance. *Academy of Management Journal*, *48*(3), 387–400.

Rich, C., Schutten, J. K., & Rogers, R. A. (2012). "Don't drop the soap": Organizing sexualities in the repeal of the US military's "Don't ask, don't tell" policy. *Communication Monographs*, *79*(3), 269–291. https://doi.org/10.1080/03637751.2012.697633

Richardson, N., & Cassop Thompson, M. (2019). A new positioning framework for organizational value: Juxtaposing organizational value positions with customer centricity. *Strategic Change*, *28*(2), 123–132. https://doi.org/10.1002/jsc.2253

Rivera, K. D. (2015). Emotional taint: Making sense of emotional dirty work at the US Border Patrol. *Management Communication Quarterly*, *29*(2), 198–228. https://doi.org/10.1177/0893318914554090

Roberge, E. M., Haddock, L. A., Oakey-Frost, D. N., Hinkson, Jr., K. D., Bryan, A. O., & Bryan, C. J. (2019). Unwanted sexual experiences and retraumatization: Predictors of mental health concerns in veterans. *Psychological Trauma: Theory, Research, Practice, and Policy*, *11*(8), 886. https://doi.org/10.1037/tra0000445

Rokeach, M. (1973). *The nature of human values*. Free Press.

Sabbir, M. (2019, April 18). Nusrat Jahan Rafi: Burned to death for reporting sexual harassment. BBC, Bengali.

Scarduzio, J. A., & Tracy, S. J. (2015). Sensegiving and sensebreaking via emotion cycles and emotional buffering. *Management Communication Quarterly*, *29*(3), 331–357. https://doi.org/10.1177%2F0893318915581647

Scarduzio, J. A., Wehlage, S. J., & Lueken, S. (2018). "It's like taking your man card away": Male victims' narratives of male-to-male sexual harassment. *Communication Quarterly*, *66*(5), 481–500. https://doi.org/10.1080/01463373.2018.1447978

Schein, E. H., & Schein, P. A. (2017). *Organizational culture and leadership* (5th ed.). Wiley.

Schoeneborn, D., Blaschke, S., Cooren, F., McPhee, R. D., Seidl, D., & Taylor, J. R. (2014). The three schools of CCO thinking: Interactive dialogue and systematic comparison. *Management Communication Quarterly*, *28*(2), 285–316. https://doi.org/10.1177%2F0893318914527000

Schwartz, S. H. (1994). *Beyond individualism/collectivism: New cultural dimensions of values*. SAGE.

Segrave, K. (1994). *The sexual harassment of women in the workplace, 1600 to 1993* (pp. 40–60). McFarland.

Seo, M., & Barrett, L. F. (2007). Being emotional during decision making—good or bad? An empirical investigation. *Academy of Management Journal*, *50*(4), 923–940. https://psycnet.apa.org/doi/10.5465/AMJ.2007.26279217

Sierra, J. J., Compton, N., & Frias-Gutierrez, K. M. (2008). Brand response-effects of perceived sexual harassment in the workplace. *Journal of Business and Management*, *14*(2), 175–197.

Smith, F., & Dougherty, D. S. (2012). Retirement and the American dream: A master narrative. *Management Communication Quarterly*, *26*(3), 453–478.

Smith, J., LaFrance, M., Knol, K., Tellinghuisen, D., & Moes, P. (2015). Surprising smiles and unanticipated frowns: How emotion and status influence gender categorization. *Journal of Nonverbal Behavior*, *39*(2), 115–130. https://doi.org/10.1080/02699931.2015.1081875

Snider, I. N. (2018). Girl bye: Turning from stereotypes to self-defined images, a womanist exploration on crooked room analysis. *Kaleidoscope: A Graduate Journal of Qualitative Communication Research*, *17*, 11–19.

Steinberg, B., & Kelly, T. (1984). *Like a virgin. On Madonna*. New York, NY: Sire Records.

Stockdale, M. S., Logan, T. K., & Weston, R. (2009). Sexual harassment and posttraumatic stress disorder: Damages beyond prior abuse. *Law and Human Behavior*, *33*(5), 405–418. https://doi.org/10.1007/s10979-008-9162-8

Suvak, M. K., Litz, B. T., Sloan, D. M., Zanarini, M. C., Barrett, L. F., & Hofmann, S. G. (2011). Emotional granularity and borderline personality disorder. *Journal of Abnormal Psychology*, *120*(2), 414–426. https://psycnet.apa.org/doi/10.1037/a0021808

Taylor, J. R. (2006). Coorientation: A conceptual framework. In F. Cooren, J. R. Taylor, E. J. Van Every, (Eds.), *Communication as organizing: Empirical and theoretical explorations in the dynamic of text and conversation* (pp. 141–156). Erlbaum.

Tinkler, J. E. (2008). "People are too quick to take offense": The effects of legal information and beliefs on definitions of sexual harassment. *Law & Social Inquiry*, *33*(2), 417–445. https://doi.org/10.1111/j.1747-4469.2008.00108.x

Trujillo, N. (1991). Hegemonic masculinity on the mound: Media representations of Nolan Ryan and American sports culture. *Critical Studies in Mass Communication*, *8*(3), 290–308. https://doi.org/10.1080/15295039109366799

Tugade, M. M., Fredrickson, B. L., & Barrett, L. F. (2004). Psychological resilience and positive emotional granularity: Examining the benefits of positive emotions on coping and health. *Journal of Personality*, *72*(6), 1161–1190. https://doi.org/10.1111/j.1467-6494.2004.00294.x

Van Quaquebeke, N., Graf, M. M., Kerschreiter, R., Schuh, S. C., & Dick, R. (2014). Ideal values and counter-ideal values as two distinct forces: Exploring a gap in organizational value research. *International Journal of Management Reviews*, *16*(2), 211–225. https://doi.org/10.1111/ijmr.12017

Vargas, E. A., Brassel, S. T., Cortina, L. M., Settles, I. H., Johnson, T. R. B., & Jagsi, R. (2020). #MedToo: A large-scale examination of the incidence and impact of sexual harassment of physicians and other faculty at an academic medical center. *Journal of Women's Health*, *29*(1), 13–20. http://doi.org/10.1089/jwh.2019.7766

Vijayasiri, G. (2008). Reporting sexual harassment: The importance of organizational culture and trust. *Gender Issues*, *25*(1), 43–61. https://doi.org/10.1007/s12147-008-9049-5

Wallace, S. (1982). Figure and ground: The interrelationships of linguistic categories. *Tense Aspect: Between Semantics and Pragmatics*, *1*, 201–223. https://doi.org/10.1075/tsl.1.14wal

Weick, K. E. (1995). *Sensemaking in organizations*. SAGE.

Willness, C. R., Steel, P., & Lee, K. (2007). A meta-analysis of the antecedents and consequences of workplace sexual harassment. *Personnel Psychology*, *60*(1), 127–162. https://doi.org/10.1111/j.1744-6570.2007.00067.x

Wolff, J. M., Rospenda, K. M., & Colaneri, A. S. (2017). Sexual harassment, psychological distress, and problematic drinking behavior among college students: An examination of reciprocal causal relations. *Journal of Sex Research*, *54*(3), 362–373. https://doi.org/10.1080/00224499.2016.1143439

Wood, J. T. (1992). Telling our stories: Narratives as a basis for theorizing sexual harassment. *Journal of Applied Communication Research*, *20*(4), 349–362. https://doi.org/10.1080/00909889209365343

Wood, J. T., & Conrad, C. (1983). Paradox in the experiences of professional women. *Western Journal of Speech Communication*, *47*(4), 305–322. https://doi.org/10.1080/10570318309374128

Wyman, L. M., & Dionisopoulos, G. N. (2000). Transcending the virgin/whore dichotomy: Telling Mina's story in Bram Stoker's *Dracula*. *Women's Studies in*

Communication, *23*(2), 209–237. https://doi.org/10.1080/07491409.2000.10162569

Ye, J. (2012). The impact of organizational values on organizational citizenship behaviors. *Public Personnel Management*, *41*(5), 35–46. https://doi.org/10.1177/009102601204100504

Yep, G. A. (2020). Towards a performative turn in intercultural communication. *Journal of Intercultural Communication Research*, *49*(5), 484–493. https://doi.org/10.1080/17475759.2020.1802325

Zorn, T. E., Page, D. J., & Cheney, G. (2000). Nuts about change. *Management Communication Quarterly*, *13*(4), 515–566. https://journals.sagepub.com/doi/abs/10.1177/0893318900134001

INDEX

C

D

E

J

K

L

M

S

www.ingramcontent.com/pod-product-compliance
Ingram Content Group UK Ltd.
Pitfield, Milton Keynes, MK11 3LW, UK
UKHW021359190726
13851UKWH00015B/134

9 781516 586356